T0406067

International Political Economy Series

Series Editors
Timothy M. Shaw
Visiting Professor
University of Massachusetts Boston, USA

Emeritus Professor
University of London, UK

The global political economy is in flux as a series of cumulative crises impacts its organization and governance. The IPE series has tracked its development in both analysis and structure over the last three decades. It has always had a concentration on the global South. Now the South increasingly challenges the North as the centre of development, also reflected in a growing number of submissions and publications on indebted Eurozone economies in Southern Europe. An indispensable resource for scholars and researchers, the series examines a variety of capitalisms and connections by focusing on emerging economies, companies and sectors, debates and policies. It informs diverse policy communities as the established trans-Atlantic North declines and 'the rest', especially the BRICS, rise.

More information about this series at
http://www.palgrave.com/gp/series/13996

Mattia Tassinari

Capitalising Economic Power in the US

Industrial Strategy in the Neoliberal Era

Mattia Tassinari
Department of Economics and Management
University of Ferrara
Ferrara, Italy

International Political Economy Series
ISBN 978-3-319-76647-8   ISBN 978-3-319-76648-5   (eBook)
https://doi.org/10.1007/978-3-319-76648-5

Library of Congress Control Number: 2018936534

This Palgrave Macmillan imprint is published by the registered company Springer International Publishing AG part of Springer Nature.
The registered company address is: Gewerbestrasse 11, 6330 Cham, Switzerland

To Marianna

ABOUT THE AUTHOR

Mattia Tassinari teaches Industrial Economics and Policy at the University of Ferrara, Italy, where he works as a research fellow. He is also a researcher at the c.MET05 (Inter-university Centre for Applied Economic Studies on Industrial Policy, Local Development and Internationalization). He is a consultant for several international organizations, such as UNIDO (United Nation Industrial Development Organization) and ECLAC (Economic Commission for Latin America and Caribbean).

Acknowledgements

A young Italian writer began one of her recent novels with these words: "I am all the people I've known, all the stories I've heard, the homes and towns I've lived in." I might say that these words are very well suited to introduce the acknowledgements for this book, which has benefited from numerous *people I've known, stories I've heard, and homes and towns I've lived in*. Indeed, there are many people with whom I shared ideas and experiences which proved useful for writing this work. A warm thanks goes to each one of them.

Among these, I would like to mention some special people. A great thanks is due to Marco Di Tommaso, who was my supervisor during my university courses and co-author of several previous works: many of the ideas on the basis of this book have grown by a continuous exchange of thoughts with him. I also thank the whole research team at the University of Ferrara: Lauretta Rubini, Elisa Barbieri, Chiara Pollio, Stefano Bonnini and, last but not least, my great friend Antonio Angelino. With all of them I have had many interesting conversations about the topics of this manuscript. I would like to thank all the participants of research initiatives organized within the c.MET05 (Inter-University Center for Applied Economic Studies on Industrial Policy, Local Development and Internationalization) and, in this context, some of the keynote speakers who have offered important ideas and reflections during the workshops and research meetings of the last year: Patrizio Bianchi, Vera Negri Zamagni, Gianfranco Viesti, Giovanni Vecchi, Ugo Pagano, Linda Weiss and John Mathews.

Thanks also to Timothy Shaw, editor of the *International Political Economy* series for Palgrave Macmillan, and Christina Brian for their generous support in the definition phase of this book.

A particular thanks is given to Alfredo Saad-Filho, both for the welcome and attention I received during the months I spent at SOAS in London, and for encouraging me to write this work: without him most likely this book would have never been written, even though I remain entirely responsible for its contents. I also thank Stuart Schweitzer from UCLA for discussing many aspects of the American reality with me.

I have to greatly thank my brother Stefano for his tireless support during the writing of this work. A special thanks cannot be missed also to my parents: my mother, who taught me to believe in great ideals, and my father, who taught me the necessary tenacity to pursue them.

Finally, there are no words to thank my wife and my son. They have stood by and encouraged me during these months of intense commitment for writing this book. Thanks to Marianna and Zaccaria.

CONTENTS

LIST OF FIGURES

CHAPTER 1

Introduction

The last 40 years have seen our everyday life increasingly influenced by the global economic dynamic. Interconnections among the world economies have resulted in new formal and informal institutions. National governments have progressively changed their role at both domestic and international level. The enlargement of the markets' scope has called for specialization, efficiency in production and new ways to do business, fostering processes of international division of labour. Innovation and technological change have determined a rise in productivity and radical processes of structural adjustment in many countries. *Globalization* has meant new life styles for many people, by varying models of consumption and working, by modifying the development *status* of societies and by defining new modalities of relation within them.

The ongoing process of global transformation has not had the same impact around the world and within societies. Competition to survive and succeed in the international marketplace, as the founding element of the contemporary global economy, has stimulated private and political actors to put in place strategic actions in order to gain competitive advantage, to reduce threats coming from competitors and to maintain economic supremacy over rivals.[1] With this setting, differences in initial endowments of resources and capabilities, in basic institutions and in modalities to participate in global production networks, have discriminated between "winners" and "losers" in the international economic game. Rising productivity,

© The Author(s) 2019
M. Tassinari, *Capitalising Economic Power in the US*,
International Political Economy Series,
https://doi.org/10.1007/978-3-319-76648-5_1

income growth and high standards of living for some groups have coexisted with unemployment, marginalization and stagnation for some others.[2]

In this context, *economic power* has been one of the fundamental forces to determine the outcome of the global economic game and its evolution over time. Economic power refers to the ability of the members (or subsystems) of the international economy to control and organize productive resources. It is the capacity of exerting an influence over the conformation and results of an organization by determining the allocation of its productive resources. Private and political actors endowed of higher economic power have prevailed in directing productive forces, according to the nature of the interest they intended to pursue.[3] Interactions among the different economic power depositaries (i.e. public governments, financial institutions, enterprises, consumers, etc.) have determined the outcome of the international system, in terms of—for example—what types of goods and services have been produced, their amount and distribution, the grade of productive efficiency and technological innovation, capabilities and freedoms made available to the society, relations of production and consumption and future consequences of this general result. Accordingly, the actual conformation of the global economy reflects, to some extent, the distribution of economic power among its members, as the condition that enforces certain interests over others, influences the individual results reached by the agents and determines the direction of the system as a whole.[4]

In this context, economic power is based upon several *individual* factors, such as existing endowments of resources, capital and capabilities of specific actors (including, for instance, knowledge, information, skills and technical competences, capacity of analysis and of defining proper goals, attitude to innovate, persuasion abilities, etc.). Moreover, interrelations among members of the system and their different capabilities create *collective* constraints and incentives that affect the individual actions, by setting a particular institutional framework of reference. Institutions constitute the rules through which economic power can exert its influence over the results of the system. Competition for obtaining and maintaining economic power stimulates the strategic efforts of the actors to gain a "rent position", by improving individual capabilities, given certain rules of the game, but also by controlling the dynamic of institutional change.[5]

Eventually, changes in the system outcome can be determined by a redistribution of economic power among the agents and by the result of the competition among vested interests. For instance, the dissatisfaction of some actors of the system for the results they achieved, a different perception of their position and role played within the system and new expectations on the outcome to be pursued, can generate internal conflicts and tensions that induce change in economic power distribution, in the fundamental institutions and in the final resources allocation of the organization.[6] Understanding how the actors of the global economy have historically achieved, maintained and exercised their economic power is an essential element to explain the results and the changes of the contemporary international system.

This book is about the US economic power in the context of the global system. It analyses the American industrial strategy from the late 1970s to the present day, what is now known as the "neoliberal era", as the way in which the protection and promotion of the American economic system has taken place in the context of the international "free market". The work provides clear evidence of how the economic power of the United States—wielded to influence the formal and informal rules of the neoliberal order—has been used as a tool for enhancing its competitive advantage against other world economies. In this perspective, the US government's role in promoting the national industrial system is a key standpoint which helps to explain the dynamic of the American economic power.[7]

This perspective, focused on public intervention in the productive system, could sound exceedingly out of place when referring to the United States, inasmuch a country where the "antipathy for government, and the corresponding belief in individualism, competition, and the marketplace, go back to the days of the founding" (Etzioni 1983: 47). And perhaps this attitude has been particularly true during the *neoliberal era*, a period characterized by a radical increase in interactions among world economies, a substantial enlargement of the extension of the markets, and a supposed withdrawal of governments in favour of laissez-faire economic liberalism. Indeed, starting from the 1980s, many governments began to change their scope for action, abandoning, to some extent, the protectionist approach that had characterized the previous decades. This neoliberal wave became particularly popular around the world just when President Reagan in the United States (and Prime Minister Thatcher in the UK) began a campaign of clear opposition to public intervention. In this context, the Americans' affection for the *free market*, as a foundation of efficient and dynamic economies, led to painting government intervention into productive dynamics as an unwelcome intrusion, more inclined to respond to rent-seekers' pressures rather than to improve economic and societal outcome. This spirit started to push the US commitment to the international promotion of free(er) trade with exceptional continuity over time.

Whilst this is the most commonly highlighted narrative in the relevant literature, there is a side of the story that most often remains in the shade. In spite of the American *rhetoric* of the last 40 years, the analysis on the *practices* of government intervention depicts the United States as moving away from the image of unconditional and genuine lovers of the *free market*.[8]

Since the days of America's independence, public intervention had occupied a strategic role in fostering the creation and development of the national economy. In this context, the government had funded, supported and protected from foreign competition American companies operating in sectors which were considered of strategic relevance. Starting from the 1980s, changes in the international scenario and the progressive acceleration of globalization processes have modified the US approach to industrial development. *Reaganomics*, at the national level, and the *Washington Consensus*, in the international arena, have become the dominant paradigms. These have been, of course, years of liberalizations, privatizations and deregulations all around the world. Nevertheless—as I am going to argue—the US government's ability to promote domestic industry has remained high and stable over time.[9] On the one hand, at a domestic level, the American political system has continued to protect and support particular firms and industries, along with the advancement of science and technology that has remained a high priority. On the other hand, America's capacity to promote domestic industry through international negotiations and trade agreements has become a central feature of the US *industrial strategy*.

In this context, the US economic power—namely the acquired supremacy in technology, the largest market put in place in the international negotiations and the political and military hegemony—has been determinant in allowing the United States to establish an institutional framework closely congenial to the interest of the national industry. In particular, the work will argue that the United States have been *capitalizing economic power* by promoting an institutional framework able, on the one hand, to pave the way for foreign markets and, on the other hand, to protect and promote the national industry. The words of the Council of Economic Advisor (CEA) of President Clinton during the 1990s can resound as the *manifesto* of this American economic strategy:

> This Administration is committed to a high-wage strategy to enable the United States to take advantage of the new opportunities and to meet the new challenges of the changing global marketplace. This strategy consists of

two distinct but interrelated parts: trade policies that will promote trade and foster more-open markets both at home and abroad; and domestic policies that will help American companies remain the most skilled and productive in the world. This two-part strategy reflects the fundamental goal of the Administration's other economic policy initiatives: higher living standards for all Americans. Realizing this goal requires that America compete not on the basis of lower wages, but on the basis of superior productivity, technology, and quality. (ERP 1994: 206)

However, despite the simplicity and linearity with which the US strategy is described by the CEA, we have to refuse from deeming public intervention in the United States a formally planned action. It is hard to think of the United States—where the electoral base has been so faithful to the idea of individual freedom and of free markets—that they could have formal institutions explicitly in charge of implementing "industrial policy" actions, like the Japanese M.I.T.I. of 1950s and 1960s or like the Chinese government in the most recent decades. For the American case, the term "industrial strategy" cannot refer (solely) to an approved formal plan for promoting industrial development. On the contrary, in order to explain the US government's role in the economy, we need to refer to (formal and informal) systemic factors, responsible for sustaining the industrial dynamic over time. These factors have been the result of the equilibrium among different domestic and international interests and forces, and the government has been the actor able to manage and direct such equilibrium.[10] From this perspective, the government actions to foster and perpetuate the domestic and international determinants of industrial development can be reasonably considered an effective "industrial strategy". From this standpoint, this work identifies the stationary elements of the US economic power which have fuelled the American industrial development over the past 40 years. They cannot be understood just as "traditional" government policies, and their effectiveness has depended on how public action has been combined with the peculiar features of the American society and of the international context of these years.

In this regard, there are at least three interconnected elements at the base of the American economic power, which—with different effectiveness over time—have made it possible to implement the American industrial strategy in the neoliberal era, as the creation of an institutional framework congenial to the national industrial interests.

First, we have a spread and almost unconditioned consent accorded to the free market regime all around the world, as the predominant economic model. In this context, the American political rhetoric played a crucial role at the beginning of the neoliberal era.[11] It served to informally create legitimization and consent at national and international level for an economic order congenial to the interest of the most competitive industries in the United States, which could benefit from a laissez-faire regime over weaker competitors. This consent has been the basis for the future promotion of neoliberal prescriptions all around the world: liberalization, fiscal austerity, reduction of the state's role and demonization of the term "industrial policy". As a result, the neoliberal proposal started sounding seductive, even among the domestic and international groups that would subsequently suffer from this regime.

The second element is given by the US ability to formally determine the rules of the international game, by capitalizing on the bargaining power in trade and public procurement agreements. In this context, for example, the capacity of negotiating favourable conditions for the US industry in bilateral and multilateral agreements has been a key leverage in determining and managing the effective American competitive advantage.

The third element is the ability, in several circumstances, of "deceiving" at domestic level the same (formal and informal) rules that the United States had been promoting at international level. In this context, despite the anti-government rhetoric and the actions to promote free(er) markets at international level, many areas of intervention in which the public role has supported and protected the national industrial system can be documented, such as public procurement, science and technology policies, protectionist trade policies and industrial bailouts.

All these elements of the US industrial strategy have created an (formal and informal) institutional framework where the American economy has been able—at least for a certain period—to take advantage from the global system, by paving the way for the international markets and promoting the domestic industry. The neoliberal institutional framework has been, to some extent, the outcome of the US economy's strategic interest, as the interest of the most influential national groups. There has been a direct relationship between the US "industrial strategy" and the *global governance* model of the last 40 years, which has impacted many economies and the life within them. American economic power and its effectiveness in promoting the national industrial system have depended, to a large extent, on the US ability to exert a strategic influence over the formal and informal global institutions. This book analyses the American industrial strategy through the various stages of the neoliberal era and questions how such a strategy will still be viable in the future global economy.

The book is organized as follows.

Chapter 2 is devoted to contextualizing from a historical perspective the American industrial strategy in the neoliberal era. The goal is to outline the key elements which have characterized the role of the government in the US industrial development before the neoliberal era. This discussion is organized considering three different "American industrial strategies" implemented during the period running from the US independence to the beginning of the neoliberal era: the Hamiltonian Strategy (1791–1861); the Oligopolistic Strategy (1861–1914); the Keynesian Strategy (1914–1973). Each "strategy" has peculiar features related to how the US government has managed, in the different historical contexts, the relationships between industry, government and civil society. It is the result of an incremental transformation process that depends on past history. Consequently, the industrial strategy in the *neoliberal era* is the result of a long-term process of economic and institutional transformation, where some elements of the previous approaches still remain, despite the paradigm can be considered changed.

Chapter 3 touches the heart of our inquiry on the American industrial strategy in the neoliberal era. It focuses on the 1980s, when in the United States—seriously threatened by the invasion of European and Japanese manufacturers into the American markets—the debate over the necessity to adopt a national industrial policy arose for the first time. In this context, an irruptive neoliberal sentiment took its first steps under the President Reagan's rhetoric. The main questions addressed in the chapter are the following: how actually did the economic role of the government change during this period? Which role did the neoliberal rhetoric of that period play? Why should we care that a possible gap between rhetoric and practice existed? Did the rhetoric itself have any causal impact on policy outcomes? Why would successive governments feel the need of embracing pro-market rhetoric? In answering these questions, the chapter describes the peculiarities of the American industrial strategy at the beginning of the neoliberal era.

Chapters 4 and 5 focus on the 1990s. In particular, Chap. 4 outlines the actions and initiatives conducted by the United States at the international level, in the context of many areas of high relevance: the establishment of the World Trade Organization (WTO); the negotiations for the North American Free Trade Agreement (NAFTA) and other important regional agreements;

the process of supranational integration in Europe; the economic transition in post-communist countries and structural reforms in developing countries. During these years, the American government played a major role as a regulator, by actively participating in the definition of supranational and international rules. The establishment of a number of multilateral and bilateral trade agreements was at the core of the American political agenda. The chapter describes the role played by the United States in shaping the new neoliberal order of the 1990s and the actions implemented in order to take advantage of the changing global system.

Chapter 5 focuses on industrial development initiatives implemented at a national level by the US government during the 1990s. The increased stability resulting from the end of the Cold War required the United States to reduce its military expenditures. Concerns about the possible negative impact on the technological and industrial development of the entire American economy of this retrenchment led the government to look for alternative ways to promote innovation. In particular, the Clinton administration was the one that proclaimed a "new approach" to the innovation policy. In this context information and communication technologies (ICTs) were considered by the government one of the top priorities, making way for the majestic wave of innovations stemmed from this sector (the so-called New Economy). The chapter describes the main changes of US science and technology policy occurred during those years.

Chapter 6 describes the economic conjuncture and the main changes in the American approach to industrial development during the Bush Junior administration, which led to the outbreak of the global financial crisis. The powerful influence, within the neoliberal order, which had characterized the United States during the 1990s, began to experience some limitations in the 2000s. With the rise of China and other emerging economies, the WTO system, as a regulatory framework of the international trade, started to struggle to multilaterally impose its rules. Furthermore, at national level, the election of Bush Junior meant important deregulation and spending cuts for new technologies. From Clinton's New Economy—which had aimed at fostering the ICT and environmental friendly technologies—the American industrial strategy seemed to return to the old economy, based on an economic growth driven by military public demand and by a growing public debt, incubating the crisis that would explode in 2008.

Chapter 7 presents the main actions taken by the Obama Administration as a short-term attempt to tackle the problems raised by the crisis, but also as an effort to restore an effective American industrial strategy by addressing the more structural problems that were affecting the US global leadership. Indeed, at the outset of the Obama presidential administration (approximately a year after the financial crisis began), the government's main objective was to bring about recovery to the American economy from the threat of a truly catastrophic economic recession. Towards this goal, the central action was represented by the American Recovery and Reinvestment Act (ARRA), enacted early in 2009. Furthermore, other important interventions at domestic and international level were promoted, consistently with the US neoliberal industrial strategy that had characterized the previous decades.

Chapter 8 traces the essential elements of the American industrial strategy in the neoliberal era, as they emerged in the historical reality of the last 40 years. The main aim of the chapter is to locate the American neoliberal strategy in the recent post-crisis context and to assess the effective possibility for the United States to continue to implement it in the future. In particular, the chapter investigates whether the ongoing global transformations—namely the changes in the distribution of economic power at the international level and in the formal and informal institutional channels of the global order—are limiting the US capacity to adopt a neoliberal industrial strategy.

Chapter 9 concludes the book. In the context of the contemporary global transformations, the chapter poses the question on what the main and more realistic options for future global governance are.

Fears, hopes and alternative paths for development and global governance are discussed and suggested. The uncertainty and ambiguity of the contemporary times seem propitious to promote a new international paradigm able to recognize the mutual interests at stake.

NOTES

1. Typically strategic actions have involved several tools, such as R&D investments, public procurement policies, bailouts, infant industry promotion, managed trade, different types of barriers to entry and industrial policy practices. See, for example, Chang (2002) and Wade (2003).
2. See, for example, Saad-Filho (2014) and Wade (2004).
3. In this context, as a pillar point of the dominant economic literature, productive resources are commonly perceived as limited compared to human needs (Robbins 1932). There would be no seduction or, for us, source of interest in economic power without the common perception that productive resources are scarce. Private property of the livelihoods, as founding

element of the contemporary economic system, stimulates competition for economic resources among the members of the society, posing the issue of the possible *scarcity*. This setting implies that there are not just private but also political implications of a particular distribution of economic power. Since economic resources are limited, their allocation for a particular purpose prevents to use them for other goals, affecting the opportunities left to the members of the organization. When such interdependency among agents is realized through the *market* institution, economic power corresponds to the *market power*, as the capacity of influencing the price and quantity of the market by controlling demand or supply and conditioning the final resources allocation. However, in this work I refer to a broader sense of economic power, as the relative capacity of the members—or *subsystems*—of controlling and organizing productive resources within any kind of organization, not just in the context of the market institution. In this framework, economic power is not referred solely to "economic" actors, but to all the agents of the system, such as governments, political parties, lobbies and trade unions, that influence the final resource allocation. Indeed, also "political" actors can be seen as "economic" agents endowed of economic power, since they compete with the other members of the system to influence the final resource allocation. The economic power of a government, for example, has to be seen in relation to the power of other social groups and it depends on the degree of autonomy that the government is able to acquire against them (see, e.g. Mann 1984). A huge literature shows how economic agents and rent-seekers can, in some circumstances, use political power to condition the allocation of resources in the direction of their interest (Hirschman 1945; Cardoso e Faletto 1979; Salamon and Siegfried 1977; Hall 1989; Khan and Jomo 2000). Accordingly, there is no reason for not considering *political* actors as a crucial part of the *economic* dynamic (as well as the vice versa), including them with full rights in our economic-power perspective.

4. One of the most popular theoretical models used to explain how productive resources are allocated in a market economy is the model of General Economic Equilibrium developed by Arrow and Debreu. Under the stringent conditions of perfect competition, an individual action produces a Pareto efficient allocation of resources (Arrow 1951; Arrow and Debreu 1954; Debreu 1959). In this case, economic power (i.e. the *market power* referring to a pure market system) is equally distributed to the members of the system and no agent prevails over the other in determining the resource allocation. However, as well known, the perfect competition model is by far inadequate to describe the economic reality of everyday life. Different initial endowments of resources and capital, bounded rationality of the agents (Simon 1957; Etzioni 1988), uncertainty (Knight 1921), asymmet-

ric information and transaction costs (Coase 1960; Knorr 1977; Keohane and Nye 1977; Williamson 1979; North 1992) can lead to significant disparities in agents' ability to influence the final allocation of social resources and in their economic power. When there is the possibility of establishing rent and dominance positions and creating barriers to entry in markets, mere individual actions expressed within the markets may be strongly inadequate to achieving satisfactory results for all members of society. Economic theory identifies as *market failures* the cases where the market is not capable of leading the system to a desirable outcome (Bator 1958), that are, in practice, all the circumstances in which the market institution, from a static or dynamic point of view, is perceived as inadequate to meet social needs (Cimoli Dosi Stiglitz 2009). In these circumstances, which strongly characterize the everyday real world, the interdependence among members of society in the use of limited resources provides important incentives to establish cooperation agreements in an effort to achieve their goals, by harmonizing their behaviours, rather than acting individually (Downs 1957; Triandis 1995). As a result, in the concreteness of economic reality, the allocation of social resources takes place through institutions based on collective dynamics, including the market institution itself. Indeed—in addition to the actions of governments and other political actors, which are the expression of collective dynamics by definition—also the market system needs to be somehow "chosen" as one among several possible institutional settings, according to the perception of the advantages that such an arrangement could generate for the different powers at stake. It is not possible, in practice, to separate the economic result from the political dynamics and from the definition of the institutional framework of reference. Eventually, the social result is predominantly determined by the expression of the prevailing economic powers at stake and by the normative value judgments of which they are representatives (Hirschman 1981).

5. There has been a growing interest in recent decades on the role of institutions in determining social outcome and economic development. Institutions—as systems of established, socially embedded rules (Hodgson 2006)—establish collective constraints and incentives by which the allocation of the economic resources of the organization is defined. In this sense, institutions can play an important role in stimulating economic development (Acemoglu et al. 2000; Acemoglu et al. 2005). Competitive markets, for example, can significantly boost productivity, investment and innovation, by developing economic and social capabilities (Sen 2001). However, considering an opposite causality, also evolution of such capabilities and improvements of economic opportunities can be crucial for institutional change. As stated by Chang (2011) "Economic development changes institutions through a number of channels. First, increased wealth due to

growth may create higher demands for higher-quality institutions (e.g., demands for political institutions with greater transparency and account-ability). Second, greater wealth also makes better institutions more affordable. Institutions are costly to establish and run, and the higher their quality the more 'expensive' they become. Third, economic development creates new agents of change, demanding new institutions. More generally, development creates economic opportunities and modifies capabilities and the perception of the position occupied by the members within the organization, thus producing new expectations on the outcome to be achieved and encouraging actions and behaviours to change the institutions themselves. In other words, development may modify the distribution of economic power among the actors of the system and generate the conditions for institutional change. As a result, it can be argued that the organizational outcome is the product of a "circular causality" relation between a particular distribution of economic power, institutions and resource allocation, where—as stated by North (1990)—"history matters". Indeed, distribution of economic power and capabilities among different groups of the society is, to some extent, the result of the quality of the past institutions and of the previous allocating outcome of the system. However, they are also relevant in determining the future institutional change and the subsequent results achieved by the organization.

6. As stated, for example, by Bianchi (2017) "Relationships within an organization are relations of power, so that to the push for the change of some, there will be others who will resist. [...] In this conflicting process, therefore, not only [the system] goes from a starting point to an arrival one, but during the transit the social relation rules are changed [...]" (Bianchi 2017). In this context, after a phase of "revolutionary upheaval" of the organization, it follows an adjustment phase in which each member finds his own repositioning, by restoring operational routines, fixing new forms of incentives and sanctions for those who will be included in the new organization, and managing the turmoil and crises of those who will remain at the margin or even outside the system (Bianchi 2017).

7. A number of contributes shows how industrial system plays a predominant role in the economic and political dynamic of a society. See, among the others, Galbraith John (1967) and Galbraith James (2008). In particular, manufacturing industries are often deemed at the base of economic growth and prosperity, thanks to peculiar features, such as high productivity of labour, dynamic economies of scale, rapid technological change and innovation and positive externalities (see, e.g. Tregenna 2009, 2014; Bianchi and Labory 2011; Chang et al. 2013; Andreoni and Scazzieri 2014).

8. See, for example, Chang (2002), Block (2008), Schrank and Whitford (2009), Block and Keller (2011), Panitch and Gindin (2012), Mazzucato

(2013), Di Tommaso and Schweitzer (2013), Tassinari (2014), Weiss (2014), Di Tommaso and Tassinari (2017).
9. On the changing role of the national states during this period see also, among others, Keohane (1989), Nye (1990), Mann (1997), Weiss (1998).
10. On this point, see, among others, Galbraith John (1970).
11. See, for example, Mirowski and Plehwe (2009) and Harvey (2005).

REFERENCES

Acemoglu, D., Johnson, S., & Robinson, J. (2000). *The Colonial Origins of Comparative Development: An Empirical Investigation* (NBER Working Paper No. W7771). Cambridge, MA: Massachusetts Institute of Technology.

Acemoglu, D., Johnson, S., & Robinson, J. (2005). The Rise of Europe: Atlantic Trade, Institutional Change, and Economic Growth. *American Economic Review, 95*(3), 546–579.

Andreoni, A., & Scazzieri, R. (2014). Triggers of Change: Structural Trajectories and Production Dynamics. *Cambridge Journal of Economics, 38*(6), 1391–1408.

Arrow, K. J. (1951). An Extension of the Basic Theorems of Classical Welfare Economics. In J. Neyman (Ed.), *Proceedings of the Second Berkeley Symposium on Mathematical Statistics and Probability* (pp. 507–532). Berkeley/Los Angeles: University of California Press.

Arrow, K. J., & Debreu, G. (1954). Existence of an Equilibrium for a Competitive Economy. *Econometrica, 22*, 265–290.

Bator, F. M. (1958). The Anatomy of Market Failure. *The Quarterly Journal of Economics, 72*(3), 351–379.

Bianchi. (2017). Il cammino e le orme. Industria e politica alle origini dell'Italia contemporanea, Il Mulino, Bologna.

Bianchi, P., & Labory, S. (2011). *Industrial Policies after the Crisis. Seizing the Future*. Cheltenham: E. Elgar.

Block, F. (2008). Swimming against the current: The Rise of a Hidden Developmental State in the United States. *Politics & Society, 36*(2), 69–206.

Block, F., & Keller, M. (Eds.). (2011). *State of Innovation: The U.S. Government's Role in Technology Development*. Colorado: Paradigm Publishers.

Cardoso, F. H., & Faletto, E. (1979). *Dependency and Development in Latin America*. Berkeley: University of California Press.

Chang, H.-J. (2002). *Kicking Away the Ladder: Development Strategy in Historical Perspective*. London: Anthem.

Chang, H.-J. (2011). Institutions and Economic Development: Theory, Policy and History. *Journal of Institutional Economics, 7*(4), 473–498.

Chang, H.-J., Andreoni, A., & Kuan, M. L. (2013). International Industrial Policy Experiences and the Lessons for the UK, Policy Report for the UK Foresight Future of Manufacturing Project, UK Government Office of Science.

Cimoli, M., Dosi, G., & Stiglitz, J. E. (2009). *Industrial Policy and Development. The Political Economy of Capabilities Accumulation*. Oxford: Oxford University Press.

Coase, R. H. (1960). The Problem of Social Cost. *Journal of Law and Economics, 3*, 1–44.

Debreau, G. (1959). *Theory of Value*. New York: Wiley.

Di Tommaso, M. R., & Schweitzer, S. O. (2013). *Industrial Policy in America. Breaking the Taboo*. Cheltenham: Edward Elgar.

Di Tommaso, M. R. & Tassinari, M. (2017). Industria, Governo, Mercato. Lezioni americane, Il Mulino, Bologna.

Downs, A. (1957). *An Economic Theory of Democracy*. New York: Harper and Row.

ERP. (1994). *Economic Report of the President*. Washington, DC: United States Government Printing Office.

Etzioni, A. (1983). The MITIzation of America?, *The Public Interest*, No. 72.

Etzioni, A. (1988). *The Moral Dimension: Toward a New Economics*. New York: The Free Press. 1.

Galbraith, J. K. (1967). *The New Industrial State*. London: H. Hamilton.

Galbraith, J. K. (1970). *American Capitalism: The Concept of Countervailing Power*. Piscataway: Transaction Publishers.

Galbraith, J. K. (2008). *The Predator State: How Conservatives Abandoned the Free Market and Why Liberals Should Too*. New York: Free Press.

Hall, P. (Ed.). (1989). *The Political Power of Economic Ideas*. Princeton: Princeton University Press.

Harvey, D. (2005). *A Brief History of Neoliberalism*. New York: Oxford University Press.

Hirschman, A. O. (1945). *National Power and the Structure of Foreign Trade*. Berkeley: University of California Press.

Hirschman, A. O. (1981). *Essays in Trespassing*. Cambridge: Cambridge University Press.

Hodgson, G. M. (2006). What Are Institutions? *Journal of Economic Issues, XL*(1), 1–25.

Keohane, R. O. (1989). *International Institutions and State Power: Essays in International Relations Theory*. Boulder: Westview Press.

Keohane, R. O., & Nye, J. S., Jr. (1977). *Power and Interdependence: World Politics in Transition*. Boston: Little, Brown.

Khan, M. H., & Jomo, K. S. (2000). *Rents, Rent-Seeking and Economic Development. Theory and Evidence in Asia*. Cambridge: Cambridge University Press.

Knight, F. H. (1921). *Risk, Uncertainty, and Profit*. Boston/New York: Houghton Mifflin Co..

Knorr, K. (1977). International Economic Leverage and Its Uses. In K. Knorr & F. Trager (Eds.), *Economic Issues and National Security*. Lawrence: University Press of Kansas.

Mann, M. (1984). The Autonomous Power of the State: Its Origins, Mechanisms and Results. *European Journal of Sociology / Archives Européennes de Sociologie / Europäisches Archiv für Soziologie, 25*(2), 185–213.

Mann, M. (1997). Has Globalization Ended the Rise and Fall of the Nation State? *Review of International Political Economy, 4*(3), 472–496.

Mazzucato, M. (2013). *The Entrepreneurial State. Debunking Public vs. Private Sector Myths*. UK and USA: Anthem Press.

Mirowski, P., & Plehwe, D. (2009). *The Road from Mont Pèlerin. The Making of the Neoliberal Thought Collective*. Cambridge, MA/London: Harvard University Press.

North, D. C. (1990). *Institutions, Institutional Change, and Economic Performance*. Cambridge, UK: Cambridge University Press.

North, D. C. (1992). "Transaction Costs, Institutions, and Economic Performance". International Center for Economic Growth, Occasional Papers, 30.

Nye, J. S. (1990). *Bound to Lead: The Changing Nature of American Power*. New York: Basic Books.

Panitch, L., & Gindin, S. (2012). *The Making of Global Capitalism: The Political Economy of American Empire*. London: Verso.

Robbins, L. (1932). *An Essay on the Nature and Significance of Economic Science*. London: Macmillan & Co.

Saad-Filho, A. (2014). The 'Rise of the South': Global Convergence at Last? *New Political Economy, 19*(4), 578–600.

Salamon, L. M., & Siegfried, J. J. (1977). Economic Power and Political Influence: The Impact of Industry Structure on Public Policy. *American Political Science Review, 71*, 1026–1043.

Schrank, A. J., & Whitford, J. (2009). Industrial Policy in the United States: A Neo-Polanyian Interpretation. *Politics and Society, 37*(4), 521–553.

Sen, A. (2001). *Development as Freedom*. Oxford: Oxford University Press.

Simon, H. A. (1957). *Models of Man: Social and Rational*. New York: Wiley.

Tassinari, M. (2014). Industrial Policy in the United States. The Theoretical Debate, the Rhetoric, and Practices in the Era of the Washington Consensus, L'Industria. *Rivista di Economia e Politica Industriale, 35*(1), 69–100.

Tregenna, F. (2009). Characterising Deindustrialisation: An Analysis of Changes in Manufacturing Employment and Output Internationally. *Cambridge Journal of Economics, 33*(3), 433–466.

Tregenna, F. (2014). A New Theoretical Analysis of Deindustrialisation. *Cambridge Journal of Economics, 38*(6), 1373–1390.

Triandis, H. C. (1995). *Individualism and Collectivism*. Boulder: Westview Press.

Wade, R. H. (2003). What Strategies are Viable for Developing Countries Today? The World Trade Organization and the Shrinking of 'Development Space'. *Review of International Political Economy, 10*(4), 621–644.

Wade, R. H. (2004). Is Globalization Reducing Poverty and Inequality? *World Development, 32*(4), 567–589.

Weiss, L. (1998). *The Myth of the Powerless State*. Ithaca: Cornell University Press.

Weiss, L. (2014). *America Inc.? Innovation and Enterprise in the National Security State*. New York: Cornell University Press.

Williamson, O. E. (1979). Transaction Cost Economics: The Governance of Contractual Relations. *Journal of Law and Economics, 22*(October), 3–61.

CHAPTER 2

Contextualizing the American Industrial Strategy in the Neoliberal Era

This book is devoted to the analysis of the American Industrial Strategy and how it has influenced global economic interactions. The temporal focus of the analysis is the period running from the 1970s to the present day, what can be identified as the *neoliberal era*. However, in order to properly explain how the US industrial strategy has taken shape during this period, we need to consider the historical context and conditions which have allowed the government to set in with such a role. For this reason, this chapter presents a reflection on the US public intervention in industrial dynamics from a long-term historical perspective. The main aim is to outline the key elements of the "American industrial strategies", which exercised their influence before the neoliberal era and represent its triggering factor.

The discussion is organized considering three different "American industrial strategies" implemented in the time span that goes from the US independence to the beginning of the neoliberal era: the Hamiltonian Strategy (1791–1861), the Oligopolistic Strategy (1861–1914) and the Keynesian Strategy (1914–1973) (see Fig. 2.1). Each "American strategy" has peculiar features related to how the US government managed, in the different historical contexts, the relationships between the diverse interests and powers at stake, interpreting the interest of the American society as whole. Changes in the relationships between industry, government and civil society, in the interests that each of these subsystems pursued and in

© The Author(s) 2019   17
M. Tassinari, *Capitalising Economic Power in the US*,
International Political Economy Series,
https://doi.org/10.1007/978-3-319-76648-5_2

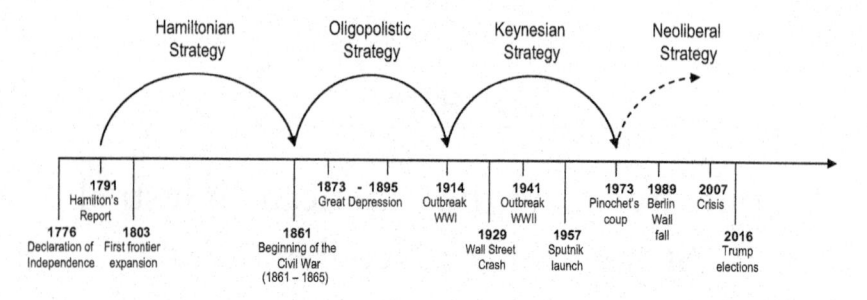

Fig. 2.1 American industrial strategies timeline (Source: Author's elaboration)

the formal and informal institutional channels through which these interests were expressed, caused transformations in the ways through which industrial development was promoted over the decades. These changes are not radical but—on the contrary—incremental, so that each industrial strategy is the result of the past history and conserves some of the elements of the previous paradigms. As a result, the industrial strategy *in the neoliberal era* is the product not just of contingent and short-term factors, but of a long-run process of economic and institutional transformation too, whereby some elements of the previous approaches remain present even though the overall general paradigm is changed.

The Hamiltonian Strategy (1791–1861)

Not many moments in American history have been as passionate as that in which the United States had just acquired their political independence. Autonomy from the European colonies projected the American population and economy towards the building of a new nation. Those were the years where the different interests of the American society confronted and clashed with each other, laying the foundations for the constitution and growth of what would become the leading actor of the global economy.

Since those days, the US government began to play a leading role in conditioning the American economic development trajectory. In particular, the idea that America should concentrate its productive forces on the creation of its own manufacturing structure started to emerge in political circles (Scheiber 1987; Chang 2007; Di Tommaso and Schweitzer 2013). After all, in those decades, radical industrialization processes had already begun, in England and in the rest of Europe, which served as an inspiration for the American political elite. Economic and social development created by the first industrial revolution became an icon of modernity, and it is not difficult to imagine how some politicians could see in these processes a path that could characterize the United States as well. What was at stake, once political independence had been gained, was the ability to conquer economic and industrial independence too.

It was the Secretary of the Treasury Alexander Hamilton who first gave concrete impetus towards industrialization. In 1791, he presented to Congress the *Report on the Subject of Manufacturing*, with which he proposed a detailed plan for American industrial development (Hamilton 1791). The document defined a clear long-term strategy for the promotion of the emerging US industry. Hamilton's prescriptions were concerned with establishing subsidies directed to strategic industries (including iron, copper, coal, cotton, glass, gunpowder and books), tariffs on imported products, tax exemption for raw materials, prohibition to export of innovative products and machineries to avoid appropriation by foreign competition, and support for the improvement of national infrastructure (Hamilton 1791; Chang 2007; Di Tommaso and Schweitzer 2013).

Initially Hamilton's plan found some resistance in Congress (Williams 1966; Scheiber 1987; Chang 2007). Indeed, the promotion and protection of American industry in the northern territories contrasted with the interest of southern farmers, who would see prices for imported products raised and an inferior quality of the manufactured goods made in America. Contrasts between north and south would become unsustainable in the subsequent decades, and would finally explode in the Civil War. In this scenario characterized by different and conflicting interests, the pressure on industry protection and manufacturing development was able to prevail and influence the American political system. As documented by Chang (2007), for example, as early as 1820, the average duty on imported products amounted to 40%. Hamilton's Industrial Plan found in those years full application, and constituted the basis for the future development and growth of American manufacturing. The increasing interventionism of the federal government during these decades played a crucial role in the organization of national production, in the dynamics of industrial development and in managing the social conflicts that these processes would generate.

In the same decades, these dynamics were also encouraged by a context of growing resources: the "expansion of the frontier", namely the acquisition of the western territories, was of crucial importance for the development of the American productive structure as a whole. The expansion to the west was supported by the government since the early 1800s. President Jefferson's expansionist strategy found its first foundation in the power that the trade relations established with the Indians could exercise in persuading them to liberate the occupied territories. In a message to the Congress on 18 January 1803 he stated:

> The Indian tribes residing within the limits of the United States, have, for a considerable time, been growing more and more uneasy at the constant diminution of the territory they occupy, although effected by their own voluntary sales: and the policy has long been gaining strength with them, of refusing absolutely all further sale, on any conditions; insomuch that, at this time, it hazards their friendship, and excites dangerous jealousies and perturbations in their minds to make any overture for the purchase of the smallest portions of their land. A very few tribes only are not yet obstinately in these dispositions. In order peaceably to counteract this policy of theirs, and to provide an extension of territory which the rapid increase of our numbers will call for, two measures are deemed expedient. First: to encourage them to abandon hunting, to apply to the raising stock, to agriculture and domestic manufacture, and thereby prove to themselves that less land and labor will maintain them in this, better than in their former mode of living. The extensive forests necessary in the hunting life, will then become useless, and they will see advantage in exchanging them for the means of improving their farms, and of increasing their domestic comforts. Secondly: to multiply trading houses among them, and place within their reach those things which will contribute more to their domestic comfort, than the possession of extensive, but uncultivated wilds.[1]

Building on these premises, the US expansionist policy would become increasingly aggressive towards the Indians, and within the time span of 50 years America would acquire most of the territories outside the frontier, covering almost all the current territory. Westward expansion gave, at this stage, a crucial impulse to American growth and development. It represented an enlargement of the American markets' scope, by providing land and productive resources. Moreover, the shifting of the western frontier stimulated industrial growth, productive specialization and economies of scale by formulating a massive new demand for infrastructure, weapons and any other good or service necessary to the expeditions and to the subsequent development of the acquired localities.

In this context, it is not a coincidence that from the early decades of the nineteenth century, the railways became one of the most strategic industries in the eyes of the American government. As the US territory was expanding, transport infrastructures played a crucial role in connecting people and goods. In these decades, the government was in charge of planning, financing and providing technical and managerial assistance to this industry (Dobbin 1994). Initially, local governments and states, in partnership with the private sector, played the main role in the development of the railroads. They allocated funds to cities that were interested in having a railway station, while private companies were in charge of building the railway lines. Financial strategies, since this first development phase of the sector, were designed and implemented by the governments, whereby the rail industry would be entrusted to private companies, even when most of the funds were allocated by the public administrations (Dobbin 1994).

THE OLIGOPOLISTIC STRATEGY (1861–1914)

The support and protection of the American infant industry, as Hamilton had suggested, along with the progressive expansion of the frontier, were factors that, in the first half of the nineteenth century, had played a decisive role in the growth and structural changes of the US economy. In this context, as early as during the years of the Civil War (1861–1865), the structure of the American economy started to be characterized by a few large corporations which had been able to strengthen their economic power in several national industries. In addition, the Great Depression of the 1870s, 1880s and 1890s would intensify market concentration by increasing the power of a number of large firms that would be able to survive the crisis and operate in a much less competitive environment. As a result, since the early 1860s, the government started to deal with the problems caused by radical processes of economic power concentration in the hands of few large industrial players (Stein 1998; Freyer 1992; Sandel 1996; Sullivan 1991). Indeed, this condition was fundamentally at risk of creating sharp contrasts within the civil society because of the high prices that the lack of competition could generate and the growing political influence that the corporations began to exercise in Congress.

The state of affairs demanded regulation of competition and the federal government commenced to play a new leading role in the dynamics of the national industry. The regulatory activity was essentially based on bargaining processes between government and large industrial groups. On the one hand, the government had to consider the role that big corporations were playing in driving the entire national productive structure, in terms of, for example, employment, demand for intermediate goods and competitiveness in international markets. These factors were at the base of the electoral consent to the government, which was consequently interested in protecting the interest of these industrial groups. On the other hand, however, the government had to be vigilant so that the abuse of market power would not become unsustainable for consumers.

This new government's role in the dynamics of economic and industrial development emerged decisively as early as the 1860s when the federal government took control of the railway sector (Dobbin 1994). While in the previous decades the local and national governments had simply managed the development of the sector, from these years on, the very dynamics of the railway industry started to be controlled centrally. The high tariffs paid by sea freight forwarders for the railway service had begun to cause tensions, demanding the intervention of the federal government for price regulation. The problem stemmed from the spread of corruption among railroad officers, and called for a sharp downsizing of local government intervention (Dobbin 1994). As stated by Dobbin (1994): "In the United States, corruption evidenced the inherent threat to political order posed by state expansion. Americans were certain that their governments had overstepped their bounds in offering aid to railroads, and forswore future, government aid to enterprise" (Dobbin 1994: 58).

However, in this new federally regulated context, the role of the government was not just limited to industry supervision and price control. It was also directed to promoting the development of the four major transcontinental lines, by providing land, guarantees and mortgages to the private industry and working in close partnership with it (Dobbin 1994). In this way, the federal government started to negotiate with an industry that had become de facto too important in the growth dynamics of the national economy. The Interstate Commerce Act of 1887 played a crucial role in establishing the government's position in regulating the railway system. This act created the first federal regulatory agency, the *Interstate Commerce Commission* (ICC), specifically in charge of managing industry-related issues (Bingham and Sharpe 1998).[2]

However, the railway sector was not an isolated case.

The steel industry is another example that clearly describes how the concentration of industrial power was, at this stage, becoming crucial in the US development dynamic and how this process closely involved the government in a managerial role of this oligopolistic power. The steel sector had played a central role in the expansion of the railways, and for this reason it had benefited from high protectionist rates since the independence. In 1855, the *American Iron and Steel Association* had been founded, with the specific aim of negotiating with the federal government protection from foreign competition (Nester 1997; Wilson 2006). In this context, inefficient companies had been able to remain in the market despite the overly high prices and low quality of their products. However, in the subsequent years, with the crisis of the second half of the nineteenth century, the actual problems of the sector started to emerge. When the demand for steel dropped, many companies were forced to close. In this situation, allowing and encouraging merger processes within this industry were considered a solution to the sector's troubles. The birth of a powerful national oligopoly was de facto accepted. In 1901, the *United States Steel Corporation* (USSC) was the first billionaire corporation in the iron and steel industry (Stein 1998: 11). At that time, the USSC held about 65% of the national market, and this position was tolerated for a long time in the name of national interest (Stein 1998).

Beyond the individual cases, these years laid the foundations for the more general institutional framework through which the government ruled its relations with the entire national industry. The Sherman Antitrust Act of 1890 and the Clayton Antitrust Act of 1914 are a central part of this institutional framework. The former aimed at controlling established monopolistic powers, whereas the latter aimed at regulating mergers and acquisitions between companies, in order to prevent further market concentration. However, whilst the logic behind these two acts was clear, the government's real capacity to intervene against economic power concentrations was rather weak (Stein 1998; Freyer 1992; Thorelli 1955). In relation to monopoly attempts (governed by Section 2 of the Sherman Antitrust Act of 1890), despite the numerous lawsuit for antitrust law breaches, the US government's wins against private companies were very few. Indeed the judges had interpreted the application of the legislation in a way that any accusation of monopolization had to be sustained by evidence of contracts, alliances or conspiracies of illegal nature (Prodi and De Giovanni 1988; Freyer 1992; Sullivan 1991; Stein 1998; Sandel 1996). This interpretation, however, was largely limitative, as market power could often be acquired by a corporation through actions that were part of normal business management and could not be considered illegal (Stein 1998; Freyer 1992; Adams and Brock 1986). As a result, this approach had de facto legitimated all the concentrations where it was not possible to prove illegal monopoly practices.[3] In the following years, this interpretation of the Sherman Act was surpassed in favour of a logic which required the verification of the existence of a real market concentration and of an excessive market power. In this new perspective, the central issue in order to apply the antitrust law became focused on the definition of the "relevant market". However, even with this new interpretation (which remained in force until the end of the 1960s), the government did not increase its real ability to contrast the monopolistic power: the federal government lost innumerable cases against some of the largest American companies, in particular because of disputes about the size of the relevant market to be considered in the legal action (Prodi and De Giovanni 1988; Stein 1998).

Also, the legislation to prevent market concentration, namely the Clayton Antitrust Act of 1914, was basically a failure. The law prohibited companies from acquiring, directly or indirectly, all or part of the shares of another enterprise if this could in any way reduce competition in the market. The law, however, was applicable only to mergers conducted by acquiring stocks and this legitimated all other purchases that took place through different channels.

As a result, the antitrust laws of these years designed an institutional framework in which ample space was left to individual negotiations between government and industry and to the tolerance towards national cartels and oligopolies.

However, the national industry and large corporations were not the only important interlocutors with which the government had to relate. Other groups of the American society played a role in counterbalancing—to some extent at least—industrial power by negotiating with the government.

In this context, the government—while it was gaining political consent by responding to industry demands—could not ignore the role of the *Labour Unions*. Indeed, if this interlocutor had not been taken into account, the whole system would have faced dangerous consequences (Williams 1966: 506). In 1886, the American Federation of Labor (AFL) was formed and it began to manage the relationship between governments and industry. It was, however, a trade union that did not question the existing order in its essence and, perhaps for this reason, it was the organization that, among others, was able to grow and enter the bargaining system. Certainly, during these years, there were some huge groups of workers that were not represented in the American negotiating framework, and whose bad conditions were functional to the prosperity of the system. In this regard, the economic growth of the nineteenth century was also fuelled by workforce who was unskilled, poorly educated and willing to do the most exhausting and badly paid jobs. There were no bargaining powers above the government for these workers. They were mainly immigrants, who were more than eight million at the beginning of the twentieth century (Briggs 1984; Daniels 2001; Ciment and Radzilowski 2012; Alexander 2009).

In short, at the end of the period running from the second half of the nineteenth century until the early 1900s, the main actors of the American economy and society had found a "functional" organization and had established their role in the system. In this framework, the equilibrium in the government-industry-civil society relationship started to constitute the base for the future economic and industrial development of the United States. In such equilibrium political and industrial interests were aligned and marched in the same direction. Large corporations had ceased to be a threat to the public order, and, rather, they had become the fulcrum of the entire economic and social system.[4] For example, in 1914 President Wilson asserted: "The antagonism between business and Government is over ... the Government and business men are ready to meet each other halfway in a common effort to square business methods with both public opinion and public law" (Wilson 1914, quoted in Crockett 2002: 114). Likewise, Herbert Hoover a few years later said: "I believe that we are, almost unnoticed, in the midst of a great revolution - or perhaps a better word, a transformation - in the whole super-organization of our economic life. We are passing from a period of extremely individualistic action into a period of associational activities" (Hoover 1922, quoted in Abend 2014: 179). This setting would continue to characterize the US political economy dynamics throughout the twentieth century.

THE KEYNESIAN STRATEGY (1914–1973)

At the beginning of the twentieth century, the productive capacity of the American economy was becoming enormous. In 1908 Henry Ford had launched the famous T-Model in the car market.[5] This car contained in itself the passage to a new industrial era. *Fordism*, which started in the automotive industry, quickly spread into many sectors of the American (and international) economy as an innovative production model. New ways of organizing economic activities and labour within factories began to exponentially increase productivity.

In this situation, the government soon realized that finding a new demand for consumption and new markets where the productive forces could be released and provide growth opportunities for the American economy as a whole was a necessity. Having reached the limit of the domestic *frontier*, the new demand for American products had to be sought in overseas expansions, by increasing the presence of the United States in international markets. The growth of the American economic system and social sustainability were based on this dynamic, and this was crystal clear to the political men of that period. For example, President Wilson, who set up at the White House in 1913, asserted:

> America's domestic market is too small: we have reached, in short, a crucial point in the process of our prosperity. It has become a question with us whether it shall continue or shall not continue. If [America] doesn't get bigger foreign markets, she will burst her jacket. There will be a congestion in this country which will be more fatal economically than any wider opening of the ports could be. (Wilson, quoted in Williams 1966: 511–2)

The outbreak of the First World War, in 1914, was a first response to the need to increase demand for American products. Belligerent economies began to formulate a new important demand for US goods and services. American exports to Europe rose, during these years, from $1.479 billion to $4.062 billion.[6] In addition, in 1917, when the United States actively took part in the war, the federal government's military spending meant a constant demand for consumption from the government to the American industry, which could therefore grow in production volumes, in efficiency of productive processes and in technological capacities, protected from foreign competition. Federal spending in the United States saw a swift increase, from $477 million in 1916 to its peak in 1918 of $8.450 billion. Various sectors were involved, including food, clothing, guns, ammunition and shipbuilding.[7]

As argued by Williams (1966),

> In sum, entry into World War I was part of the transformation of the American society that had already begun... American leaders had turned to overseas economic expansion as the strategy of recovery and future prosperity *before* the United States became involved in the conflicts as either a non-fighting belligerent or an active military protagonist... the system began to produce welfare and a sense of community only as a by-product of warfare. (Williams 1966: 415–6)

Indeed, the First World War was only the beginning of an industrial growth dynamic based on the war economy. The United States—for the decades to come and until the present—would be committed in a long series of armed conflicts and in the Cold War, establishing a model of growth and technological development based on military public demand.

However, at the end of the First World War it was clear that the problem of the lack of an adequate market demand, able to keep up with the growing productivity and investment of the US manufacturing capacity, was not solved. Income and wealth inequalities generated insufficient domestic consumption. One of the toughest overproduction crisis—the Great Depression—would overwhelm the United States, and the government would soon be called upon to play a decisive role in formulating demand for goods and services to the American private sector. The growing expansion in productive capacity, not adequately supported by domestic consumption and international demand, was accompanied by stock market speculation, which led to an increase in the value of shares not supported by a real increase in sales of goods and services. The Wall Street Crash of October 1929 destroyed the stock value of many savers who, in the uncertain climate, withdrew their bank deposits, denying liquidity to the industrial system. Moreover, consumption started to reduce with the consequent increasing of the unemployment rate. The recession triggered a vicious circle that involved the whole American economy, spreading eventually to the international level (Krugman, 2008; Gjerstad and Smith 2009; Allen and Moessner 2012).

During the Great Depression years, the government had to necessarily intervene to respond to the economic and social issues that arose from the system. This context contributed to deeply root in the American system a model of development in which the government was a crucial actor in formulating a massive demand for goods and services to the domestic industry, and not just in war times. Not only did this kind of intervention, of *Keynesian* inspiration, serve the interest of the American industry, but—at that time—it did represent a strategy able to reconcile the different interests of the US society. Indeed, Roosevelt's New Deal cannot be described simply as a response to the economic crisis. It had the ability to link the interests of the industrial class to a more general collective interest. As Keynes had suggested, the expansion of the demand and consumption of the mass of workers could revitalize the economy and foster the system as a whole (Shonfield 1965).

In this framework, jobs and public procurements were promoted in order to boost employment and support domestic demand. The whole American industry was subsidized. The National Industrial Recovery Act of 1933 established the Public Works Administration for the implementation of a large public works programme. The Buy American Act of 1933 had the goal of stimulating domestic demand by imposing limits on the purchase of foreign products in public contracts, thus supporting a great part of the national industry (Frank 1999). At the same time, the government further alleviated the antitrust pressure for companies, which established new trusts and monopolies recognized of national interests (Dobbin 1993). In the context of the *New Deal*, the Reconstruction Finance Corporation (RFC)—a national development bank created to subsidize companies and industries—was central. The RFC was proposed by Hoover in 1932 to replace the War Finance Corporation (WFC), which had been created by President Wilson in 1918 to fund the war industry during the First World War. At the end of the Hoover legislature, the RFC had provided $1.6 billion in mortgages to numerous financial institutions and to the railway industry. During the New Deal years, from 1932 to 1935, the RFC distributed over $2 billion to businesses unable to obtain credit from the private sector (Bingham and Sharpe 1998).

The Roosevelt Administration then decided to promote an ambitious reform of the national banking sector that had shown, in those years, obvious frailties and weaknesses. The Banking Acts of 1933 and 1935 defined a series of actions to protect banks. In 1933, the Federal Deposit Insurance Corporation was created, separating commercial banks from investment banks. The Glass-Steagall Act of 1933 introduced the Regulation Q, which imposed limits on interest rates and a zero interest rate on current accounts, which essentially constituted a permanent subsidy accorded by the government to the sector (Bingham and Sharpe 1998). In those years, the Federal Reserve System was also reformed. A new internal organ was created, the Federal Open Market Committee, whose board of directors was charged to define the monetary policy.

During the 1930s, some specific sectors were particularly favoured by government interventions.

The steel industry was once again the subject of particular attention by the administration, which operated by responding to the demand of industrialists and considering the interest of the masses of workers employed in the sector. In this framework, the Smoot-Hawley Act of 1930 and the Reciprocal Trade Act of 1934 were crucial to save the industry from collapse (Di Tommaso and Schweitzer 2013).

The Roosevelt Administration also intervened in the agricultural sector. A central measure was the Agricultural Adjustment Act of 1933, which had the main purpose of guaranteeing farmers greater income levels. During these years of crisis, the Department of Agriculture was in charge of planning the agricultural production at a central level. Since 1938, the

Commodity Credit Corporation—a federal agency regulating agricultural commodity prices—began to grant loans by accepting as guarantees the garnered agricultural products (Bingham and Sharpe 1998).[8]

Another industry in which the US government intervened decisively during the 1930s was air transportation. Since 1925 the Congress had authorized the privatization of the airmail service, and in a short time private distribution had gained the main role. While initially the government had paid the private sector on the basis of the amount of mail delivered, in 1930 the government changed policy and began to pay transporters according to plane size and whether the aircraft also had seats for passenger transport. This mode of payment provided an incentive to the development of the passenger transport service. This resulted in an increase in demand for new and larger aircrafts, which encouraged innovation in the industry and the development of new business services. Moreover, in 1938, the Civil Aeronautics Act was enacted. It was a regulation system that, through the Civil Aeronautics Board (CAB), promoted a more structured postal, commercial and military air transport (Bingham and Sharpe 1998). At any rate, in the following years this emerging industry would find new sources of public support in the context of a country involved in the Second World War.

Indeed, the American economy was progressively returning to be driven by military necessities. The National Defence Act of 1920 had already predisposed that the War Department should set up a plan to mobilize the entire economy to prepare it for a possible war. Subsequently, various detailed plans for industrial mobilization were elaborated (in 1930, 1933, 1936 and the last in 1939 when the war was approaching) (Nester 1997). In 1940 Roosevelt formed the National Defence Advisory Commission Board, which in 1941, was replaced by the Office of Production Mobilization (later renamed the War Production Board). This agency cooperated with the Production Executive Committee and the Office of War Mobilization, involving government officials, military leaders and private industry managers in order to coordinate and manage the entire national industrial productive capacity to meet military needs. In this framework, with the Berry Amendment of 1941, foreign competitors were excluded from the supply of goods and services to the defence sector (Weiss and Thurbon 2006).

The growing public demand for goods and services to the private sector and government funds for military-led research and development (R&D) stimulated the development of economies of scale and learning in particular industries.

In the automobile industry, for example, the American Automobile Manufacturers Association was transformed, during the war years, into the Automotive Council for War Production. In this context the government purchased from the national automotive industry for a value of about $30 billion (Bingham and Sharpe 1998). Then, at the end of the war, the Office for War Mobilization and Reconversion was founded. It authorized the public purchase of 100,000 cars in 1945 to start conversion to the civilian market (Bingham and Sharpe 1998). In addition, the car industry further benefited from a massive federal programme for building the national highway network (governed by the Interstate Highway Act of 1956) (Williamson 2012).

The naval sector was another industry strongly affected by government intervention during these years. The industry had already been involved in the government's industrial plans during the First World War. The war had provided the opportunity to protect and finance the construction of an American fleet that could compete globally, not only in war time but also in supporting foreign trade. When the war ended, most ships were sold to private companies at prices far below market rates. The effects of this policy had turned out to be disastrous: the demand for new ships had collapsed and in 1928, the government had been forced to save the national industry by allocating new subsidies and granting the protection from foreign competition (ABMC 1938; Bingham and Sharpe 1998). During the Second World War, the government essentially repeated what had happened in the First World War. The administration supported a large programme for the construction of warships. At the end of the conflict, the American naval industry was no longer able to compete autonomously on private markets, remaining dependent on the federal government's demand and subsidies (Bingham and Sharpe 1998).

At any rate, when the Second World War ended, new and attractive perspectives arose for the American economy. Many of the world economies that had taken part in the war had to face important reconstruction processes. In this context, American aid, granted under the "Marshall Plan", was undoubtedly a decisive factor to a rapid economic recovery in Europe, as well as it represented a crucial element for the US economy itself, by fuelling demand for American goods and services (Hogan 1987). Of the 13 billion dollars allocated by the United States until 1951, a great part of it was spent for American productions (3.4 for raw materials and semi-finished products, 3.2 for food and fertilizers, 1.9 for machinery and vehicles, 1.6 for fuel) (Hogan 1987). However, the Marshall Plan also had long-term effects. A strong relationship between some European countries and the American industry was established and this would link European demand for goods, services and technology to the US economy for many decades to come.

In this context, the United States was progressively acquiring global leadership, and not just under the economic profile. The end of the war puts—de facto—the United States in the position of coordinating the construction of the international institutional framework of the following decades. With the Bretton Woods Conference, a system of fixed exchange rates was set up to tie international currencies to the value of the dollar. The International Monetary Fund, the World Bank and the General Agreement on Tariff and Trade were also created. As this book is going to point out in the following chapters, these international institutions would maintain a preferential relationship with the United States in the decades ahead, favouring the emergence of a global governance under American influence.

Furthermore, in the context of Post-Second World War, a new threat could once again justify the US intervention in the domestic *military-industrial complex*. The *Cold War* was rapidly invading the international scene and the federal government decided to step up military and technological efforts to assert its supremacy globally (Block 2008; Mazzucato 2013; Weiss 2014). Competition with the Soviet Union was principally based on the ability to prove military and technological superiority, as a deterrent for the adversaries of the war. This dynamic basically legitimated the continuity with the model of economic and industrial development of the Second World War, expanding its scope. Federal government's expenditure fuelled an important and growing public demand for goods, services and technologies. The US private companies could rely on the government as costumer and, protected from foreign competition, they started to increase production volumes, to develop economies of scale and learning and to improve their innovative capacity. The massive R&D activity conducted for military purposes—and funded by public resources (as the Vannevar Bush's report of 1945 prescribed)—became the source of important innovations and dual-use technologies, which were subsequently applied and commercialized in private markets. It was estimated that the Cold War stimulated military spending programmes for a total value of about $16 trillion, of which $4 trillion was spent on nuclear weapons (Nester 1997: 149; Schwartz 1998; Mowery 1998).

At the beginning of the Cold War, the institutional framework concerning national security was strengthened. In 1948, the National Security

Council (NSC) and the Central Intelligence Agency (CIA) were created. In the following years, public commissions in the military field as well as many other public spending programmes dedicated to specific issues progressively increased. A decisive turning point in this direction was in 1957, the year when the Soviets launched the *Sputnik*, the first satellite orbiting around the Earth (Weiss 2014). It was an event that—highlighting the Soviet Union's progress in the field of technology—pushed the United States to drastically intensify their military and technological efforts. In 1958 the Advanced Research Projects Agency (ARPA) (later renamed the Defence Advanced Research Projects Agency [DARPA]), National Aeronautics and Space Administration (NASA) and the Small Business Investment Corporation (SBIC) were created, with the specific aim of promoting technological innovation in military and civil fields (Block 2008; Fuchs 2010; Weiss 2014). At the end of the 1960s, government spending in the defence sector was close to 9% of the US GDP, while R&D expenditure increased from 1.5% of US GDP to over 3% (Weiss 2014; Block and Keller 2011; Mazzucato 2013).

In this context, *software* and computer industries benefited of massive public investments (Markusen et al. 1991; Abbate 1999; Fong 2001; Lazonick 2008; Breakthrough Institute 2010; Mazzucato 2013). A growing amount of computers was demanded by a number of US departments and agencies, such as the Department of Defence (DoD), Air Force, Army Signal Corps, Atomic Energy Commission, NASA, US Weather Bureau and National Institute of Health and Social Security Administration. This massive public demand encouraged private companies to develop new products and new technologies while enjoying protection from foreign competition (Mazzucato 2013; Block 2008).[9] For example, during the 1960s, DARPA funded the research that led to the birth and development of Internet, paying private partners to develop a network capable of connecting each other's computers operating in different locations: in 1969, two computers were connected for the first time from the University of California Los Angeles (UCLA) to Stanford through a telephone line (Abbate 1999; Ceruzzi 2003; Kenney 2003; Rand 2011; Di Tommaso and Schweitzer 2013).

Similarly, the memory chip industry rapidly evolved, during this period, thanks to the growing demand from the Air Force and NASA, which in 1960s and 1970s implemented the Apollo Program for space exploration (Ceruzzi 2003; Mazzucato 2013; Di Tommaso and Schweitzer 2013).

The development of nuclear energy for civil purposes also sprang up from national security and military necessities. The Manhattan Project began the study of nuclear energy in 1941. Four years later, the American aviation released the atomic bombs on Hiroshima and Nagasaki. At the end of the war, the federal government began to support some research centres for the development of nuclear energy for civil purposes. The Atomic Energy Commission became responsible for coordinating the research activities in this field, which were entrusted to the Argonne National Laboratory at the University of Chicago. In 1954, with President Eisenhower, the Atomic Energy Act was approved. It encouraged technological progress for nuclear power generation. In the same year, the Atomic Energy Commission announced the Power Demonstration Reactor Program, which was based on the cooperation between the federal government and two private companies for the production of the first generation of nuclear reactors (The US Joint Committee on Atomic Energy 1955). Between the late 1950s and the early 1960s, the federal government further funded this sector. In these years, the first nuclear power plant was inaugurated by President Eisenhower in the framework of his *Atom for Peace Program*. Starting from this first decisive public effort, this industry would see, during the 1970s, a rapid development due to the need to increase US domestic energy production to face the two oil crises of 1973 and 1979. Of course, the problem of how to satisfy the domestic demand for energy still remains today one of the major issues that affect American political economy and its international relations in many areas of the world.

Another example of industry that saw its development in the Cold War circumstances is the biotechnology sector. In 1969, President Nixon converted the national programme for the construction of biological weapons into scientific research activities for the development of the biomedical sector: in 1974, the National Institute of Health had already funded a total of 123 new biotechnology projects, encouraging academic research in this field and the development of important collaborations between businesses and universities (Hurt 2011).

In this scenario—where the Soviet threat was legitimizing a constant and massive public demand for goods, services and technologies to the private industries—the American economic growth became exponential. In this context, the US industry could rely on a growing domestic market and on a post-war international framework where competition with foreign firms was weak. 1950s and 1960s were the years of a massive economic boom, in which millions of Americans improved their life standards.

However, not all social groups benefited in the same way from this particular conjuncture. While the American middle class grew along with the productive capacity of the industry, the degradation of some metropolitan areas was evident, especially in the southern states. Modernization and mechanization of agriculture since the early 1930s had progressively created unemployment and mass migration towards metropolitan areas in search for jobs. In other words, while automation in manufacturing sectors such as steel, automobile and mining had meant new industrial products, rising demand of skilled workers and higher wages, agriculture-based territories were releasing unqualified manpower (Stein 1998). After all, it was quite obvious that the American development model, which placed the war tensions at the foundation of its economic progress, risked to be overly unbalanced towards the pursuit of industrial and defence-related interests, raising serious concerns about the protection of minorities. During Lyndon Johnson's presidency, at the White House from November 1963 after Kennedy's assassination, it was clear that the American system had, in some ways, failed in producing adequate living conditions for all Americans:

> The United States has long been a rich country. The abundance of our material output is one of the wonders of the world. [...] Yet we know that our society is imperfect. The President has sounded the keynote for a new effort to address ourselves to social problems which have been in our consciousness but which we have failed to attack with the full use of the great technical, social, and economic resources that we possess. World War II, and the long cold war diverted our effort to other matters. (ERP 1965: 145)

The social policies implemented by President Johnson, which took the name of *Great Society* policies, somehow tried to address poverty, degradation and racial marginalization, which were characterizing many large cities. The Great Society was a series of federal programmes (some of which had been launched by President Kennedy but remained locked in Congress after his assassination), aimed at promoting education, health, welfare services, social security and poverty reduction (ERP 1965: 153). From 1960 to 1967, this kind of social programmes increased from 132 to 379, with an increase in spending from $8.6 billion in 1963 to $20.3 billion in 1969 (Reischauer 1986). These programmes remained operative for many years, and some of them, like Medicaid, Medicare, Older Americans Act, still are (Zelizer 2015).[10]

Nevertheless, the Great Society's initiatives had short life. The Johnson administration soon found strong resistance in Congress due, in particular, to its resolutions about the Vietnam War, which had raised important protests in the civil society. Following the loss of the Democratic majority in Congress in 1966 mid-term elections, the Great Society project lost much of its initial strength, and the remaining part of Johnson's mandate was dedicated to managing the pressure from Republicans seeking austerity and cuts in public spending (Helsing 2000). Indeed, from these years industrial interests started to dedicate more and more attention to private investments and capital accumulation. In this context the Keynesian approach began to decline, foreshadowing the oncoming neoliberal era (see, e.g. Harvey 2005).

CONCLUSION

This chapter has presented from a long-term perspective the historical context of the American industrial strategy in the neoliberal era. In particular, this chapter has considered the main features of the role of the government in the US industrial dynamic, which have exercised their influence before the neoliberal era. The discussion has been organized considering three different "American industrial strategies", each of which was implemented in a period of about 60 years, in the time span that goes from the US independence to the beginning of the neoliberal era: the Hamiltonian Strategy (1791–1861), the Oligopolistic Strategy (1861–1914) and the Keynesian Strategy (1914–1973).

The first approach to industrialization, after the American political independency, saw the government committed to promoting the main infant industries of that time, such as railroad, iron and steel, textile, coal and weapons. In this context, the strategy was essentially to subsidize and protect the US productive system from foreign competition, as Alexander Hamilton had outlined in his *Report on the Subject of Manufacturing* (1791). In the same decades, this dynamic was strengthened by the expansion of the *frontier*, which provided a context of growing resources; this element proved to be of crucial importance for the development of the American productive structure as a whole. In over about 50 years, the United States acquired most of the territories outside the frontier. These are the years of conflict among different interests, in which American industrial vocation is still challenged by contrasts with farmers in the south of the country.

With the Civil War (1861–1865), the divergences between industrialists and farmers exploded. From these years, a new phase of the government role in the American economy started. In the second half of the nineteenth century, the US productive system became progressively characterized by few large corporations in several national industries, and the government assumed the primary role of regulating the economic power in the hands of few large industrial players and managing potential conflicts caused by increasing industrial concentration. We refer to these years as characterized by an Oligopolistic strategy, as the government allowed the birth and development of national cartels and oligopolies, by negotiating and regulating their role in the framework of the different interests present in the national system. These were the years in which the institutional and organizational structure of the American economy and society found its order, as a base for the future economic and industrial development of the United States.

At the beginning of the twentieth century, the productive capacity of the American economy was becoming enormous. Fordism was changing the organization of the production within factories and in the US society. The American industry started to increasingly require new demand in order to release its productive forces. This context opened a season whereby the government began to be one of the most important customers of the US private sector. The First World War, Great Depression, Second World War and Cold War were the circumstances which constantly justified massive programmes of public procurements and R&D financing, fostering innovation, economies of scale and learning in the US industry. As suggested by Keynes, the expansion of the public demand triggered a virtuous circle for rising wages, booming consumptions and fostering the growth of the economy as a whole.

In the early 1970s, the American political and industrial system already had in its "arsenal" a long list of tools for supporting national industry, whose use was gradually becoming familiar to US companies and had been tested during the past industrial stages: subsidies and protectionist policies dating back to the Hamiltonian approach, the capacity and habit of the government to negotiate and regulate the large industrial power concentrations acquired since the second half of the nineteenth century, bail-outs and public procurement policies typical of the Keynesian strategy that had worked during the years of the Great Depression and of military conflicts.

Nevertheless, during the 1970s, the conditions started to change. The enormous impact on the US economic growth of public and domestic demand started to decline, while international competition was increasing from the economies which had recovered after the Second World War. At the beginning of the 1970s, the economic growth collapsed and unemployment and inflation started to increase. Demand-side policies and Keynesian approach had led to the saturation of the productive capacity of the industrial system and were no longer working. The response that emerged from the economic crisis of this decade was to reduce the fiscal pressure and the burden of public intervention in the economy, in order to restore private investments and create new productive capacity able to improve competitiveness on international markets and decrease unemployment.

A new great transformation was knocking on the door. The new neoliberal era would be built on " the assumption that individual freedom are guaranteed by freedom of the market and of trade ..., [with] a state apparatus whose fundamental mission was to facilitate conditions for profitable capital accumulation on the part of both domestic and foreign capital ... [reflecting] the interests of private property, owners, businesses, multinational corporations, and financial capital" (Harvey 2005: 7).

The beginning of the neoliberal era can be traced back to the Pinochet's coup of 1973, who—thanks to the support of the US government, American corporations and CIA—took power in Chile. Pinochet's economic policy applied the neoliberal economic prescriptions to the letter under the advice of the "Chicago boys", namely a group of economists from the Chicago University, devotees of the neoliberal theories taught by Milton Friedman (Harvey 2005). Whilst the Chilean "experiment" with neoliberal policies was deemed a disaster by many, from the late 1970s, the neoliberal approach started to be adopted (with different modalities) almost everywhere around the world. Indeed, international consent to neoliberal policies, encouraged by the industrial interests of those years, will become one of the fundamental institutional elements of the neoliberal global system. The American "free-market" rhetoric would play a crucial role in establishing such a consensus. The next chapter will show how in the United States this rhetoric has started to exert its influence and has favoured the rise of the neoliberal ideology in the early 1980s, with the establishment of the Reagan Administration.

Notes

1. See Library of Congress, https://www.loc.gov/exhibits/lewisandclark/transcript56.html, last accessed 9th March 2017.
2. In the subsequent years, with the Transportation Act of 1920, the role of the ICC was further strengthened, acquiring both the authority to set tar-

iffs on the railroads market and the more general task of maintaining adequate levels of quality of the railway service (Bingham and Sharpe 1998). The ICC, however, did not deal only with the railroads. From the first half of the twentieth century, and for many decades to come, the entire transport sector was regulated by this Commission. The Motor Carrier Act of 1935 entrusted the ICC with the control of entry of the entire American transport market, managed through concessions, licences and regulation of the tariffs (Cochran 1950; Hill 1951; Carter 1968; Lloyd 1982; Dobbin 1994; Bingham and Sharpe 1998; Di Tommaso and Schweitzer 2013; Di Tommaso and Tassinari 2017).

3. For example, in 1920 the *U.S. Steel Corporation* (quoted above), despite its lowered weight on the domestic market (which had fallen to 40%), was accused of *predatory pricing*. However, the indictment dropped soon because the Supreme Court ruled that the Attorney General had failed to demonstrate that the Company had adopted illegal monopoly practices. No sanctions or punitive actions were taken against the *U.S. Steel Corporation*, though the government demonstrated to the counterpart to be vigilant and ready to open up a new phase of negotiation (Stein 1998).

4. It has to be considered that at the end of the First World War, 31% of all manufacturing was in the hands of the corporations, giving work to 86% of the entire workforce (Williams 1966: 536).

5. In those years, the automotive industry began to occupy a central position for the development of the entire American economy, thanks to the high demand that it formulated to the backward-linked sectors. Thus, this industry was becoming subject of government's attention by remaining publicly supported on several occasions throughout the Twentieth century (Vlasic 2011; Ingrassia and White 1995). From 1913 to 1934, import product tariffs in the sectors fluctuated from 25% to 50%, to stabilize at a level of about 10% in subsequent years (Nester 1997). With the Federal Highway Act of 1916 and 1921, the car industry was further supported by the massive financing of transport infrastructures that these programs provided (Bingham and Sharpe 1998; Williamson 2012). During these years the "Big Three" American car manufacturers (Ford, Chrysler and General Motors) established their relevance in the American economy.

6. See, for example, https://sites.google.com/site/wartoendallwarscom/home/industry-during-ww1 (last accessed June, 2017).

7. See, for example, https://sites.google.com/site/wartoendallwarscom/home/industry-during-ww1 (last accessed June, 2017).

8. Even in the decades following the Great Depression, the agricultural sector continued to be supported by the government. For example, with President Eisenhower (1953–1961), farmers were further subsidized to reduce pro-

duction and to implement the rotation of the productions over the years (Bingham and Sharpe 1998).

9. *Apple*—that is today one of the global giants in consumer electronics and computer software—was among the companies that benefited from these public programs. During the start-up phase in 1970s, the company received public funds for an amount of $500,000 from the Small Business Investment Company (SBIC) program (Mazzucato 2013; Audretsch 1995). In the subsequent years, technologies used by Apple in its products (microprocessors, memory chips, hard disks, touch-screen, GPS, LCD screens, lithium batteries) were created thanks to DoD support, and in particular within the DARPA-funded Spintronics project of 1995, with an investment of $100 million. Likewise, years later, DoD's activism explains a lot about the development of the iOS products (iPod, iPhone, iPad) launched by Apple. For more details on the Apple case, see Mazzucato (2013), Dediu and Schmidt (2012), Adner (2012), Prestowitz (2012), McCray (2009), Brodd (2005), Irwin and Klenow (1996).

10. Policies inspired by the ideals of the Great Society were directed, in most cases, to mitigate the problems that characterized the urban environment. These were actions aimed at improving the quality of life in the metropolitan areas, which were the most degraded ones, and especially where differences in living conditions of the population had long been accentuated. In this context, social issues such as juvenile delinquency (with the Juvenile Delinquency and Youth Offenses Act of 1963), mental illness (with the Community Mental Health Centers Act of 1963), poverty (with the Economic Opportunity Act of 1964), the degradation of neighbourhoods (with the Demonstration Cities and Metropolitan Development Act of 1964) were addressed. These programs were especially directed at the populations of the central areas of the cities, which had become, in many cases, insecure, unhealthy and incredibly poor, while the middle class had chosen new peripheral districts (Piven and Cloward 2005). The Great Society project was also interested in training and education (ERP 1966, Chapter 3): along with (primary, secondary and higher) education funding programs, specific initiatives were launched to improve the skills and productivity of the workforce. At the same time, efforts were made to make the mechanisms for meeting the demand and supply of job more efficient. The programs developed under the Manpower Development and Training Act (MDTA) provided, for instance, basic training and education for unemployed people with previous work experience, in order to upgrade their professional skills. Between the adoption of the law, in 1962, and the end of its effectiveness, in 1965, these programs had reached a total of 370,000 subscribers (ERP 1966: 99). Furthermore, Healthcare programs had important implications on workforce productivity, as well as on the devel-

opment of the health sector's supply chains. In this context, for example, the Great Society project promoted an important increase in funding for medical research. Total health-related spending in 1965 was around $1.9 billion, which corresponded at almost 9% of the total national research and development expenditure. This sum was more than ten times higher than that of 1950, with an annual increase of almost 18%. Public investment in health research was channelled mainly through the National Institute of Health (NIH), whose overall research, structure and training budget grew over ten years from less than $100 million to over one billion in 1965. NIH's spending in this year represented two-fifths of the total medical research expenditure in the United States (ERP 1966: 104).

References

Abbate, J. (1999). *Inventing the Internet.* Cambridge, MA: MIT Press.

Abend, G. (2014). *The Moral Background: An Inquiry into the History of Business Ethics.* Princeton: Princeton University Press.

ABMC – American Battle Monuments Commission. (1938). *American Armies and Battlefields in Europe.* Washington: US Government Printing.

Adams, W., & Brock, J. W. (1986). *The Bigness Complex.* New York: Patheon.

Adner, R. (2012). *The Wide Lens: A new Strategy for Innovation.* New York: Portfolio/Penguin.

Alexander, J. G. (2009). *Daily Life in Immigrant America, 1870–1920: How the Second Great Wave of Immigrants Made Their Way in America.* Chicago: Ivan R.Dee.

Allen, W. A., & Moessner, R. (2012). The International Propagation of the Financial Crisis of 2008 and a Comparison with 1931. *Financial History Review, 19,* 123–147.

Audretsch, D. B. (1995). *Innovation and Industry Evolution.* Cambridge, MA: MIT Press.

Bingham, R. D., & Sharpe, M. E. (1998). *Industrial Policy American Style: From Hamilton to HDTV.* New York: Armonk.

Block, F. (2008). Swimming Against the Current: The Rise of a Hidden Developmental State in the United States. *Politics & Society, 36*(2), 169–206.

Block, F., & Keller, M. (Eds.). (2011). *State of Innovation: The U.S. Government's Role in Technology Development.* Boulder: Paradigm Publishers.

Breakthrough Institute. (2010). *Where Good Technologies Come From: Case Studies in American Innovation.* Oakland: Breakthrough Institute.

Briggs, V. (1984). *Immigration Policy and the American Labor Force.* Baltimore: John Hopkins University Press.

Brodd, R. J. (2005). *Factors Affecting US Production Decisions: Why are there No Volume Lithium-Ion Battery Manufacturers in the United States?,* National

Institute of Standard and Technology, ATP Working Paper Series, Working Paper 05-01.

Carter, G. (1968). *State in, State Out: A Pattern of Development Policy*. Journal of Economic Issues, *2*(4), 365–383.

Ceruzzi, P. (2003). *A History of Modern Computing*. Cambridge, MA: MIT Press.

Chang, H. J. (2007). *Bad Samaritans: The Myth of Free Trade and the Secret History of Capitalism*. New York: Random House Business Book.

Ciment, J., & Radzilowski, J. (2012). *American Immigration: An Encyclopedia of Political, Social, and Cultural Change*. London/New York: Routledge.

Cochran, T. C. (1950). *North American Railroads: Land Grants and Railroad Entrepreneurship*. The Journal of Economic History, *10*, 53–67.

Crockett, D. A. (2002). *The Opposition Presidency: Leadership and the Constraints of History*. College Station: Texas A&M University Press.

Daniels, R. (2001). *American Immigration*. Oxford: Oxford University Press.

Dediu, H. & Schmidt, D. (2012). *You Cannot Buy Innovation*, Asymco, 30 gennaio, su http://www.asymco.com/2012/01/30/you-cannot-buy-innovation/ (ultimo accesso 5 settembre 2014).

Di Tommaso, M. R., & Schweitzer, S. O. (2013). *Industrial Policy in America. Breaking the Taboo*. Cheltenham, UK/Northampton: Edward Elgar.

Di Tommaso, M. R. & Tassinari, M. (2017). Industria, Governo, Mercato. Lezioni americane, Il Mulino, Bologna.

Dobbin, F. (1993). *The Social Construction of the Great Depression: Industrial Policy During the 1930s in the United States, Britain and France*. Theory and Society, *22*(1), 1–56.

Dobbin, F. (1994). *Forging Industrial Policy*. Cambridge: Cambridge University Press.

ERP. (1965). *Economic Report of the President*. Washington, DC: United States Government Printing Office.

ERP. (1966). *Economic Report of the President*. Washington, DC: United States Government Printing Office.

Fong, G. (2001). *ARPA Does Windows: The Defense Underpinning of the PC Revolution*. Business and Politics, *3*(3.) Taylor & Francis.

Frank, D. (1999). *Buy American: The Untold Story of Economic Nationalism*. Boston: Beacon Press.

Freyer, T. (1992). *Regulating Big Business: Antitrust in Great Britain and America 1880–1990*. Cambridge: Cambridge University Press.

Fuchs, E. R. H. (2010). *Rethinking the Role of the State in Technology Development: Darpa and the Case for Embedded Network Governance*. Research Policy, *39*, 1133–1147.

Gjerstad, S., & Smith, V. L. (2009). *Monetary Policy, Credit Extension, and Housing Bubbles: 2008 and 1929, A Critical Review*. Journal of Politics and Society, *21*(2–3), 269.

Hamilton A. (1791). *Report on the Subject of Manufactures.* Republished by Cosimo, New York, 2007.

Harvey, D. (2005). *A Brief History of Neoliberalism.* Oxford/New York: Oxford University Press.

Helsing, J. W. (2000). *Johnson's War/Johnson's Great Society: The Guns and Butter Trap Praeger.* Connecticut/London: Westport.

Hill, G. F. (1951). *Government Engineering Aid to Railroad before the Civil War. Journal of Economic History, 11*(3), 235–246.

Hogan, M. J. (1987). *The Marshall Plan: America, Britain, and the Reconstruction of Western Europe, 1947–1952.* Cambridge: Cambridge University Press.

Hurt S. L. (2011). The Military's Hidden Hand: Examining the Dual-use Origins of Biotechnology in the American Context, 1969–1972. In Block F. & Keller M. R. (a cura di), *State of Innovation: The U.S. Government's Role in Technology Development.* Boulder: Paradigm Publishers.

Ingrassia, P., & White, J. B. (1995). *Comeback: The Fall & Rise of the American Automobile Industry.* New York: Touchstone Book.

Irwin, D. A., & Klenow, P. J. (1996). *Sematech: Purpose and Performance. Proceedings of the National Academy of Sciences of the United States of America, XCIII*(23), 12739–12742.

Kenney, M. (2003). The Growth and Development of the Internet in the United States. In B. Kogut (Ed.), *The Global Internet Economy* (pp. 69–108). Cambridge, MA: MIT Press.

Krugman, P. (2008). Partying Like It's 1929. *New York Times,* March 21, 2008.

Lazonick, W. (2008). *Entrepreneurial Ventures and the Developmental State: Lessons from the Advanced Economies,* Unu-Wider, Discussion Paper 1, Helsinki.

Lloyd, J. M. (1982). *Railroads and Land Grant Policy: A Study in Government Intervention.* New York: Academic Press.

Markusen, A., Hall, P., Campbell, S., & Deitrick, S. (1991). *The Rise of the Gunbelt: The Military Remapping of Industrial America.* New York: Oxford University Press.

Mazzucato, M. (2013). *The Entrepreneurial State. Debunking Public vs. Private Sector Myths.* UK and USA: Anthem Press.

McCray, P. W. (2009). From Lab to iPod: A Story of Discovery and Commercialization in the Post-Cold War Era. *Technology and Culture,* L, 1, 58–81.

Mowery, D. C. (1998). *The Changing Structure of the US National Innovation System: Implication for International and Conflict in R&D Policy. Research Policy, 27,* 639–654.

Nester, W. R. (1997). *American Industrial Policy.* London: Macmillan.

Piven, F. F. & Cloward, R. A. (2005). *The Politics of the Great Society* in *The Great Society and the High Tide of Liberalism.* Milkis S. M. & Mileur J. M. (Ed.). Amherst: University of Massachusetts Press, pp. 253–269.

Prestowitz, C. (2012). *Apple Makes Good Products but Flawed Arguments*. Foreign Policy, 23 gennaio.

Prodi, R. & De Giovanni, D. (1988). Mutamenti concorrenziali e regole del gioco. In Bianchi P. (Ed.), *Antitrust e gruppi industriali*. Il Mulino, Bologna.

Rand (Research and Development). (2011). *Paul Baran and the Origins of the Internet*, 23 December, su www.rand.org/about/history/baran.html (ultimo accesso 05 settembre 2014).

Reischauer, R. (1986). Fiscal Federalism in the 1980's: Dismantling or Rationalizing the Great Society. In M. Kaplan & P. Cuciti (Eds.), *The Great Society and Its Legacy*. Durham: Duke University Press.

Sandel, M. J. (1996). *Democracy's Discontent: America in Search of a Public Philosophy*. Cambridge, MA: Belknap Press.

Scheiber, H. N. (1987). State Law and Industrial Policy in American Development, 1790–1987. *California Law Review*, Articolo 18, Vol. 75, Issue 1.

Schwartz, S. I. (1998). *Atomic Audit: The Costs and Consequences of U.S. Nuclear Weapons Since 1940*. Washington, DC: Brooking Institute Press.

Shonfield, A. (1965). *Modern Capitalism*. London: Oxford University Press.

Stein, J. (1998). *Running Steel, Running America: Race, Economic Policy and the Decline of Liberalism*. Chapel Hill: The University of North Carolina Press.

Sullivan, E. T. (1991). *The Political Economy of the Sherman Act. The First One Hundred Years*. Oxford: Oxford University Press.

The US Joint Committee on Atomic Energy. (1955). *Current statement of the Atomic Energy Commission on the Five-Years Power Reactor Development Program*. The United States of America Government Printing Office: Washington.

Thorelli, H. E. (1955). *The Federal Antitrust Policy: Origination of an American Tradition*. Baltimore: The Johns Hopkins Press.

Vlasic, B. (2011). *Once Upon a Car: The Fall and Resurrection of America's Big Three Automakers – GM, Ford, and Chrysler*. New York: HarpersCollins.

Weiss, L. (2014). *America Inc.? Innovation and Enterprise in the National Security State*. New York: Cornell University Press.

Weiss, L., & Thurbon, E. (2006). *The Business of Buying American: Government Procurement as Trade Strategy. Review of International Political Economy."*, Routledge, *13*(5).

Williams, W. A. (1966). *The Contours of American History*. Chicago: Quadrangle Books.

Williamson, J. (2012). *Federal Aid to Roads and Highways Since the 18th Century: A Legislative History*. Congressional Research Service, 7-5700. www.crs.gov R42140.

Wilson, M. R. (2006). *The Business of Civil War: Military Mobilization and the State, 1861–1865*. Baltimore: JHU Press.

Zelizer, J. E. (2015). *The Fierce Urgency of Now: Lyndon Johnson, Congress, and the Battle for the Great Society*. New York: Penguin Press.

CHAPTER 3

The Rise of the Neoliberal Rhetoric: *Reaganomics* and Its Contradictions

This chapter enters the heart of our inquiry on the American industrial strategy in the neoliberal era. As it is well known to most, the 1980s marked the beginning of a new era in the approach to public intervention in the socio-economic sphere. While, during the post-war period, public intervention had greatly interfered with the functioning of the economies through protectionist policies and by targeting the promotion of specific companies and sectors, starting from these years the flag of the *free market* was raised in the name of more efficient and dynamic economies. Many governments substantially changed their scope for action, under a public rhetoric that painted public administrations as more inclined to respond to rent-seekers' pressures rather than to improve economic and societal outcomes. As that is the narrative commonly accepted by the "social scientists", regardless of their background, what is certainly mostly debated concerns the actual nature of these changes, the forces that have driven them and the normative implications drawn from their analysis. In this perspective, some questions may be raised concerning the peculiarities of the American industrial strategy as this was located in the economic, political and rhetorical context of the 1980s: how did actually the economic role of the government change? Which role did the neoliberal rhetoric of that period play? Why should we care that a possible gap between rhetoric and practice existed? Did the rhetoric itself have any causal impact on the policy outcomes? Why would successive governments have felt the need of embracing pro-market rhetoric?

© The Author(s) 2019
M. Tassinari, *Capitalising Economic Power in the US*,
International Political Economy Series,
https://doi.org/10.1007/978-3-319-76648-5_3

This chapter gathers these questions and, through them, it will attempt to draw the main characteristics of the American industrial strategy at the beginning of the neoliberal era. They also represent the base to understand how this strategy has lasted in the subsequent decades.

THE AMERICAN DEBATE ON INDUSTRIAL POLICY AND *REAGANOMICS*

In order to zoom in on the economic conjuncture that would see an unheard-of neoliberal rhetoric take its first steps in the United States, we have to start from the late 1970s, when European and Japanese manufacturers were making serious inroads into the American markets. At that time, concerns about whether or not America was experiencing a substantial deindustrialization were at their peak (Blueston and Harrison 1982; Norton 1986; Graham 1992; Panitch and Gindin 2012). From 1979 to 1982, the rate of unemployment grew from 5.8% up to 9.7%, the Real GDP was stagnant, while trade deficit was stably worsening, reaching $114 billion per year in 1985 (data from the ERP 2013). This context of growing unemployment, rampant inflation and high trade deficit raised the question of a renewed commitment of the government to the economy. Although policies for industrial development had been well rooted in the American history since Hamilton times (Hamilton 1791), it was only starting from these years that the words "industrial policy" formally entered the American political discussion, stimulating a wide debate inside and outside academic circles (Reich 1982; Dumke 1984; Eisinger 1990; Bingham and Sharpe 1998; White 2007), as revealed by the literature of those years:

> Since the late 1970s, the term "industrial policy" has come to figure more and more prominently in American political debate. The apparent decline of America's competitive position in the world economy, widespread concern over the deterioration of such basic industries as steel and automobiles, and increasing uneasiness about the potential of the United States to maintain its pre-eminence in high technology have led to many calls for a broad reappraisal of government's role in economic life. (Dumke 1984: ix)

In this context of strong political and economic turmoil, both, at domestic and international level, Carter established an Economic Policy Group explicitly instructed to formulate a proposal for a National Industrial

Policy (NIP) (ERP 1981; Graham 1992). However, the group produced no formal documents until 1980 when Carter, in a speech during the election campaign, announced an Economic Revitalization Program (Bingham and Sharpe 1998).

At a general level, Carter's industrial policy plan proposed the establishment of specific institutions: a federal agency to formulate industrial policy strategies, a tripartite council composed by representatives of government, business and workers that would be responsible for collecting information on the status of domestic industry, and a federal development bank. On the one hand, the idea was to finance those industries which were considered not having an adequate access to capital. This was the case, for example, for some emerging industries in which private investors appeared to be too risk-averse. On the other hand, the goal pursued by the administration was to provide support and temporary protection from imports to declining or threatened industries, in order to buy time for adjustments in the productive system and change the competitive conditions (ERP 1984). According to the NIP proponents, these measures were necessary to structural adjustment and growth of the American economy. President Carter, however, lost the elections and the Economic Revitalization Program was doomed to fall.

Nevertheless, public discussion on the need for the United States to officially adopt an industrial policy continued in the 1980s. Two distinct schools of thought gradually emerged in America. The first supported an active role of the government in the industrial dynamics by defining industrial policy strategies (Reich 1982). At an academic level, this position was supported, in particular, by the Harvard School, more inclined to recognize the need for public intervention. The second, in contrast—built mainly on the Chicago School—claimed positions in line with *supply-side economics*, favouring substantial freedom of markets' functioning and professing a greater confidence in the ability of the markets to achieve an efficient allocation of resources within the economy (Van Horn and Mirowski 2009).

During these years, it was clear that the outcome of the dispute between the two positions would lead to a new emerging model of public intervention. This was a time during which the United States rethought the role that the government should play in the economy and the general principles which should guide political action (Reich 1982; DiLorenzo 1984; Dorn 1984; Johnson 1984). Reich (1982: 74), for example, stated:

Two broad policies are available, both of which focus squarely on stimulating investment rather than demand. One goes the name "supply-side economics"; the other, "industrial policy". Neither has as yet been put to the full test in the United States, but it is reasonably certain that one of them, or a combination of both, will form the basis of American economic policy during the next decade.

Advocates of industrial policy nourished the national debate focusing on some key issues (Reich 1982, 1984). First, given that the government was already affecting industrial development through public procurement and by funding military R&D programmes, a "better" government planning was deemed necessary to a rational use of this massive amount of resources, along with a rigorous assessment of the public programmes on the competitiveness of the national industrial system. Second, trade protection and costly benefits were too often accorded to particular industries, due to lobbying pressure on the government, while the need was for interventions guided by a broader and long-run-oriented strategy of industrial development, as the rise of Japanese and European industries seemed to require. Third, it was thought paramount to restore industries that were losing their competitive advantage in international markets. The decline in labour-intensive industries, for example, would cause the loss of many jobs, high social costs and the formation of protectionist coalitions opposed to economic change, since the relocation and acquisition of new labour force skills were slow and expensive processes. An industrial policy was considered necessary because banks and private investors were seen as reluctant to finance activities that offered poor short-term profits. Fourth, industrial policy would have to respond to the competitive strategies of other advanced industrialized nations, by promoting infant industries that presented the best opportunity to compete in international markets. Finally, the government would also have to increase the investment in public goods, particularly in infrastructure, education and health, necessary for the future competitiveness of the American industry.

Meanwhile, advocates of supply-side economics were arguing that the government should not replace the market by "picking the winners" (ERP 1981). Indeed, the concept of *industrial policy* that emerged in America in the 1980s was primarily associated with a narrow set of policy tools (such as subsidies, tax relief and trade protectionism for particular industries) in favour of particular companies and industries. Quite the reverse, supporters of industrial policy focused on industrial policy goals by perceiving public policy as an opportunity to pursue broader economic and societal goals, which exceeded the narrow interests of the industries or companies involved in the intervention (White 2007; Ketels 2007). Building on this different interpretation of the concept of *industrial policy*, many American scholars were inclined to consider industrial policy as a poorly justified "intrusion" of the government in market dynamics.

In this context, the role of the government should have been limited to the definition of the "rules of the competitive game", through property rights' protection and by preserving the price system. Thus, consistent with this framework was a policy of reduction of federal expenditures accompanied by a cut of the tax burden for businesses and investors, in order to encourage private investments. Such a reduction in government regulation would also mitigate distortions of government involvement in the market system. In this conceptual framework, at least in principle, there was no room for industrial policy (DiLorenzo 1984). The reasons for this line of thinking were primarily drawn from the literature on *government failures*,[1] which presented at least two main elements.

First, the government was condemned to fail because of the enormous difficulties in finding and processing the information required for the development and implementation of an industrial policy. The information asymmetries characterizing government activities resulted in costs which could exceed the expected benefits (DiLorenzo 1984; Etzioni 1983; Schultze 1983). As clearly pointed out by Etzioni (1983: 49):

> To identify a winning industry requires predicting the future, determining what product line will succeed, taking into account future technological developments, changes in the general level of economic activity, actions by our competitors, and so on. The fact is that American industries that in the past were considered sure losers – textiles, shoes – have become winners, without industrial policy, and an industry that until recently seemed an American winner – airplane manufacturing – may turn sour (and then again may not). It is hard to foretell ... successful long-run identification of winners or losers is beyond our current intellectual and technical capacity.

Secondly, government interventions were, by definition, destined to fail since they were inclined to trigger non-virtuous mechanisms of rent-seeking, clientelism and corruption. Here, at stake was the effective ability of the government to represent the collective interest. The main assumption was that the politicians and bureaucrats were in no way different from other people in pursuing their own interests, by maximizing variables such as wages, public reputation, and power of their office, and by diverting government activities from promoting the public interest (see, e.g. Dorn 1984; Krueger 1990; Le Grand 1991; Chang 1994).

In 1980, as Ronald Reagan won the elections, after a political campaign of sharp opposition to public intervention, it was immediately clear which of the two positions the Americans had—at least ideally—chosen. Since his first presidential inaugural speech, President Reagan intended to show that he genuinely mistrusted the government. Being it intrinsically inefficient and ineffective, the government was, famously, not considered "the solution" but it was described as "the problem".[2]

The high stagflation of those years—high inflation combined with high unemployment—was soon attributed by the Reagan administration to the government interference in the economy, which pumped up money supply and unnecessary regulatory activities (ERP 1982). The line of economic policy that Reagan claimed would have promoted for economic recovery, baptized as "Reaganomics", was clearly described by the administration (ERP 1984). Reagan embraced the basic principles of *supply-side economics*—aimed at increasing the overall level of investment—and was favourable to the ideas at the basis of monetarism, which advocated for a reduction of the money supply in circulation in order to reduce inflation. The strategy of the US government seemed to be of letting markets operate as freely as possible. Obviously, by embracing this rhetoric line, President Reagan took, at the same time, a clear position in the public debate that was running in those years. The Economic Report of the President (ERP) in 1984 devoted an entire chapter to industrial policy issues, openly rejecting all proposals made by the supporters of government intervention in industry (ERP 1984, chapter 3):

> It is true that many Federal policies affect industrial output. But the argument about whether they constitute industrial policy, like all arguments about definitions, is pointless. What is relevant is whether the proposals of industrial policy advocates are a good idea. Should the U.S. Government have a larger role than it now has in deciding the composition of U.S. industry? The answer is "no". An industrial policy would not solve the problems faced by U.S. industry and would instead create new problems. ... The best way to deal with the many changes in demand that occur in a dynamic economy is to allow investors and workers to reserved respond to such changes. ... Government allocation of investment that ignores market signals usually you stunts growth by diverting labour and capital from blackberries productive uses. (ERP 1984: 88)

According to the Reagan administration, the United States was not facing a problem of competitiveness of the entire industrial system (a "deindustrialization"). Quite the reverse, the problem was seen in the decline of a few industries, and the solution had to be sought in direct aids to workers, encouraging the workforce to move to new jobs. Industrial policy, it was stated, would have discouraged the adjustment to more efficient productive processes, while protecting inefficient firms. Likewise—concerning the infant industries that were not able to receive adequate private financial capital—according to the administration there were no reasons to believe that private investors were mistaken in their risk assessment, and there were no reasons to think that government funding could have improved capital allocation compared to the private sector. The policy solutions, rather, had to be found in increasing tax cuts and in strengthening intellectual property rights' protection through patents and copyrights (ERP 1984). The justifications to support this "anti-government" policy line were explicitly based on the *government failures* literature (ERP 1982: 37–42).

At any rate, it is important to highlight that, since the 1980s, *government failure* assumptions started to play a role that went well beyond the boundaries of a mere theory on public administration. It did not simply turn the spotlight on the weaknesses of government action in order to genuinely look for solutions; it mainly served to fuel the idea that public intervention was per se not desirable and hopelessly doomed to fail. The political impact of this ideology at a national and international level would be impressive in the following decades.

From the actual issue of defining the better line of economic policy in order to solve the problems of the American economy, the positions rapidly tended to polarize around the more general State-versus-Market dispute, both in academic and policy-maker circuits. Furthermore, the clang that this debate had in the American society led eventually the discussion to the ideological level, resilient to any pragmatic idea concerning the necessary actions to heal the economy.

As Reagan was spreading his anti-government rhetoric, at the same time the neoliberal ideology was getting stronger. No doubt, in fact, that the Reaganian rhetoric was prodding the deepest American beliefs on individual freedom, finding a civil society ready to welcome it (and, of course, to vote at the presidential elections) (Harvey 2005: 39). Indeed, as stated by Etzioni (1983: 47), "the American antipathy for government, and the corresponding belief in individualism, competition, and the marketplace, [went] back to the days of the founding."

Moreover, it is useful to recall that the historical circumstances could per se greatly explain why the Americans were so responsive to the neoliberal proposal. The Cold War was still far to be over and the stoutly neoliberal rhetoric took hold as an anti-communist response, by strengthening the national identity and character against the competing Soviet Bloc (Engelhardt 1995).

In short, the American debate on industrial policy in the 1980s was discussed on a soil which was fertile of ideological prejudices and misunderstandings, well exploited by politicians to justify public actions with a music that the civil society liked to listen. Moreover, as ideological positions are generally harder to undermine than pragmatic ones, the industrial policy debate during these years was founding and reinforcing a long-run consent for making government intervention in economy an anathema. As a result, the words "industrial policy" have been banned from the American political debate until the present day, or used instrumentally by politicians for polarizing political positions.

Trade Policy Between Protectionism and *Aggressive Unilateralism*

Trade policy was naturally one of the fields where *Reaganomics* should have greatly resounded. Consistently with the general line of thought adopted by Reagan, the rhetoric concerning trade policy emphasized the idea of an unconditional liberalization of the international markets: "Our policy toward other nations' barriers to trade and to investment or export subsidies is one of strong opposition. Our trading partners must recognize that it is in their own interest, as well as ours, to assure that international trade and investment remain a two-way street" (ERP 1982: 176).

Of course, such a fundamentalist approach implied important consequences for the US economy. If foreign economies had a competitive advantage over the United States, as it could appear in the early 1980s, American industry had to find the way to improve by "itself" its competitive capacity or to shift its productive forces to other economic activities (Baldwin and Richardson 1987). This option however was not (perhaps quite obviously) possible in practice.

In the United States, a protectionist trade policy generally took shape from the pressure exerted by a domestic industry on the Congress through a petition. The US International Trade Commission (USITC) was the independent federal agency with a mandate to collect the information necessary to the Congress, the President and the Office of the United States Trade Representative (USTR) (that is part of the Executive Office of the President) to decide on the proper trade policy to adopt. It was voted by the Congress, but the President could eventually veto it. As a matter of fact, President Reagan, facing the hard realities of international competition and of the national politics, was not as fundamentalist as his theoretical principals and rhetoric suggested. The excessive trade deficit created a strong political pressure for protectionist policies to limit the economic problem, save jobs and protect the declining industries of those times, such as auto industry, textile, steel and semiconductor (ERP 1986). Analysing the auto case, for example, Baldwin and Richardson (1987: 137) stated:

> The President might have held to a strong liberal trade position and threatened to veto any restrictive bill emerging from Congress, but it would have been politically difficult to do so in view of his own stated position and the generally recognized fact that increased Japanese imports were an important cause of injury in this politically powerful industry.

In short, what emerged in the 1980s in America was a strong discrepancy between what Reagan was rhetorically professing and the actual policy which was implemented. Clear traces of this can be found all over the literature of those years. Richman (1988), for example, entitled an article on Reagan's trade policy "The Reagan Record on Trade: Rhetoric *vs.* Reality". In an article published a few months later, William Niskanen (1988), a member of the Council of Economic Advisors during the first term of the Reagan presidency, was launching quite the same message: "U.S. trade policy turned sharply protectionist during the Reagan years. Moreover, all of the new trade restraints imposed were initiated or approved by the administration, despite a general endorsement of free trade in its public rhetoric." Likewise, Baldwin and Richardson (1987: 136) stated: "On the basis of its 'Statement on U.S. Trade Policy', one would have expected the administration to follow a very tough stance against import protection. However, on the surface at least, the administration's actual performance in granting import relief does not seem to differ significantly from the varied record of other recent administrations."

Analysing the policy practices of those years, a series of protectionist interventions was implemented in favour of those sectors threatened by international competitive pressure. These interventions were generally justified by the government as actions for dealing with the commercial practices of foreign countries considered in some way unfair. Curiously, in what cases these practices were to be considered "unfair" was decided by the United States only, under the guidance of their Office of the USTR. The result was that the international trade had to be "free", but there could be "exceptions" for implementing national protectionism policies, *unilaterally* decided by the United States according to the condition of their domestic industry. In this context, public intervention was substantially a specialized form of "functional problem solving", targeted at remedying problems of specific industries and, therefore, having the value of an active *industrial policy* (Bingham and Sharpe 1998: 70). This form of intervention in the international trade arena was a relatively new approach in the 1980s, and it was encouraged by the injuries that the international trade was causing to the American economy. Indeed, as stated by Bingham and Sharpe (1998: 71):

> The United States was in an enviable economic position immediately following World War II. Europe and Japan were devastated. The United States was in a position to sell far more abroad than the rest of the world could sell her in return. Liberal trade policy (freer trade) made practical sense. And trade policy could be subordinated to the broader American foreign policy of reconstructing the free world. But in the early 1960s, after the formation of the New European Economic Community, the Congress began having doubts about the wisdom of subordinating trade to foreign policy within the State Department and established … a Special Representative for Trade Negotiations [the current USTR] … to administer the American system of trade remedies to those industries and company seriously injured by imports or unfair foreign trade practices.

In this context, the most "traditional" American trade policy instruments were anti-dumping interventions or applications of countervailing duties. The anti-dumping measures were implemented in cases where the price of goods imported into the United States was lower than its production cost. In these cases, the US government was acting substantially by bridging this difference—the *dumping*—through the imposition of a duty on the imported product. Similarly, through the countervailing duty, the government applied a duty on imports that were subsidized by foreign governments, in order to "compensate" the subsidy.

However, during the 1980s, Reagan's trade policy went beyond the rationale of unfair practices of foreign countries. Indeed, in the United States there were also other remedies of trade policy permitted by the law, which did not find any justification in the practices of governments of competing economies. These interventions were simply aimed at temporarily protecting special American industries when the foreign competitive pressure was too high. In this scenario, "Section 201" of the Trade Act of 1974 established the procedures and conditions for which it was possible to provide temporary protection to industries that were seriously damaged by imports from abroad. Since the application of this measure did not require a demonstration of unfair practices by foreign countries, this statute was also called "escape clause". In this context, the International Trade Commission had the task of establishing the existence of the institute's applicability and of possibly recommending to the President the appropriate remedies to promote the adjustment of the domestic industry. Subsequently, the President considered whether the proposal was consistent with the national interest—for example by assessing the policy effects on consumers, other industries and exports—and decided the eventual amount and type of protection. The protection could not, in any case, be guaranteed by statute for a period of more than eight years.

The number of anti-dumping, countervailing duty cases and Section 201 investigations initiated from 1979 to 1994 was more than 1200 (Destler 2005: 149). During the five years from 1982 to 1986, the use of these investigations was at its peak, with 620 cases examined overall. In 1982, for example, there were 65 anti-dumping cases, 140 countervailing duty cases and 3 Section 201 cases investigated. The escape clause (Section 201 cases) was sparingly used. Only 25 cases were investigated in 16 years, and most of them were concentrated before 1986. Although during this period, on average, only 50% of the cases were successful in providing protection for petitioner industries (Bingham and Sharpe 1998: 84), investigations and applications of these remedies show how, in realty, during the 1980s, the US trade policy was greatly inconsistent with the ideal free market hankered by President Reagan.

Furthermore, beyond these legal measures, other less-orthodox remedies were applied by the Reagan administration in the realm of the so-called managed trade. In this context, one of the most common remedies adopted was the negotiation with foreign governments for "Voluntary" Export Restraints (VERs) involving some foreign exports directed to the United States. In these cases, the administration did not pass any legislation concerning trade remedies, but the restraints to foreign exports were imposed by the foreign governments themselves.

In 1981, for example, the US administration put pressure on the Japanese government in order to reduce the sales of cars from Japan to the

United States through a programme of VER. In March 1982, the Japanese government restricted its exports to 1.68 million cars. The threshold gradually shifted upward over the following years, but remained present until 1985, with 2.3 million cars exported (Niskanen 1988; Richman 1988; Bingham and Sharpe 1998). In this case, the restraints were imposed by the Japanese themselves. There were no formal trade actions, no demands, no bilateral trade negotiations and no technical violation of international trade law. The White House simply signalled to the Japanese that they must restrain their auto shipments (Reich and Donahue 1985, quoted in Bingham and Sharpe 1998: 67).

In the textile and clothing sector, the Reagan administration renewed the Multi-Fiber Agreement, a system of quotas on exports from industrialized countries, adopted in order to regulate the importation of a large number of products and change the rules on exports in the exporting countries (Niskanen 1988).

Similarly, in 1982, the administration promoted other VERs on steel coming from European companies, included as anti-dumping penalties. However, the agreement fixed a general limit on exports of steel from Europe of 5.5% of the US market, regardless of the amount of subsidies that European goods had received. A similar threshold was also set on the import of pipes. In 1984, the US government started negotiations to restrict exports from all the major steel-producing countries. From 1984 to 1986, steel imports in the United States decreased from 26.4% to 23% of the market (Niskanen 1988).

Furthermore, in the semiconductor industry, in 1986 the US government persuaded Japan to establish a "fair" market price (determined by the US Department of Commerce) for memory chips used in computer production. Japan had also to set the same price even in third-country markets, and increase the sales of US chips in its own market. Japan respected the first point, and raised the price to the fixed level, but it was accused by the US government of not setting that price to third countries and not increasing the sales of American chips in the Japanese market. The United States responded to these gaps by imposing a tariff of 100%, to a value of $300 million, to other Japanese imports (Niskanen 1988; Richman 1988).

The VERs would be entirely banned in the subsequent years under the Uruguay Round of the General Agreement on Tariffs and Trade (GATT).

At any rate, a part from import remedies, in the 1980s a similar approach also characterized the US export promotion policy. One of the main laws regulating export promotion was "Section 301" of the Trade Act of 1974. This clause stated that the Office of the USTR was obliged to take all appropriate actions in order to remove any act, policy or practice which violated an international agreement or unjustifiably posed restrictions on American exports. The Omnibus Trade and Competitiveness Act of 1988, signed by President Reagan, introduced two variants of Section 301, called "Special 301" and "Super 301", reinforcing the USTR's role in defence of US exports. The export promotion policy of those years was labelled as *aggressive unilateralism* (Bingham and Sharpe 1998: 68), to highlight how the United States imposed on foreign economies reductions of barriers to US exports and investments under threats of trade retaliations (so "aggressively") without any reciprocal concession (so "unilaterally"). In this regard William Niskanen wrote:

> The Administration stepped up pressure on other governments to open their markets to U.S. goods. The general tactic was to threaten limits on their exports to the United States in order to induce them to reduce their limits on U.S. sales in their markets. The Reagan administration initiated 10 such cases during its first term and 22 such cases after September 1985, when trade policy became markedly more *aggressive*. These measures had some success. Japan reduced or eliminated tariffs on aluminium products, cigarettes, and leather products, and substituted high tariffs for very restrictive quotas on beef and citrus. Korea reduced its barriers on U.S. movies and television programming. Taiwan opened its market to beer, wine, and cigarettes. Europe reduced restraints on imports of corn and citrus. And so on. (Niskanen 1988: 5, emphasis added)

It has been assessed that of 72 Regular, Special and Super 301 cases completed between 1975 and 1992, the US objectives had a 49% rate of success (Bayard and Elliott 1994, quoted in Bingham and Sharpe 1998). This average value was given by a growing rate of successes (from 30% before 1985 to 60% after that year), thus highlighting how the US negotiation power was increasing during the first decades of the neoliberal era.[3]

BAILOUT OF THE AUTO INDUSTRY

The auto industry was one of the most affected by the crisis in the late 1970s. Imports of cars in the United States had reached 30% of the market and, in particular Chrysler, one of the "Big Three" American auto producers, had already fired 40% of its employees, and it was risking bankruptcy.

Chrysler was soon considered *too big to fail*. It was the Carter administration to plan the first interventions to bail out the company. At an early stage, the administration collected all the necessary information for action by assessing the impact of the possible failure of the company and seeking solutions to the problems that may have arisen. The approach that Carter had intended to adopt provided for direct government involvement in managing the company that would be saved by public money. In particular, the administration wanted to prevent Chrysler from receiving financial aid without adopting measures that would improve the company's competitive capacities (Graham 1992). In 1979 the Congress passed the Chrysler Corporation Loan Guarantee Act and, in 1980, Chrysler received $1.5 billion as collateral on loans from the Federal government and $3.5 billion as additional capital and concessions from trade unions (Di Tommaso and Schweitzer 2013).

Since 1981, when President Reagan settled in the White House, the administration continued to manage the relationship between Chrysler and the Federal government. Whilst the intervention was led by the same goal to bail out the American company—whose bankruptcy would have had serious social consequences on employees, suppliers and the entire metropolitan area of Detroit—Reagan's approach was radically different from that held by Carter. The new administration basically decided to adopt the same line that characterized the action in other sectors. The interventionist approach established by Caret for controlling the management of the company was abandoned in favour of a widespread protection of the whole auto industry. As we have already shown in previous pages of this chapter, the general strategy of the Regan administration was to negotiate VERs with the Japanese government, in order to reduce the sales of cars from Japan to the United States (Niskanen 1988; Richman 1988; Bingham and Sharpe 1998).

National Security and Science and Technology Policy

As we have shown in Chap. 2, at a general level, from the Second World War, the American industrial development had been markedly characterized by two main levers in the hands of the federal government: public procurements and government-funded R&D. Public procurements (regulated at a national level by the Buy American Act of 1933)[4] had pursued industrial development through a massive public demand, able to exploit economies of scale and "learning by doing" and, at the same time, to protect national industry from foreign competition, since American programmes excluded foreign companies as potentially suppliers of the American public administrations (Weiss and Thurbon 2006). On the other side, the support for R&D activities had been aimed at the promotion of technological innovation, mainly through public funds for research in specific areas.

In this context, several departments and agencies of the US government (but above all the Department of Defence [DOD]) had purchased goods and services from the American industry and had financed R&D in order to achieve the agencies' specific objectives (i.e. national defence). However, at the same time and as a sort of "unintended" consequence, such spending programmes had finally impacted on the development of companies and technologies involved in the private markets. In this way, the American government had fostered the development of different industries, including the railway, shipbuilding, automotive, airline industry, semiconductor, biotechnology, nuclear and so on.[5]

An interventionist approach to industrial development had been, after all, common also to the other industrialized economies. While in the United States public procurements had prevailed, Japan had favoured practices for targeting specific sectors, and Europe had generally resorted to state-owned enterprises (SOEs) and direct subsidies to private companies (Buigues and Sekkat 2009).

However, at the beginning of the 1980s, this US "defence-centred" model of national innovation and development seemed to be losing its effectiveness. The Vietnam War was concluded and, during the 1970s, the demand for military equipment and technologies had quickly decreased its weight in the American economy (see Fig. 3.1).

Likewise, also the federal share of total R&D expenditures was decreasing during those decades (see Fig. 3.2). In short, as pointed out by Weiss (2014: 39), "from the late 1970s, the enormous leverage that the federal government once exercised in terms of market pull began to weaken. Two structural changes that underpinned that process could not be reversed: the diminution in relative size of the government procurement market (dwarfed by commercial markets by the 1970s) and the falling federal share of total R&D spending (overtaken by private R&D outlays by the late 1980s)." As a consequence of this changing context, the "innovation system", characterized by the cooperation based on military interests between private business and government, was reducing its effectiveness since it was withdrawing incentives for innovative companies to work on DOD's projects.

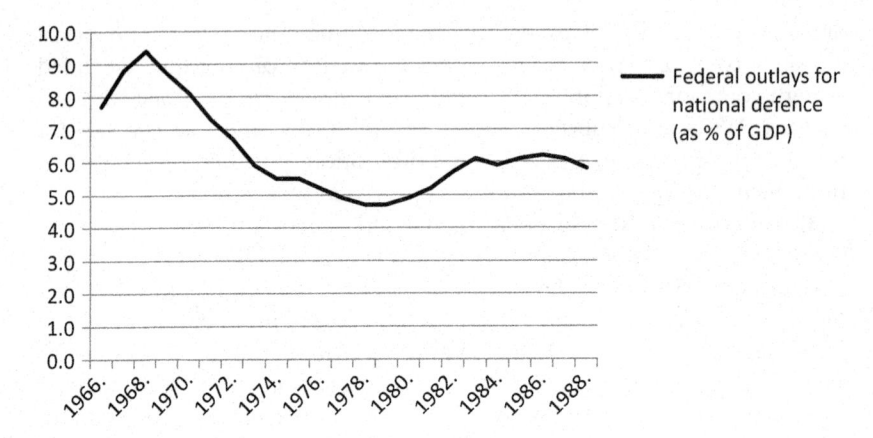

Fig. 3.1 Federal outlays for national defence (as % of GDP) (Source: Author's elaboration based on Table B–79—E.R.P. 2013/Department of Commerce)

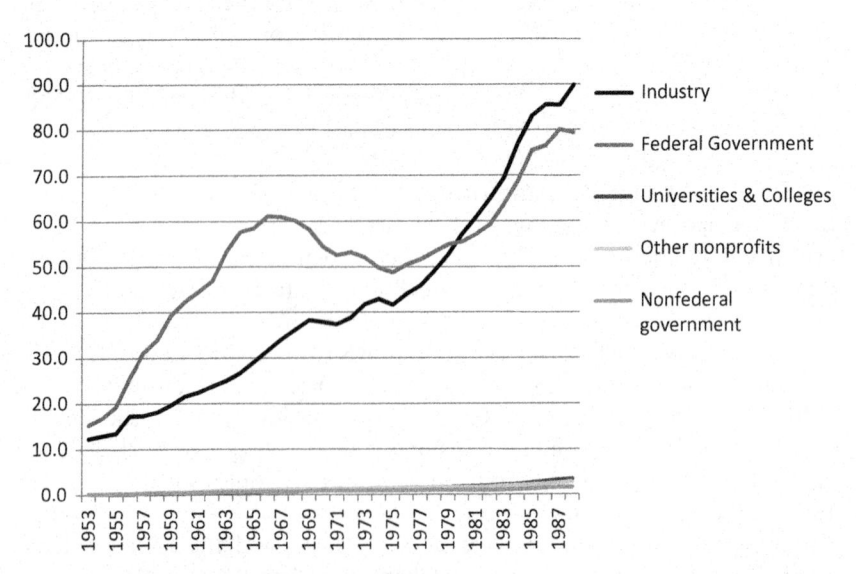

Fig. 3.2 US R&D expenditures: 1953–2007 (2000 const. $ billions) (Source: Author's elaboration based on data from National Science Foundation, Division of Science Resources Statistics, National Patterns of R&D Resources [annual series])

Of course, a liberal administration, as the Reagan administration had claimed to be, could not promote industrial development and innovation by *directly* financing the private sector. According to President Reagan, the scarcity of information and incentives that the government held in determining the most productive allocation of capitals in the economy would have led to dramatic *failures* in R&D policies, because it was not possible to predict in advance what would the commercial use of the results obtained be (ERP 1988: 185–186). However, this *information asymmetry* was avoided when it was the government itself, and not a private company, to be the main user of the research results (i.e. in the case of research used by federal agencies for their own purposes). Therefore, government intervention in the fields of science and technology was generally held appropriate when aimed at the development of traditional *public goods* or in response to common *market failures*. Most of the government funding for R&D were justified as meeting specific societal goals, and federal funds were allocated to the agencies for those research activities that pursued these goals.

In this perspective, "national security", as a *public good*, still remained at the centre of the R&D policy, and with it the DOD, as its promoter. More than half of the federal funds for R&D were allocated to this department. In 1987, the defence sector absorbed 69% of the total expenditure of the government in R&D (which was 60 billion dollars, equivalent to almost half the national total) (ERP 1988). More generally, during the 1980s, Reagan was able, not without political complications, to significantly increase the total level of military expenses, as an attempt to "remilitarise" technology. As stated by Reich (1985): "... blackberries important to high tech is President Reagan's military buildup. Since 1981, about $400 billion has been channelled into new weapons – most depending on advanced technologies. This demand for state-of-the-art products has pulled these emerging industries down the 'learning curve' to the point where commercial spinoffs are attainable."

However, the crucial change that occurred during the 1980s had to do with the fact that the Reagan administration was able to give a new life to this "defence-centred" innovation system. The transformations promoted by the government in this field aimed essentially at giving new incentives for private businesses to cooperate with the government, in order to promote innovation technology. This meant substantially to allow private companies to use technology breakthroughs (publicly financed) for commercial purposes (Weiss 2014). As a result, the official rhetoric of the

Reagan administration was telling that public funding was necessary for promoting national security, while the real actions of the government were oriented to transforming the system in order to promote the competitiveness of the national industry. The main objective pursued was national security; however, the effects of public research were not to remain confined into the purposes of the federal agencies, but spill over into the private sector as new processes or new commercial products.

As a part of this transformation, policies to encourage technology transfer started to play a crucial role. These had an impact not just on the DOD, but on many government agencies involved in public R&D activities, such as the Department of Energy (DOE), NASA, the National Science Foundation (NASF) and the National Institutes of Health (NIH), along with university laboratories. These agencies commissioned research activities to universities and private laboratories in the fields of their interest, and research findings could have led to commercial spin-offs in the private sector. In this context, the so-called Bayh-Dole Act was the first important law that encouraged these processes.

Before 1980 the federal agencies' research findings were leased to the private sector through non-exclusive licences. The demand for these licences appeared to be poor. The University and Small Business Patent Procedures Act of 1980 (also known as the Bayh-Dole Act) created the possibility for private universities, small businesses and non-profit private institutions to have, as an exclusive property right, the patent for the results of the publicly funded research. In 1983, the Reagan administration extended that possibility to private companies of all sizes and, in the following year, to non-profit institutions and public universities. This policy seemed to increase both the research activities and the use of public research results for commercial purposes through an increased university-industry cooperation (ERP 1989). The numbers of university patents rose from 230 in 1976 to approximately 900 in 1987, of which universities were licensing almost one-third to private firms for development and potential commercialization (ERP 1989: 245). Today virtually every research-oriented university has an "Office of Intellectual Property".

Other important policy initiatives to encourage technology transfer from federal laboratories to private enterprises were the Technology Innovation Act of 1980 and the Federal Technology Transfer Act of 1986. The laws essentially allowed the federal laboratories to establish a cooperative research with private companies. Of particular interest was the fact that, thanks to the law of 1986, federal laboratories began, through the negotiation of licensing agreements, to retain a portion of the royalties paid by the private sector for the use of research findings (ERP 1989).

At the same time, the cooperation between government and private sector was encouraged through direct public financing of research consortiums and of a list of public-private initiatives, as a "merging of public and private innovation efforts" (see Weiss 2014: 43; Block 2008: 179–182). In this scenario, for example, the machine tools industry and the semiconductor industry represented two relevant cases. Both sectors were, in those years, threatened by the competition with foreign firms, and they were losing considerable market shares. In the machine tools industry, in 1986, a research consortium was constituted for the development of new production technologies, the National Center for Manufacturing Sciences (NCMS), for which the DOD allocated approximately $5 million per year (ERP 1989). Similarly, but with a definitely larger budget, in the semiconductor industry, a consortium of American manufacturers and users of semiconductor was founded, for the development of new productive processes. This initiative was named Semiconductor Manufacturing Technology Initiatives (SEMATECH) and, in 1989, it was supported with $100 million allocated by the DOD (ERP 1989; Browning and Shetler 2000; Block 2008; Wade 2012). The words reported in the ERP of 1989 clarify that, in both cases, the primary objective of the government had little to do with national security:

> The existence of NCMS and SEMATECH raises fundamental questions about DOD's role in supporting civilian commercial technologies. The Department clearly needs semiconductors and advanced machine tools and, in special circumstances, may not want to rely on foreign suppliers. But DOD's demand for these products is only a small portion of the total market, and DOD alone does not need and cannot support a large domestic production base. Requiring DOD to provide R&D support for an industrial base larger than it needs, however, diverts its resources from military technologies that the private sector would never fund on its own. (ERP 1989: 248)

Furthermore, other initiatives were implemented by the administration during the 1980s in the field of science and technology. They were related to antitrust policies used to promote business cooperation in research, tax credits for private sector and policies for intellectual property protection.

Antitrust legislation had an important role in encouraging cooperation among businesses in the field of the R&D. In this case a "lightening" of antitrust legislation could allow private companies to exploit economies of scope and scale by conducting joint research. The National Cooperative

Research Act of 1984 allowed companies to cooperate on research in the early stage of product development, before beginning the competition for the sale of the finished product. More than one hundred research consortia were founded during the Reagan administration from the enactment of the law (ERP 1988, 1989).

Tax credits were established to encourage private sector investments. The Economic Recovery Tax Act of 1981 provided for businesses a tax credit of 25% on the amount of research spending which would exceed the average level of spending of the previous three years. However, since it was a tax credit on increased spending on research, the impact of the subsidy was quite limited. Furthermore, the tax credit was valid only from 1981 to 1986, although the Tax Reform Act of 1986 protracted it until 1989 (ERP 1989).

Finally, another crucial element where the administration could boost the research activities of the private sector was represented by the improvement of intellectual property protection. The need for private companies to make their investments in R&D profitable required a legal regime to regulate intellectual property rights through copyright, patents, trademarks, trade secret laws and licences. However, the effectiveness of these tools was related to the ability to enforce property rights not only at a national level but also abroad. Thus, with the beginning of the Uruguay Round negotiations in 1986, the US government started to pursue the improvement of intellectual property protection overseas. Likewise, the Omnibus Trade and Competitiveness Act of 1988 reinforced, for the American patent holders, the legal right to block imports from a foreign country or to claim damages from foreign companies that had sold products made by using US patented processes.

As we are referencing the interventions implemented by the Reagan administration for promoting the US science and technology, it seems more than appropriate to conclude this section by quoting the resonant words pointed out by Weiss that stated:

> In the realm of science and technology at least, the Reagan administration's actions belied its small government, antistatist rhetoric, in keeping with the fact that it is in the S&T domain that both parties, in competing for the national security mantle, have generally reached across the partisan divide. (Weiss 2014: 44)

DECENTRALIZING INDUSTRIAL POLICY

One of the problems met in putting forward an industrial policy at the beginning of the 1980s was associated with sceptical positions about its effectiveness in a contest characterized by political decentralization, namely strong separation of powers and federalism (Whitford and Schrank 2011; Dubnick 1984; Magaziner and Reich 1982). Indeed, a common perception was that an effective industrial policy required political centralization and authoritative decision-making in order to make public interventions, on one side, consistent to each other, and, on the other side, homogeneous and widespread across the national territory. A solid and centrally directed industrial strategy would have allowed public resources for industrial development to be efficiently and effectively spent, because it is focused on consistent goals and targeted on the entire national territory. However, the American politico-institutional system was characterized—then as now—by (a) a strong separation of powers between executive, legislative and judiciary; and (b) a strong separation of powers between federal, state and local levels (Wade 2014; Ketels 2007; Hall and Soskice 2001; Mann 1997). These conditions could limit the efficiency and effectiveness of industrial policy because federal government investments would have competed with Congress priorities and with state and local government's autonomy.

Concerning the relationship between government and Congress, at a federal level, the President could establish a political agenda by identifying specific problems and he/she could have a good chance to implement policies only in a few areas deemed of high priority, investing the political capital of the presidency. On the other hand, the Congress was responsible for ensuring that the general actions of the administration would meet the specific interests of the voters, through the influence on the definition of the remaining policies on industry. This generated a set of uncoordinated different interventions: a few key policies established by the President, and many small individual actions, in favour of local industries, decided by the Congress (Ketels 2007). Moreover, this kind of inconsistency characterized, to some degree, also the actions of the several agencies that played a role in different fields of economic development, such as the Small Business Administration (SBA), the Economic Development Administration (EDA), the Department of Agriculture (DoA) and the Department of Housing and Urban Development (HUD).

Focusing on the separation between federal, state and local powers, the problem of inconsistency was similar. Indeed, local governments and state seemed to exert a direct and strong influence on industrial development dynamics that could compete with federal action. From this perspective, some authors argued that some American states had an industrial policy to encourage, subsidize and guide private investment, compared to the one implemented, at a national level, by many other states, such as France or Japan. In other words, whilst at the federal level, the American industrial policy was highly controversial, at a local and state level public interventions in favour of the industry assumed a value difficult to refute. Eisinger (1990: 511), for example, stated: "(...) the United States may not have an industrial policy, but to varying degrees many of the individual states do, and their industrial policies draw on the tradition of vigorous, self-conscious, planned micro-economic intervention generally regarded as foreign to the American political economy." Therefore, during the 1980s, state and local governments were already autonomously intervening to address specific "market failures", such as underinvestment in R&D, underinvestment in training the workforce, difficulties of access to the capital market, underproduction of public infrastructure and scarcity of industrial land availability (Bartik 2004). In this context, local governments could on their own encourage the analysis of the needs and potentialities of a given territory and define ad hoc interventions, for example, for attracting new businesses, influencing location decisions through incentives (tax credits, subsidies, loans and guarantees), providing the availability of areas with appropriate infrastructure, skilled workforce and consulting services and so on (Bartik 2004).

It is clear that this high dynamism of the state and local governments could meet serious difficulties to coordinate itself with a central industrial strategy defined by the federal government, especially in the absence of specific institutions responsible to address this problem. More generally, the problem of "inconsistency" regarded the lack of institutions in coordinating and supporting the cooperation among a plurality of public and private economic agents, which was a key element to make the federal public investment "prolific", but that was deemed alien to the American *variety of capitalism* (Hall and Soskice 2001).

Nevertheless, in keeping up with the change that was occurring in policies for science and technology discussed in the previous section, the Reagan administration promoted, despite once again the neoliberal rhetoric of those years, several innovative initiatives that would begin to mitigate coordination and inconsistency problems among public and private economic actors.

Of course the cooperation between public and private agents, as well as between federal, state and local government, was not unheard of in the American industrial system. For example, since the years of the American industrial independency and during the nineteenth century, the industrial policy had encouraged the development of the rail industry, considered one of the most important sectors of that time. In this context, the development of the local and national railway system required a strong partnership between local, state and federal governments and the private sector in planning and financing the railway lines (Dobbin 1994).

During the 1980s however, some specific new programmes started to operate at a "meso" level, aimed at overcoming *network failures* (Whitford 2005; Whitford and Schrank 2011; Wade 2012) and favouring cooperation among a plurality of actors, such as companies, scientists, engineers, venture capitalists, local governments, state economic development agencies, private enterprise development centres, organizations that provided services for businesses, universities and so on. Programmes such as the Small Business Innovation Research (SBIR) and the Manufacturing Extension Partnerships (MEPs) started to foster cooperation and exchange of information among the agents of an increasing complex system of innovation and production (Wade 2012; Block 2008; Schrank and Whitford 2009)

The SBIR of 1982 created a consortium between the SBA and other government agencies (including the DOD, the DOE and the Environmental Protection Agency). The government agencies were directed to allocate a fraction of their research budget to support initiatives promoted by small private companies and to develop innovative start-ups (Lerner 1999; Audretsch 2003; Mazzucato 2013). In general, the programme was crucial in strengthening the innovation system based on a network of institutions and organizations able to provide assistance and financial capital to entrepreneurial innovation (Mazzucato 2013; Block and Keller 2011). [6]

The MEP, sponsored by the National Institute of Standards and Technology (NIST), started to exert an important role in the extension of management and technical assistance services for small businesses (Shapira 2001). It was launched in 1988 to improve productivity, competitiveness and technological capacities of American SMEs through the establishment of state and local centres. The MEP operated by creating a network of local economic relations for providing consultancy services to businesses related, for example, to access to new markets, financing, investment in physical capital and innovation and skilled workforce. The provided consultancy services were often notably superior to the one that small local communities could acquire individually, thanks to the economies of scale developed by the MEP (Shapira 2001; Hallancer 2005).

All in all, leaving aside any definitional issue concerning the concept of *industrial policy*, during the 1980s the Reagan administration was actually a promoter of a new approach to industrial development. As stated by the words of Hallancer (2005: 3–4):

> (...) weaknesses in the traditional model of technological innovation combined with a perceived industrial competitiveness crisis resulted in emergence of a new science policy paradigm during the 1980s, aimed at linking publicly funded research performers with private industry to address a perceived national economic competitiveness crisis.

Conclusion

We began this chapter by asserting that the 1980s are regarded as the beginning of a new era, as far as the role of the government in economy is concerned. Indeed that was the case. However, our analysis has shown that, conversely to what is believed by many, the change did not regard the withdrawal of the government from economic dynamics, but rather its *renovation*. Indeed, some important changes occurred in policy practices. On the one hand, the Japanese invasion of the US markets and the crisis of the American economy of those years stimulated a more *aggressive* stance in trade policy, both in protecting specific domestic industries and in promoting American export. The strategy of the Reagan administration was basically to negotiate "voluntary" favourable conditions for American imports and exports with foreign economies, leveraging on US economic power. On the other hand, the crisis of the "defence-centred" model of innovation encouraged President Reagan to find new ways for relaunching the relationship between government and private industry on the base of military interest. Here, policies for technology transfer and for private-public cooperation were implemented by reorganizing the American system of innovation.

At any rate, whilst these changes are important and alone can mark the beginning of a new approach in promoting industrial development in the United States, they cannot entirely explain the radical fracture with the past that happened in those years. To more appropriately understand the nature of the socio-economic transformation that gradually happened during the 1980s, we must refer to the relationship between economic policy and political rhetoric and, in the specific case of the Reagan administration, to the gap between them. This stance could sound uncanny to some: why should we even care about a possible gap between rhetoric and practice? There is nothing surprising to social scientists in recognizing that politicians are better looked at for what they do rather than for what they say. And perhaps this would have been the case during the Reagan administration. Indeed, the President could have been genuinely passionate with the concept of *free market*, but—beyond the ideological and theoretical level—the pure *Reaganomics* could have never been implemented. The reason is pretty clear, and it is explained by the fact that any theoretical stance, even though useful as "ex-ante" hermeneutical mechanism, has good chances to collide with the hard realty, within or outside social sciences (see, e.g. Kuhn 1962). Furthermore, as it is well known, in the case of social sciences the uncertainty of the theory is perhaps even larger, as human *rationality* could be—perhaps fortunately—imaginative and unpredictable (Knight 1921; Simon 1947; Spender 2012). Thus, coming to the concrete case, it was not surprising that the Reagan "paradigm", claimed in his rhetoric, was in the practices excessively fundamentalist. Indeed, political pressure for an interventionist approach of the administration became very soon unsustainable, displaying a strong discrepancy between the rhetoric and reality (and showing, of course, the inadequacy of the theoretical base adopted by the administration in explaining the hard reality of the international competition).

At any rate, we believe that the reason for considering the gap between rhetoric and realty can reasonably exist. This is the case in which the rhetoric has a casual impact on the policy outcome. The relevance of Reagan's rhetoric in fact was not in the rhetoric itself. On the contrary, its importance depended on the value that the civil society was giving to it. In other words, it was the fertile soil that the neoliberal idea was finding that made such rhetoric so powerful in influencing Reagan consent to govern. More specifically, it was the shifting to an ideological stance of the neoliberal idea and its resilience in civil society that gave Reagan a steady consent to implement potentially any policy justified in the name of free(er) markets. This idea started to find room during the 1980s, opening the neoliberal era, but it would be crucial to understand the *political economy* of the American industrial strategy in the subsequent decades when the neoliberal consent would exercise its influence at international level under the better-known name of "Washington Consensus" (Williamson 1989).

Indeed, while Reagan cultivated neoliberal ideas in the civil society, the future American administration "was learning" the lesson on how to get consent from Americans: *do not advertise government intervention in the economy*. Naturally, there were some minorities that, in fact, rejected the neoliberal proposal, not least the influential industries that were knocking on Washington's doors asking for trade protection.

In short, it was in these years that the American industrial strategy started to capitalize the US economic power by promoting an institutional framework able, on the one hand, to pave the way for foreign markets and, on the other hand, to protect and promote the development of the national industry.

NOTES

1. See, for example, Schultze (1983), Chaudhuri (1990), Krueger (1990), Le Grand (1991), Chang (1994), Khan (2000), Lerner (2009), Di Tommaso and Schweitzer (2013).
2. Reagan R., 20 January 1981, Inaugural Address, http://www.reaganfoundation.org/pdf/Inaugural_Address_012081.pdf. (Last accessed February 2016).
3. In those years another measure of export promotion was introduced by the Administration Reagan through the Export Trading Company Act of 1982. The Act essentially allowed certain types of banks to charge interest rate subsidies to exporting companies and also allowed to export specific activities a partial exemption from antitrust laws (Baldwin and Richardson 1987: 135).
4. For a summary of the contents of the Buy American Act of 1933 and subsequent amendments see for example Luckey (2009).
5. See Nester 1997; Bingham and Sharpe 1998; Mowery 1998; Chang 2008; Block 2008; Weiss 2014.
6. For further details see Block (2008); Schrank and Whitford (2009); Wade (2012); Weiss (2014).

REFERENCES

Audretsch, D. B. (2003). Standing on the Shoulders of Midgets: The US Small Business Innovation Research Program (Sbir). *Small Business Economics, 20*(2), 129–135.

Baldwin, R., & Richardson, D. (1987). Recent U.S. Trade Policy and Its Global Implications. In C. I. Bradford Jr. & W. H. Branson (Eds.), *Trade and Structural Change in Pacific Asia* (pp. 121–156). Chicago: University of Chicago Press.

Bartik, J. T. (2004). Economic Development. In R. J. Aronson & E. Schwartz (Eds.), *Management Policies in Local Government Finance* (pp. 355–390). Washington, DC: International City/County Management Association.

Bayard, T. O., & Elliott, K. A. (1994). *Reciprocity and Retaliation in U.S. Trade Policy.* Washington, DC: Institute for International Economics.

Bingham, R. D., & Sharpe, M. E. (1998). *Industrial Policy American Style: From Hamilton to HDTV.* New York: Armonk.

Block, F. (2008). Swimming against the current: The Rise of a Hidden Developmental State in the United States. *Politics & Society, 36*(2), 69–206.

Block, F., & Keller, M. (Eds.). (2011). *State of Innovation: The U.S. Government's Role in Technology Development.* Colorado: Paradigm Publishers.

Blueston, B., & Harrison, B. (1982). *The Deindustrialization of America. Plant Closings, Community Abandonment, and the Dismantling of Basic Industry.* New York: Basic Books Publisher.

Browning, L. D., & Shetler, J. C. (2000). *Sematech: Saving the U.S. Semiconductor Industry.* College Station: Texas A&M University Press.

Buigues, P. A., & Sekkat, K. (2009). *Industrial Policy in Europe, Japan and the USA. Amounts, Mechanisms and Effectiveness.* London: Palgrave Macmillan.

Chang, H. J. (1994). *The Political Economy of Industrial Policy.* New York: St Martin's Press.

Chang, H. J. (2008). *Bad Samaritans: The Myth of Free Trade and the Secret History of Capitalism.* New York: Bloomsbury Press.

Chaudhuri, D. M. (1990). Market Failure and Government Failure. *The Journal of Economic Perspectives, 4*(3), 25–39.

Destler, I. M. (2005). *American Trade Politics* (4th ed.). Washington, DC: Institute for International Economics.

Di Tommaso, M. R., & Schweitzer, S. O. (2013). *Industrial Policy in America. Breaking the Taboo.* Cheltenham: Edward Elgar.

DiLorenzo, J. T. (1984). The Political Economy of National Industrial Policy. *Cato Journal, 4*(2), 587–607.

Dobbin, F. (1994). *Forging Industrial Policy.* Cambridge: Cambridge University Press.

Dorn, J. A. (1984). Planning America: Government or The Market? Introduction. *Cato Journal, 4*(2), 365–380.

Dubnick, M. (1984). American States and the Industrial Policy Debate. *Review of Policy Research, 4*(1), 22–27.

Dumke, G. (1984). Preface. In C. Johnson (Ed.), *The Industrial Policy Debate.* California: Institute for Contemporary Studies.

Eisinger, P. (1990). Do the American States Do Industrial Policy? *British Journal of Political Science, 20*(4), 509–535. Reprinted in Hawdon, J. E. (1990). *Industrial Policy and Competitive Advantage.* Edward Elger Publishing Limited.

Engelhardt, T. (1995). *The End of Victory Culture: Cold War America and the Disillusioning of a Generation*. New York: Basic Book.

ERP. (1981). *Economic Report of the President*. Washington, DC: United States Government Printing Office.

ERP. (1982). *Economic Report of the President*. Washington, DC: United States Government Printing Office.

ERP. (1984). *Economic Report of the President*. Washington, DC: United States Government Printing Office.

ERP. (1986). *Economic Report of the President*. Washington, DC: United States Government Printing Office.

ERP. (1988). *Economic Report of the President*. Washington, DC: United States Government Printing Office.

ERP. (1989). *Economic Report of the President*. Washington, DC: United States Government Printing Office.

ERP. (2013). *Economic Report of the President*. Washington, DC: United States Government Printing Office.

Etzioni, A. (1983). The MITIzation of America?, *The Public Interest*, No. 72.

Graham, O. L. (1992). *Losing Time: The Industrial Policy Debate*. Cambridge, MA: Harvard University Press.

Hall, P., & Soskice, D. (Eds.). (2001). *Varieties of Capitalism*. Oxford: Oxford University Press.

Hallacher, P. M. (2005). *Why Policy Issue Networks Matter: The Advanced Technology Program and the Manufacturing Extension Partnership*. Lanham: Rowman & Littlefield Publishers Incorporated.

Hamilton, A. (1791). *Report on the Subject of Manufactures*. Republished by Cosimo Inc., New York, 2007.

Harvey, D. (2005). *A Brief History of Neoliberalism*. New York: Oxford University Press.

Johnson, C. (1984). *The Industrial Policy Debate*. California: Institute for Contemporary Studies.

Ketels, C. H. M. (2007). Industrial Policy in the United States, *Journal of Industry, Competition and Trade*, 7(3/4), 147–167.

Khan, M. H. (2000). Rent Seeking as a Process. In M. H. Khan & K. S. Jomo (Eds.), *Rents, Rent-Seeking and Economic Development. Theory and Evidence in Asia*. Cambridge: Cambridge University Press.

Knight, F. H. (1921). *Risk, Uncertainty, and Profit*. Boston/New York: Houghton Mifflin.

Krueger, A. O. (1990). Government Failures in Development. *The Journal of Economic Perspectives*, 4(3), 9–23.

Kuhn, T. S. (1962). *The Structure of Scientific Revolutions*. Chicago: The University of Chicago Press.

Le Grand, J. (1991). The Theory of Government Failure. *British Journal of Political Science*, 21(4), 423–442.

Lerner, J. (1999). The Government as Venture Capitalist: The Long Run Impact of the Sbir Program. *Journal of Business, LXXII*(3), 285–318.

Lerner, J. (2009). *Boulevard of Broken Dreams: Why Public Efforts to Boost Entrepreneurship and Venture Capital Have Failed and What to Do About It.* Princeton: Princeton University Press.

Luckey, J. R. (2009). *The Buy American Act: Requiring Government Procurements to Come from Domestic Sources.* Washington, DC: Congressional Research Service.

Magaziner, I. C., & Reich, R. B. (1982). *Minding America's Business: The Decline and Rise of the American Economy.* New York: Vintage Books.

Mann, M. (1997). Has Globalization Ended the Rise and Fall of the Nation State? *Review of International Political Economy, 4*(3), 472–496.

Mazzucato, M. (2013). *The Entrepreneurial State. Debunking Public vs. Private Sector Myths.* UK and USA: Anthem Press.

Mowery, D. C. (1998). The Changing Structure of the US National Innovation System: Implication for International and Conflict in R&D Policy. *Research Policy, 27*, 639–654.

Nester, W. R. (1997). *American Industrial Policy.* London: Macmillan.

Niskanen, W. A. (1988). *U. S. Trade Policy.* The Cato Review of Business & Government.

Norton, R. D. (1986). Industrial Policy and American Renewal. *Journal of Economic Literature, 24*(1), 1–40.

Panitch, L., & Gindin, S. (2012). *The Making of Global Capitalism: The Political Economy of American Empire.* London: Verso.

Reich, R. B. (1982). Why the US Needs an Industrial Policy. *Harvard Business Review, 60*(1), 74–81.

Reich, R. B. (1984). *The Next American Frontier.* New York: Penguin Books.

Reich, R. B. (1985). Reagan's Hidden "Industrial Policy", *New York Times,* August 4, 1985.

Reich, R. B., & Donahue, J. D. (1985). *New Deals: The Chrysler Revival and the American System.* New York: Times Books.

Richman, S. L. (1988). The Reagan Record On Trade: Rhetoric Vs. Reality. *Cato Policy Analysis,* No. 107.

Schrank, A. J., & Whitford, J. (2009). Industrial Policy in the United States: A Neo-Polanyian Interpretation. *Politics and Society, 37*(4), 521–553.

Schultze, C. L. (1983). Industrial Policy: A Dissent. *The Brookings Review, 2*(1), 3–12.

Shapira, P. (2001). US Manufacturing Extension Partnership: Technology Policy Reinvented? *Research Policy, 30*(6), 977–992.

Simon, H. A. (1947). *Administrative Behaviour.* New York: Macmillan.

Spender, J. C. (2012). Strategizing. In J. D. Wright (Ed.), *International Encyclopedia Social and Behavioral Sciences* (2nd ed.). Amsterdam: Elsevier.

Van Horn, R., & Mirowski, P. (2009). The Rise of the Chicago School of Economics and the Birth of Neoliberalism. In P. Mirowski & D. Plehwe (Eds.), *The Road from Mont Pèlerin. The Making of the Neoliberal Thought Collective.* Cambridge, MA/London, UK: Harvard University Press.

Wade, R. H. (2012). Return of Industrial Policy? *International Review of Applied Economics, 26*(2), 223–239.

Wade, R. H. (2014). The Paradox of US Industrial Policy: The Developmental State in Disguise. In J. M. Salazar-Xirinachs, I. Nübler, & R. Kozul-Wright (Eds.), *Transforming Economies: Making Industrial Policy Work for Growth, Jobs and Development.* International Labour Office: Geneva.

Weiss, L. (2014). *America Inc.? Innovation and Enterprise in the National Security State.* New York: Cornell University Press.

Weiss, L., & Thurbon, E. (2006). The Business of Buying American: Government Procurement as Trade Strategy. *Review of International Political Economy, 13*(5), 701–724.

White, L. J. (2007). *Antitrust Policy and Industrial Policy: A View from the U.S.* Presented at the Second Lisbon Conference on Competition Law and Economics, Lisbon.

Whitford, J. (2005). *The New Old Economy. Networks, Institutions, and Organizational Transformation of American Manufacturing.* Oxford: Oxford University Press.

Whitford, J., & Schrank, A. (2011). The Paradox of the Weak State Revisited: Industrial Policy, Network Governance, and Political Decentralization. In F. Block & M. Keller (Eds.), *State of Innovation: The U.S. Government's Role in Technology Development.* Boulder: Paradigm Publishers.

Williamson, J. (1989). What Washington Means by Policy Reform. In J. Williamson (Ed.), *Latin American Readjustment: How Much has Happened.* Washington: Institute for International Economics.

CHAPTER 4

The End of the Cold War and the New Neoliberal Order

As shown in the previous chapter, the 1980s saw an irruptive neoliberal rhetoric take its first steps in the United States, by the hands of President Reagan, and very soon became the theoretical and ideological model of reference in many countries at the international level.[1] At the beginning of the 1990s, the neoliberal ideology was already well spread and rooted on global ground. Under the pressure of this new ideological wind, the international political and economic order was changing radically, fostering an important acceleration of the globalization process. Some main elements were part of this radical institutional restructuring around the world.

First of all, 1989 was signed by the fall of the Berlin Wall and, along with it, by the end of the Cold War. During the 1980s, President Reagan, the US CIA and the US trade union, with the support of the Vatican and the Catholic Church, had contributed to develop an international political pressure and a system of economic aid that favoured the opposition of the Polish people to the communist regime of Moscow. The events which took place in Poland in those years—including the first strikes of workers employed in the regime's industries, the creation of the Polish union (*Solidarnosc*) and the resistance to Moscow's martial law—prepared the final conditions for the fall of the Berlin Wall in November 1989, the symbol of the communist regime downfall and the end of the Cold War. The new political equilibrium would soon be translated into a "new international economic order", where the United States appeared as the only

© The Author(s) 2019
M. Tassinari, *Capitalising Economic Power in the US*,
International Political Economy Series,
https://doi.org/10.1007/978-3-319-76648-5_4

leader left in the global scenario. This context meant that the transition from a collectivized economy to a market economy for many post-communist states and the US government, along with the international institutions, found abundant space to manage this transition by promoting a rapid liberalization of the markets (Stiglitz 2002).

Another prominent element of these years that was substantially altering the global economic scenario was related to the processes of definition of common international economic rules. The negotiations in the context of the Uruguay Round led to the creation of the WTO in 1994, replacing the GATT. This new international institution started, in those years, to represent the supreme authority placed to guarantee the maximum extent of the markets at the international level. Even if the negotiations for the establishment of economic rules under the WTO were formally carried out at a multilateral level, the United States benefited from an undisputed political and economic leadership and from their stronger bargaining power compared to the other countries. There is little doubt, in fact, that the birth of the WTO coincided with a historical period characterized by a substantial identity of views between the American government and the main economic international institutions.

As a part of this neoliberal scenario, several other trade initiatives took place during the 1990s as regional and supranational integration. The NAFTA, signed in 1992, represented the most remarkable resolution for the establishment of a free trade zone in North America. Similar processes were happening in Europe, which, in the same year, saw the signature of the Maastricht Treaty for the economic and political integration in the context of the European Union. This event represented (and it still represents today) a prominent challenge for the future of Europe as a unified entity, where important economic and political interests were at stake for the whole Union. However, the realization of the integration was not only a matter for the Europeans. Obviously this issue importantly aroused the interest of the United States, that were involved in the process because of the existing trade relations between the two blocks, looking at Europe as a larger and unified potential market for American products (and also as a potential stronger competitor).

Another important element in order to understand the international institutional context of the 1990s concerns the "Global South". Indeed, the 1980s and 1990s coincided with a growing debt crisis in many developing economies. This circumstance opened up important spaces for the definition and implementation of economic and institutional reforms in the debtor countries. Also in this case, reforms meant the establishment of a neoliberal setting in the economic and political activity in debtor countries, whereby the role played by the United States and the international institutions based in Washington was prominent.

These major changes in the global institutional framework of the 1990s occurred along with the emergence of new global competitors such as South Korea, Taiwan, Hong Kong, Singapore—the so-called Asian tigers—and Malaysia, Thailand and Indonesia and, a little later, China. In America, the perception of these new competitors suggested that more effort should be put in order "to enable the United States to take advantage of the new opportunities and to meet the new challenges of the changing global marketplace" (ERP 1994: 206).

All the above-mentioned circumstances were radically changing the global institutional and competitive framework. The ideas of market liberalization, privatization and fiscal austerity promoted during the 1980s by President Reagan spread out rapidly and exerted its impact all around the world as the dominant economic and political model: this was the decade in which the neoliberal paradigm started to have its greatest influence under the auspices of the *Washington Consensus* (Williamson 1989). In this context, the ability of domestic firms to enter the global networks of suppliers and customers gained increasing importance, and the economic policy approach seemed to change substantially in all industrialized economies. Protectionism and national policies, which had a vertical impact on economic sectors during the previous decades, were replaced by policies aimed at regulating and managing trade with global economies, which brought about economic integration and the signing of several multilateral and bilateral agreements. The ability of national governments to significantly influence negotiations of supranational and international agreements (such as WTO and NAFTA) became a central feature of the national economies' industrial strategies.[2]

During these years, the American government took the lead as a regulator by actively participating in the definition of supranational and international rules. The establishment of a number of multilateral and bilateral trade agreements was at the centre of the American political agenda. This chapter describes the role played by the United States in shaping the new neoliberal order of the 1990s and the actions implemented in order to take advantage of the changing global system.

Industrial Strategy in the Context of the World Trade Organization (WTO)

In the early 1990s, it was clear that the new neoliberal order was born under long-term auspices of the US administrations, which for decades had adopted a clear trade policy strategy: liberalizing foreign markets. This was the imprinting that American governments had given to the global economic changes for decades, as Clinton administration's words openly asserted:

> This Administration, like its predecessors, has responded to these changes by pursuing liberalization and the promotion of exports at a variety of negotiating levels. The American approach has been of nondiscrimination: negotiated reductions in trade barriers should apply to all trading nations; individual nations should not cut deals that benefit themselves at the expense of others. (ERP 1995: 203)

Historical reasons were brought forward by Clinton administration for justifying the adoption of a neoliberal perspective, which stemmed from an analysis of past economic policy mistakes. The protectionist policy, economic isolationism and the reduction of international trade of the 1920s were held responsible for the aggravation of the Great Depression's consequences (ERP 1994, 1996, 1997, 1998). With President Franklin Delano Roosevelt (1933–1945), the New Deal policies and, in particular, the Reciprocal Trade Agreements Act of 1934, international trade seemed to come back to life (ERP 1998). From the Second World War, the United States was described as the promoters and defenders of free trade and of market liberalization. During the 1990s, the Clinton administration felt the task of continuing the mission of liberalizing international trade, which had historically characterized American economic thinking (ERP 1995). This was the standpoint from which the United States approached the great changes that were taking place in the 1990s.

The United States' commitment to shape the international institutional context was primarily focused on the multilateral initiatives ongoing in those years. Among these initiatives, one of the most important ones was undoubtedly represented by the Uruguay Round, namely the GATT negotiations which led to the creation of the WTO in 1995. The importance that the United States attributed to these negotiations was central:

As global integration advances and competition intensifies, the United States must increase its efforts to lead the world toward a system of free trade and open markets. The Administration remains strongly committed to those efforts and staunchly opposed to managed trade. That commitment means actively removing trade barriers and resisting inevitable calls for protection – thereby opening markets, not closing them. The President's highest priority in trade policy is to further the role of the General Agreement on Tariffs and Trade (GATT) as a rules-based system for liberalizing trade and settling trade disputes. (ERP 1990: 30)

The GATT was born at the end of the Second World War with the aim of establishing a system of basic rules for international trade. It was initially signed by 23 countries that attended the Geneva Conference of 1947, and became effective in 1948. The number of participating countries grew in subsequent decades and in the early 1990s the GATT was signed by 96 countries representing about 80% of the World Trade (ERP 1990). Within the GATT, the acceding countries had conducted several rounds of negotiations. The Uruguay Round, which was the last of the GATT negotiations, was certainly one of the most significant. It began in 1986 with the Reagan administration, involved the following Bush administration and ended during the Clinton administration in 1994, with the establishment of the WTO.

The Uruguay Round pursued several fundamental objectives, such as the reduction of trade barriers, the extension of GATT rules to new sectors and the adaptation of international rules to new commercial realities. Other measures were related to the regulation of foreign investments (through the Agreement on Trade-related Investment Measures—TRIM), the protection of intellectual property (through the Agreement on Trade-related Aspects of Intellectual Property Rights—TRIP), uniform quality standards for products, regulation of safeguard measures (e.g. the so-called voluntary export restraints and anti-dumping measures) and the adoption of a dispute settlement system between member states (ERP 1991, 1995). These were crucial areas of action in regulating global competitive dynamics.

In this context, the liberalization of the international markets of those years took place under the influence of the United States on the reduction and elimination of the trade tariffs around the world. The Bush Senior administration demanded cutting tariffs on "thousands of specific products", particularly in the agricultural, textiles and services sectors (ERP 1991). In this process of liberalization, the "safeguard measures" represented a crucial step of the Uruguay Round negotiations. These were trade measures for the temporary restriction on imports of goods from abroad in order to allow the weaker economies to adapt their national industries to the changing global competitive environment. In this area, however, the new regulation provided the possibility for the countries affected by safeguard measures (i.e. countries forced by these measures to reduce their exports) to claim compensation from the countries adopting these measures. Such a framework de facto discouraged the use of this formal instrument in favour of more informal bilateral agreements on import restrictions (ERP 1991: 251). This fact meant that the safeguard of the weaker economies, which were unable to stand for international competition, was entrusted to bilateral negotiations, whose outcome depended on the mutual bargaining powers at stake. In this scenario, the United States appeared as the country with an unquestioned negotiating power, due to the vast internal market they controlled, with the possibility to take advantage from the negotiations (ERP 1995: 212–213). In this scenario, it was clear that international rules favoured the most competitive economies, which did not need trade protection, harming the weakest ones, to whom the possibility of implementing protectionist policies was legally denied (see, in particular, Weiss 2005).

Indeed, the establishment of the WTO (along with the other trade agreements of that period) gradually imposed strong constraints on the member states on the implementation of protectionist industrial policies, by providing a uniform framework of trade rules. As highlighted, for example, by Pack and Saggi (2006), from this historical period, characterized by a substantial acceleration of globalization processes, the whole economic and institutional mechanism of the international trade started to change. On the one hand, enterprises were increasingly buying their inputs from global-based suppliers, creating international manufacturing networks. On the other hand, national companies started to distribute their products through articulated global retail chains. In this context, the ability of companies of being internationally integrated into these trade networks with suppliers and customers gained more and more importance, increasing efficiency in organizing the production processes and reducing their costs. According to Pack and Saggi (2006), with the creation of this new competitive environment, industrial policies based on the protection of specific sectors or companies lost much of their significance for the advanced economies, leaving to the market system a wider space in the definition of the national productive structure. The new government task was that of fostering the integration of the national economy into the complex international supply networks (Pack and Saggi 2006).[3]

As a consequence, in this new context, the "old" protectionist policy appeared only as an impediment to the growth of the more dynamically and globally interconnected economies, and it was largely banned by the rules imposed by the WTO regime. From the 1990s, however, the role of the government as a *regulator* was noteworthy, not just in the domestic economy (i.e. by providing *public goods* to strengthen the competitiveness of national companies, such as research activities and infrastructures), but also at the international and supranational level, by contributing to the definition of trade rules under the multilateral and bilateral agreements of that period. In the case of the United States, in particular, the ability to exercise significant influence within the WTO played a central role in the implementation of the US trade policy strategy. Initially, the establishment of the WTO system as a set of international trade rules, aroused concern in the United States about the relationship between the rules imposed by the international organization and domestic sovereignty (ERP 1995: 212). The raised issues in particular concerned the possibility of undermining national interest (e.g. in terms of less stringent health and safety standards) by deregulating or liberalizing some American markets. The Clinton administration responded to these resistances to the US participation in the WTO, by clearly showing how international rules would not harm American sovereignty at the national level (ERP 1995). Indeed, trade agreements established within the WTO would have a limited legal force in the United States. If there was a risk of undermining the national interest, the United States could have refrained from applying certain laws by offering trade liberalization in other areas as compensation, or by accepting commercial barriers to the US exports in sectors of interest for other countries (ERP 1995). The outcome of trade agreements within the WTO was therefore essentially determined by bargaining dynamics, which allowed the prevailing interests to be expressed and the predominant powers to impose their will.

In conclusion, despite the fact that the WTO was a goal pursued in a formally multilateral climate, the United States, as the main economic and military power of those years, was the counterpart with the best chance of conducting the negotiations in a way that could put American national interest before that of other trading partners.[4] As a result, the bargaining dynamics through which the agreements were reached, led, in the 1990s, to a substantial identity of views of the US government and the WTO in shaping the conformation of the global system. In this regard, the Economic Report of President (ERP) of 1995 asserted:

> Although the principle of one country, one vote as always characterized the GATT, in fact GATT votes were almost never taken; decisions were reached on the basis of consensus among members. In practice, the United States has always had a major influence over the course of GATT policy, not because it has had a larger formal vote but, in baldest terms, because it brought the largest market to the table. [...] Of course, Uruguay Round agreement and the WTO do place obligations on the United States, but the balance of obligations in this accord is favorable, both because the United States had considerable influence on the Uruguay Round outcome, and because this country has a transparent, rules-based system and the WTO represent a convergence toward a system of this type. (ERP 1995: 212–213)

TACTIC IN THE INTERNATIONAL PUBLIC PROCUREMENT

The fact that the United States undoubtedly had the power to influence international rules and their effectiveness in creating actual constraints to the American economy was clearly reflected also in international public procurements. As argued in the previous chapters, public procurements had been an important tool for the US industrial strategy, capable of fulfilling the dual objective of promoting industrial development and trading protection of certain sectors. In particular, this policy (regulated at a national level by the Buy American Act of 1933) had pursued industrial development through a massive public demand, able to exploit economies of scale and "learning by doing" and, at the same time, it had protected the national industry from foreign competition, since American programmes excluded foreign companies as potentially suppliers of the American public administrations (Weiss and Thurbon 2006).

In the 1990s, the Uruguay Round addressed the issues of the regulation of public procurements at international level, with the main aim of liberalizing public procurement markets. In reality, the international regulation in this area had already begun at the end of the 1960s under previous GATT's Rounds. The first two Government Procurement Agreements (GPAs) had come into force respectively in 1981 and 1988. However, the Uruguay Round conducted from 1986 to 1994 introduced a more structured regulation, with the signing of the WTO-GPA in 1994 (which came into force in 1996). The agreement was initially signed by the United States, Canada, 15 EU Member States, Japan, Israel, Korea, Norway and Switzerland.[5]

Nevertheless, the path towards a substantial resolution of the problem of the discrimination of foreign companies in accessing national public procurement markets—still unfinished[6]—was particularly tortuous during the 1990s, leaving (once again) a wide space for disputes and agreements conducted at a bilateral level.

In this context, the "trade war" between the United States and the European Community (EC) of the early 1990s is an emblematic case. In 1993, the EC Directive on public procurement in the utilities sector (the Directive 93/38/EEC, also called the "Utilities Directive") required that the EC operators gave a 3% price preference to EC suppliers over third-country suppliers. The United States felt that this Directive would lead to unwarranted discrimination against US telecom equipment suppliers. Accordingly, in May 1993, the US government reacted by imposing unilaterally sanctions under Title VII of the 1988 Omnibus Trade and Competitiveness Act against most EC Member States. In particular, sanctions were applied to: contracts for goods, services and constructions whose value had fallen below certain thresholds; all service contracts purchased by the Tennessee Valley Authority and Power Marketing Administrations of the DOE; a list of 14 services given as procurement by federal agencies, including broadcasting, R&D, legal services, health and telecommunications. In direct response to these sanctions, the EC imposed equivalent countermeasures in June 1993.[7]

A similar case was raised by trade relations with Japan (which in the 1990s was the second most important American trading partner). The success of Japanese companies in American markets and the difficulties of American suppliers to enter Japanese markets prompted the United States to accuse Japan of unfair trade practices. Some measures were taken under the GATT, but other initiatives were carried out under the aforementioned "Super 301" of the Omnibus Trade and Competitiveness Act in order to liberalize the public procurement market for computers and satellites (ERP 1990).[8]

The cases presented above show that, in the 1990s, the WTO public procurement regulation, as a means of opening up public procurement markets, left to individual states a considerable margin for autonomy in the implementation of national purchase programmes, which were discriminatory against foreign suppliers. As a result, even in a renewed neoliberal context, public procurements continued to be a strategic tool used by a country to promote industrial development strategies. On the one hand, within the international regulation, it provided the opportunity to leverage on the government's ability to influence the opening of foreign public procurement markets (relying on the rules of the WTO-GPA or through bilateral agreements). On the other hand, within the national regulation, it provided the opportunity to exploit the capacity to close the domestic public procurement market to foreign companies, by circumventing international law.

According to Weiss and Thurbon (2006), the ability of the United States to strategically manage these two levels of intervention was a fundamental feature of American approach to public procurements. Indeed, the US government adopted an aggressive policy of opening foreign public procurement markets, through the influence exercised in the definition of the WTO-GPA. In this field the United States had the ability to spread the WTO regulation to an increasing number of countries and to negotiate, at a bilateral level, better conditions of access to the foreign markets. At the same time, American administration was able, in many circumstances, to close to foreign suppliers the domestic market of public procurement, by claiming national law (*Buy American*) through legal loopholes or other types of informal barriers (Weiss and Thurbon 2006). Through this trade policy strategy, the American industrial system could benefit from domestic and foreign public demand, with important positive effects on the development of the productive skills and capacities. In this regard, Weiss and Thurbon (2006) state: "no other state has been as globally active in driving open procurement markets; and no other state has been as nationally protectionist in legally mandating 'buy national' policies" (Weiss and Thurbon 2006: 705).

The NAFTA and Other Regional Trade Agreements

In addition to the WTO multilateral agreements, the US commitment to the creation of the neoliberal institutional framework of those years was focused on a number of regional initiatives. Among these initiatives, the NAFTA—the agreement between the United States, Canada and Mexico—was one of the most important. Already President Reagan, at the beginning of his mandate, had proposed a "North American Agreement". From Reagan's proposal, after a number of negotiations, the 1988 US-Canada Free Trade Agreement was signed, which involved exclusively the United

States and Canada. From this first agreement a series of negotiations led the Bush Senior administration to the official NAFTA signature in December 1992 (just a few days before the end of his mandate) (ERP 1992, 1993). The Clinton administration, in 1993, ratified the 1992 agreement and integrated the NAFTA with subsidiary agreements, in particular on issues concerning labour and environment: the NAFTA and these subsidiary agreements came into force on 1 January 1994.

The main points discussed in the negotiations for the establishment of the NAFTA were: the elimination of most (tariff and non-tariff) trade barriers; the definition of a system of common rules for investments; the liberalization of the financial sector, land transportation and telecommunications services; the consolidation of laws on the labour market and environment; the establishment of a dispute resolution mechanism and of a system for the protection of intellectual property rights. In 1993, the Clinton administration, by integrating the NAFTA with some subsidiary agreements, defined guiding principles and institutions to address issues related to environmental deterioration, to the standards required for workers' rights and to the damage caused by an excessive competitive pressure among member countries. Concerning the latter point, the potential risk that some sectors of the US economy could be threatened by rising imports from Mexico and Canada led the Clinton administration to predispose the adoption of "adjustment" measures. It was established that liberalization would take place over 10 years for industrial products and over 15 years for agricultural products. Also, safeguard measures were envisaged to temporarily limit imports when they constituted an excessive threat to the national economy. Finally, the Transitional Adjustment Assistance (TAA) programme was implemented in order to mitigate the costs of the adjustment on workers, through employment and training services, unemployment insurance and reimbursement benefits. In 1994, the NAFTA-TAA programme provided assistance to approximately 12,000 workers (ERP 1995). The underlying motives of the NAFTA agreement were clear in President Clinton's words:

> I believe that NAFTA will create 200,000 American jobs in the first 2 years of its effect. I believe if you look at the trends – and President Bush and I were talking about it this morning – starting about the time he was elected President, over one-third of our economic growth and in some years over one-half of our net new jobs came directly from exports. (...) I believe that NAFTA will create a million jobs in the first 5 years of its impact. (...) NAFTA will generate these jobs by fostering an export boom to Mexico, by

tearing down tariff walls which have been lowered quite a bit by the present administration of President Salinas but are still higher than Americas'. Already Mexican consumers buy more per capita from the United States than other consumers in other nations. Most Americans don't know this, but the average Mexican citizen, even though wages are much lower in Mexico, the average Mexican citizen is now spending $450 per year per person to buy American goods.[9]

The goal of maximizing the export of American products to increase domestic wealth was the key reason that drove the US trade strategy in the 1990s. With this perspective, in addition to the NAFTA, the United States launched other two important regional initiatives in those years.

The first one, the Free Trade Area of the Americas (FTAA), launched in December 1994 by the Clinton administration, was a plan to establish a free trade area with Latin American countries by 2005 (33 were the countries that participated in the discussion on the initiative at the first summit in Miami in 1994). The idea behind the FTAA was to begin standardizing subregional trade agreements through common rules to facilitate the path towards the establishment of the largest free trade area (ERP 1996). From the first meeting in Miami, a long series of Summits of Americas and of negotiations between the countries involved in the FTAA project began: Santiago (1998), Quebec (2001), Monterey (2004), Mar de la Plata (2005). There were also Trade Ministerial Meetings: Denver (1995), Cartagena (1996), Belo Horizonte (1997), San Jose (1998), Toronto (1999), Buenos Aires (2001), Quito (2002), Miami (2003). Permanent working groups were formed on numerous areas: agriculture, government procurement, investment, competition policy, intellectual property rights, services, dispute settlement, subsidies, anti-dumping and countervailing duties. In this context, the main issues at stake were the elimination of tariff and non-tariff barriers, the reform and homogenization of custom regimes, investment promotion, sanitary standards and anti-dumping measures. The potential benefit for the United States from the establishment of the FTAA was clearly highlighted by the 1996 ERP:

> The United States should reap significant benefits from establishment of the FTAA. It will create a market of over 850 million consumers with a combined income of roughly $13 trillion [...] The FTAA will also level the playing field for U.S. exporters, reducing Latin American trade barriers that are currently three times higher on average than U.S. barriers. (ERP 1996: 241)

In reality, the FTAA negotiations progressively became more and more complex and lengthy. Summits of Americas and Trade Ministerial Meetings continued, although in some Latin American countries a strong opposition to the project arose, highlighting the disparities in economic and political power that characterized the countries involved in the FTAA. The FTAA project did not therefore successfully reached completion in 2005, as initially planned. However, the activities and negotiations implemented in this context played an important role in the neoliberal climate of those years, succeeding in influencing the policies of many Latin American governments in the direction taken by President Clinton.

The second initiative was the Asia-Pacific Economic Cooperation (APEC). It was launched in 1989 to boost economic cooperation with Asian economies (initially there were 12 countries involved). Since the beginning of his mandate in 1993, President Clinton was firmly committed to further develop the opportunities offered by this cooperation, which in the meanwhile had been expanded to 18 countries (including China, Singapore, South Korea, Malaysia and Thailand). In particular, a number of meetings were held between the leaders of the participating countries in order to make the role of the APEC more substantial in solving the concrete trade problems in the region, which represented about 30% of the world trade. The first meeting was in 1993 in the State of Washington, the second in 1994 in Indonesia and the third in 1996 in Japan. Following these meetings, the leaders of the countries involved in the project decided to adopt an Action Agenda to achieve the goal of the markets liberalization by 2020. In particular, the objective of the initiative was related to market access issues, such as quotas and tariffs, services, investment, competition and deregulation policies (ERP 1996). The nature of the Action Agenda was strongly oriented to concrete action:

> The principles embodied in the Action Agenda ensure that liberalization in each country will be comprehensive, covering all products, services, and investment, and require each country to achieve results that are balanced and comparable to those of other APEC members. In the coming months, each member will detail the specific steps it will take to begin implementing the Action Agenda. (ERP 1996: 242)

The Situation in Europe

In the 1990s, regional integration processes similar to NAFTA were also taking place in Europe. Since the Treaty of Rome (1957) the economic integration and the creation of a single market among member countries had been the main objectives pursued by the European Economic Community (EEC). The goal was to gradually promote free movement of goods, services, people and capitals, in order to increase efficiency, competitiveness and opportunities for specialization for European economies (Treaty of Rome, 1957). As broadly documented, the process of liberalization within Europe—still not fully concluded—was complex and gradual.[10]

The 1970s were characterized by a vertical and protectionist industrial policy implemented by single member states and by the Community to address the crisis. This policy approach, rather incompatible with a single market, changed quite radically during the mid-1980s. The White Paper of 1985 emphasized the importance of reducing not only tariff barriers, already significantly reduced during the 1960s, but also non-tariff ones, that continued to make the movement of goods within the European market unsatisfactory. In this context, a process of harmonization of national legislation in the field of technical standards and of removal of administrative barriers to trade began (Cecchini et al. 1988; Emerson et al. 1989). As a matter of fact, the European industrial policy assumed a connotation mainly horizontal (Bianchi and Labory 2011). The selective policies in favour of particular industries were drastically reduced, while the emerging literature on *government failures* was exposing the difficulties for public administrations in "picking the winners" and being immune to lobbies' pressures (Schultze 1983; Krueger 1990; Le Grand 1991; Chang 1994).

In this new framework, a growing attention was given to encourage markets' competition and efficiency. The new industrial policy was aimed at developing the ability of economic agents to participate in the competitive game by improving the "institutional environment", in which businesses operated. Thus, the creation of the single market and the definition of the rules for its proper functioning became the first European industrial policy (Bianchi and Labory 2011). One of the main priorities which the European treaties focused on was the protection of competition through the coordination of antitrust regulations of the member countries (Pelkmans 2006). It was in this context that the EC, in 1993, concluded the path towards the establishment of the European Union.[11]

The interest of the United States in the realization of this European integration process was obviously particularly high during the years of the Bush administration, because of the existing trade relations. In particular, the United States was looking at Europe as a larger and unified potential market for American products (and also as a potential stronger competitor). In this regard, the ERP of 1992 stated:

> For both U.S. exporters and investors, EC 92 offers potential benefits, partly because it creates an integrated market, and partly because the process of integration could promote growth. As trading partner, the United States could gain through increased EC demand for imported products. The realization of these benefits, however, depends on the EC market's openness to external trade and how much more competitive European companies become. (ERP 1992: 224)

In the context of these opportunities and challenges, for example, there was the signing of the Airbus Agreement, in July 1992, a bilateral agreement between the United States and the EC to provide restrictions to government subsidies and other forms of support to the civil aviation industry (ERP 1991). Furthermore, in June 1997, there was the US-EU Agreement on Mutual Recognition of Product Testing or Approval Requirements. This agreement essentially established that the governments of the two countries had to mutually recognize the validity of product testing and certification, eliminating, by so doing, the need to duplicate controls and inspections on requisites, with considerable savings for the exporting companies. In this context, barriers to trade in telecommunications, medical equipment, electromagnetic compatibility, electrical safety, pleasure craft and pharmaceuticals were reduced (ERP 1998).

PUSHING STRUCTURAL REFORMS: POLICIES IN TRANSITION ECONOMIES AND IN DEVELOPING COUNTRIES

In November 1989, the fall of the Berlin Wall signed the end of the communist regime and of the Cold War. The new political equilibrium would soon be translated into a "new international economic order", where the American capitalism appeared triumphant, as an economic model from which to draw example. This context meant the transition from a collectivized economy to a market economy for many post-communist states.

During these years, the United States—under the Bush Senior administration—had a clear idea of the direction that the economic transition of the "Soviet Bloc" had to take: "A renewed commitment to open markets and policies that encourage competitive and undistorted markets and greater productivity are keys to growth – for both industrial countries and economies in transition" (ERP 1992: 233).

Following this perspective, the Bush administration—in combination with the role played by international institutions and multilateral agreements—pursued a number of bilateral initiatives to promote the opening of markets in transition economies.

The Enterprise for Americas Initiative (EAI) of 1990, for example, was a legislation that laid the foundations for the expansion of free trade zones in the Western Hemisphere. It pursued three main goals: to establish trade agreements between North and South America, to expand investments and to reduce debt for Latin American and Caribbean countries. In the context of this initiative, the negotiations on the liberalization of markets and investments were conducted in Mexico, which led to the signing of NAFTA. Subsequently, the United States began negotiations with many other countries, including Bolivia, Colombia, Chile, Ecuador, Honduras, Costa Rica, Venezuela, Peru, Nicaragua, Argentina, Brazil, Uruguay, Paraguay (ERP 1991).

Furthermore, the Trade Enhancement Initiative (ERP 1992) established the main framework through which the United States massively intervened in Central and Eastern Europe. In order to foster economic transition, the United States allocated $944 million in subsidies and over $1 billion in other assistance programmes to the countries in the area. A special fund for $360 million was formed for the development of the private sector in Poland, Hungary and Czechoslovakia. Furthermore, the United States allocated other $200 million for technical assistance in a variety of areas, such as management training, market economics education, privatization, legal and financial reforms, strengthening democratic institutions. They also allocated $260 million for food aid (of which $112 million were destined to Romania). Finally, in 1992, with the Freedom Support Act, another $2 billion was allocated by the United States Agency for International Development (USAID) for Russia (ERP 1997).[12]

In the context of the interventions in Central and Eastern Europe, the influence of the United States was also exercised indirectly, through the participation in the activities of international institutions. Indeed, the

International Monetary Fund (IMF) allocated around \$5 billion in 1991, the World Bank \$9 billion (between 1991 and 1994), while the European Bank for Reconstruction and Development between 1991 and 1996 granted loans for \$7 billion.[13]

The main interest of the American economy in providing these aids was, in the vast markets, that the transition to capitalism opened to goods and services from the United States: "These multilateral and bilateral arrangements have two-way benefits. By encouraging growth abroad, they increase exports and growth in the United States" (ERP 1992: 234).

Another important element to understand the changes in the international context of the 1990s concerns the structural reforms in the "Global South". Since the mid-1970s, many developing countries began to be indebted to the major banks in the industrialized countries, when loan conditions and repayment prospects were particularly favourable. In the early 1980s, however, interest rates on loans began to grow considerably, placing many countries in the impossibility of repaying their debts. The major American commercial banks and other industrialized countries that had lent money to developing countries began to drastically reduce the issuance of new loans to the debtors, in order to avoid significant losses and consolidate their financial position. Many nations in Latin America and Africa began to suffer from severe economic stagnation (ERP 1990).

The international response to the "debt crisis" was to promote macro-economic stabilization policies in developing countries and coordinate the provision of new loans. Among these programmes, implemented under the supervision of the IMF and the World Bank, there were, for example, the Extended Fund Facility (promoted by the IMF since 1974) and the Structural Adjustment Loan Program (promoted by World Bank in 1980)— (ERP 1993). These programmes were specifically aimed at promoting fiscal rigour, by reducing public subsidies, improving government revenue, slowing monetary growth, devaluing exchange rates and promoting exports. These policies had the effect of stabilizing international financial markets and maintaining liquidity in countries with the debt problem, although the results in terms of economic recovery were virtually null (ERP 1990).

In the subsequent years, the role played by the United States in dealing with the problems of developing countries was part of this broader international framework:

> The United State continues to take a leadership role in developing and implementing a strategy of coordinated debt restructuring and support for economic policy reforms in indebted countries, consistent with reviving growth and restoring their access to world capital markets. (ERP 1990: 235)

The history of the US "leadership role" in supporting reforms and debt restructuring in developing countries began during the Reagan presidency. The first initiative was the "Baker Plan" of 1985, launched by the Secretary of the Treasury James Baker. The programme aimed at supporting economic growth in developing countries and promoted the issuance of new loans for a total of $20 billion through international commercial banks and an increase of 50% in loans from multilateral development banks for the years 1986–1988. The programme also specifically worked in order to lead the World Bank to play a more active role in supporting institutional and sector reforms, and promoting market liberalization policies (ERP 1990).

However, the persistence of serious problems in debtor countries led the United States to new interventions. In particular, the Bush Senior administration continued to underline the need to implement market-oriented economic reforms. In 1989, the "Brady Initiative" was launched—by the Secretary of the Treasury Nicholas Brady. The programme constituted the main framework for the debt renegotiation of those years: new loans would be granted only if the debtor countries were committed to implement the economic reforms deemed necessary (ERP 1990). Under this framework, debtors and commercial credit banks could negotiate a menu of options for converting and reducing existing loans and extending new loans. The key condition for debtor countries was a commitment to implement economic adjustment programmes, defined in cooperation with the IMF and the World Bank, aimed at encouraging foreign investment. These reforms included, in particular, the reduction of government deficits (in order to reduce inflationary pressures), devaluation of exchange rates (to restore the competitiveness of exports in foreign markets), the removal of the ceilings on interest rates paid on financial investments (for stimulating national savings), the reduction of trade barriers to imports from abroad and of government regulation (in order to increase foreign investment) and the privatization of SOEs (ERP 1990).

In this context, the US aids, during the 1990s, were directed to Egypt, Israel, Haiti, India, South Africa, Turkey, Ukraine and several other countries in Sub-Saharan Africa and Latin America (ERP 1997).[14] In reality, in most cases, aids and policies directed to developing countries did not produce the expected results, and the effects of structural reforms and of the unconditional market opening were, in some cases, disastrous (Stiglitz 2002). At any rate, regardless of the effective impact that the interventions had on the recipient countries, it was evident that the economic return for the United States and American companies from the operations carried out in the Global South was undeniable:

> When our aid helps countries grow, we benefit from increased exports. For example, 20 countries have achieved a sufficient level of development to graduate from lending programs of the International Development Association (the World Bank affiliate that lends to the poorest countries on a concessional basis). These countries bought $61 billion in U.S. exports in 1995, or 6.3 percent of our total exports. And by deepening our economic relationship with developing country through aid, we also make it more likely that they will turn to U.S. firms for products in the future. (ERP 1997: 260–261)

CONCLUSION

This chapter has outlined the actions and initiatives conducted by the United States during the 1990s in many areas of international relevance: the establishment of the WTO; the negotiations for the NAFTA and other important regional agreements; the process of supranational integration in Europe; the economic transition in post-communist countries and structural reforms in developing countries. Overall, the involvement of the US government in trade agreements and structural reforms during the 1990s had an almost global reach. This evidence has suggested that the American influence in shaping the rules of the new global order during this decade has been prominent. Indeed, the end of the Cold War gave the United States an almost absolute international leadership. In this context, the US economic power has been used with the aim of creating a global institutional framework that was closely congenial to the interests of American economy. In particular, the American strategy has been to pave the way for foreign markets through the promotion of international market liberalization policies, in order to support US exports and economic growth.

The words of the US administration leave little doubt about the fact that the construction of the neoliberal international system of the last 40 years has been the fruit of the American leadership, which was able of *capitalizing its economic power* to pursue the national interest:

We are looked to for leadership in part because our economy remains the largest in the world, and in part because we are the sole remaining superpower. How do we intend to exercise that leadership? Among the most important objectives of U.S. economic policy are to ensure that the United States itself benefits fully from the integration of these emerging markets into a globalized economy [...] One way in which the United States has led the pursuit of these objectives has been by promoting an international economic system that reflects our values of openness, competition, and private enterprise. (ERP 1997: 257)

Notes

1. In reality, very few countries have been able to apply the neoliberal prescriptions to the letter, approaching this model without never completely achieving it. Perhaps Chile after the structural reforms implemented by Pinochet during the 1970s represents the most extreme attempt to embrace the neoliberal paradigm. See also the discussion on this point in Chap. 2.

2. In this context, despite the liberalization of international markets led to the reduction of public intervention at national level in many industrialized countries, the shrinking of the government role was focused particularly on protectionist trade policies. Indeed, during the neoliberal era, science and technology policies remained a high priority, continuing to value increased productivity and technological innovation, in order to assure competitiveness at the international level. The next chapter is devoted to discuss, in particular, science and technology policy during the 1990s.

3. For further details on these aspects see, for example, Elms and Low (2013), Pietrobelli and Rabellotti (2011), Gibbon et al. (2008), Gereffi et al. (2005).

4. In this context, the bargaining power of the United States during the 1990s was of the same nature which had allowed Reagan administration to negotiate *voluntary export restraints* and to adopt an "aggressive unilateralism" in trade policy during the 1980s (see Chap. 3).

5. See, among others, Trionfetti (2000), Hoekman and Mavroidis (1997).

6. For example, the *Buy American* has been relaunched in recent times, in the context of the *stimulus package* implemented by Obama in 2009 in response to the crisis, raising a lot of criticism (Hufbauer and Schott 2009).

7. Public procurement sanctions remained in force for both parties until 2006, when the substantial liberalization of the European telecommunications market rendered the US sanctions unjustified. See the Proposal for a Council Regulation (EEC) n. 352/2006, repealing Council Regulation (EEC) n. 1461/93 concerning access to public contracts for tenderers from the United States (http://eur-lex.europa.eu/legal-content/IT/ALL/?uri=CELEX:32006R0352, last accessed September 2017).

8. More generally, in addition to public procurement issues, in the same years, a broader set of issues related to the national structure and institutions was addressed with Japan through bilateral negotiations, called "Structural Impediments Initiatives", focused mainly on six areas: savings and investment; territorial planning policy; price mechanism; distribution system; antitrust policy; *Keiretsu*'s relationships (companies holding each other's capital) (ERP 1990). Further agreements also pursued the specific objective of reducing trade barriers that were restricting access to the market for American products (such as semiconductors, wood products, mobile phones and constructions) and those of structural nature (e.g. related to distribution systems, excessive regulation and lack of transparency in public procurements). With the Clinton administration, under the framework of the 1993 US-Japan Framework for a New Economic Partnership Agreement, in 1998 the United States had already negotiated 33 trade agreements with Japan, regarding both "structural issues" (such as intellectual property rights, deregulation and investment) and "sector issues" (in automotive and spare parts industry, financial services, telecommunications and medical, pharmaceutical and glass technologies) (ERP 1998).

9. Clinton W.J., Remarks at the Signing Ceremony for the Supplemental Agreements to the North American Free Trade Agreement, 14 September 1993, http://www.presidency.ucsb.edu/ws/?pid=47070 (last accessed September 2017).

10. For an overview of the European industrial policy, see, for example, Geroski (1989), Foreman-Peck and Federico (1999), Bianchi and Labory (2011), Grabas and Nützenadel (2014).

11. However, one of the main issues that the "Industrial policy in an open and competitive environment" (European Commission 1990) had to address was the *cohesion* between the different European countries. The ability of the different European territories to adequate their productive structure to the growing extent of the market and the growing competition has increasingly become fundamental for participating to the benefits of the single market. *Cohesion policies* (namely *structural adjustment policies*, or *innovation policies*, or *regional policies*—all these terms, in different historical stages, have replaced the old term "industrial policy" used during the 1970s, that was understood as synonymous of vertical and protectionist intervention) began to be implemented to stimulate innovation and the creation of complementary productive specializations in lagging regions. The Single European Act (SEA) of 1986 defined the first cohesion policies, and *structural funds* were provided to finance development projects in poorer geographical areas. Later, the structural funds were declined under other regional development programmes, including *Agenda 2000* and the *Lisbon Strategy* (Bianchi and Labory 2006). In particular, the Lisbon

Strategy, launched in 2000, was important to fix a distinctive feature of the current European industrial policy. In the prevailing approach at the beginning of the new century, the European Commission assumed the role of coordinator of the single industrial policy actions, which were defined in detail at national and regional level. In this context, the industrial policy had to be implemented at local level with a *horizontal* approach, through general interventions able to develop the competitiveness of the whole regional system, not with mere subsidies to compensate for efficiency gaps (Bianchi and Labory 2009). In this manner, the ability of the local economic actors to create networks and to share *knowledge* for innovation has today become a central element of the European industrial policy. In line with the Lisbon strategy's approach, *Europe 2020* strategy, of 2010, has encouraged the adoption of Research and Innovation Strategies for Smart Specialization (RIS 3) to promote *smart, sustainable* and *inclusive* growth (European Commission 2010). The dominant role in the managing of structural funds is played by individual states and regions (see the "Guide to Research and Innovation Strategies for Smart Specialization—RIS 3" on https://www.researchitaly.it/uploads/4692/RIS3%20Guide%20March%202012final_0204.pdf?v=048101c, last accessed September 2017). Nevertheless, today, despite the cohesion policies implemented at European level, the economic crisis and the growth of emerging industrial powers seem to have exacerbated regional disparities between the "centre" and the European "periphery" (Bianchi and Labory 2011; Pianta 2014; Fazi 2014). These internal challenges to the structural adjustment of the single countries are leading to the formation of regressive coalitions which demand protectionist policies from the national governments. Under these conditions, the European economic integration is seriously threatened.

12. On the scenarios in Russia of that period see Rice (2000), Sakwa (2008), Dunlop (1993).
13. See, White House Statement, 12 July 1991, on https://www.cambridge.org/core/journals/foreign-policy-bulletin/article/trade-enhancement-initiative-for-central-and-eastern-europe/B291ED6B52FD4CE9796F00BE81A9F392 (last accessed September 2017).
14. In 1996, for example, the Clinton administration authorized a spending of $6.7 billion, requesting subsequently an increase of 10% in the 1998 budget.

REFERENCES

Bianchi, P., & Labory, S. (Eds.). (2006). *International Handbook on Industrial Policy*. Cheltenham: E. Elgar.
Bianchi, P., & Labory, S. (2009). *Le nuove politiche industriali dell'Unione Europea*. Il Mulino: Bologna.

Bianchi, P., & Labory, S. (2011). *Industrial Policies after the Crisis. Seizing the Future.* Cheltenham: E. Elgar.

Cecchini, P., Catinat, M., & Jacquemin, A. (1988). *The European Challenge: The benefits of a Single Market.* Aldershot: Wildwood House.

Chang, H.-J. (1994). *The Political Economy of Industrial Policy.* New York: St. Martin's Press.

Dunlop, J. B. (1993). *The Rise of Russia and the Fall of the Soviet Empire.* Princeton: Princeton University Press.

Elms, D. K. & Low, P. (Eds.). (2013). *Global Value Chains in a Changing World.* Geneva: Fung Global Institute (FGI), Nanyang Technological University (NTU) and World Trade Organization (WTO).

Emerson, M., et al. (1989). *The Economics of 1992: The EC Commission's Assessment of the Economic Effects of Completing the Single Market.* Oxford: Oxford University Press.

ERP. (1990). *Economic Report of the President.* Washington, DC: United States Government Printing Office.

ERP. (1991). *Economic Report of the President.* Washington, DC: United States Government Printing Office.

ERP. (1992). *Economic Report of the President.* Washington, DC: United States Government Printing Office.

ERP. (1993). *Economic Report of the President.* Washington, DC: United States Government Printing Office.

ERP. (1994). *Economic Report of the President.* Washington, DC: United States Government Printing Office.

ERP. (1995). *Economic Report of the President.* Washington, DC: United States Government Printing Office.

ERP. (1996). *Economic Report of the President.* Washington, DC: United States Government Printing Office.

ERP. (1997). *Economic Report of the President.* Washington, DC: United States Government Printing Office.

ERP. (1998). *Economic Report of the President.* Washington, DC: United States Government Printing Office.

European Commission. (1990). Industrial Policy in an Open and Competitive Environment (Bangemann Memorandum), Bruxelles, Working paper December 14.

European Commission. (2010). *Europe 2020. A Strategy for Smart, Sustainable and Inclusive Growth.* COM: 2020.

Fazi, T. (2014). *The Battle for Europe. How an Elite Hijacked a Continent and How We Can Take It Back.* London: Pluto Press.

Foreman-Peck, J., & Federico, G. (1999). *European Industrial Policy: The Twentieth Century Experience.* Oxford: Oxford University Press.

Gereffi, G., Humphrey, J., & Sturgeon, T. (2005). The Governance of Global Value Chains. *Review of International Political Economy, 12*(1), 78–104.

Geroski, P. A. (1989). *European Industrial Policy and Industrial Policy in Europe.* Oxford Review of Economic Policy

Gibbon, P., Bair, J., & Ponte, S. (2008). Governing Global Value Chains: An Introduction. *Economy and Society, 37*(3), 315–338.

Grabas, C., & Nützenadel, A. (Eds.). (2014). *Industrial Policy in Europe after 1945: Wealth, Power and Economic Development in the Cold War.* London: Palgrave.

Hoekman, B. M., & Mavroidis, P. C. (1997). *Law and Policy in Public Purchasing.* Ann Arbor: Michigan Press.

Hufbauer, G. C., & Schott, J. J. (2009). *Buy American: Bad for Jobs, Worse for Reputation* (Peterson Institute for International Economics, Policy Brief number PB09-2). Washington, DC: Peterson Institute for International Economics.

Krueger, A. O. (1990). Government Failures in Development. *The Journal of Economic Perspectives, 4*(3), 9–23.

Le Grand, J. (1991). The Theory of Government Failure. *British Journal of Political Science, 21*(4), 423–442.

Pack, H., & Saggi, K. (2006). Is There a Case for Industrial Policy? A Critical Survey. *World Bank Research Observer, 21*(2), 267–297.

Pelkmans, J. (2006). *European Integration: Methods and Economic Analysis.* London: Prentice Hall.

Pianta, M. (2014). An Industrial Policy for Europe. *Seoul Journal of Economics, 27*, 3.

Pietrobelli, C., & Rabellotti, R. (2011). Global Value Chains Meet Innovation Systems: Are There Learning Opportunities for Developing Countries? *World Development, 39*(7), 1261–1269.

Rice, C. (2000). Promoting the National Interest. *Foreign Affairs, Washington, Council on Foreign Relations, 79*, 45.

Sakwa, R. (2008). *Russian Politics and Society.* London: Routledge.

Schultze, C. L. (1983). Industrial Policy: A Dissent. *The Brookings Review, 2*(1), 3–12.

Stiglitz, J. E. (2002). *Globalization and its Discontents.* New York: Norton.

Trionfetti, F. (2000). *Discriminatory Public Procurement and International Trade.* Oxford: Blackwell Publishers.

Weiss, L. (2005). *Global Governance, National Strategies: How Industrialized States Make Room to Move Under the WTO. Review of International Political Economy, 12*(5), 723–749.

Weiss, L., & Thurbon, E. (2006). The Business of Buying American: Government Procurement as Trade Strategy. *Review of International Political Economy, 13*(5). Routledge.

Williamson, J. (1989). What Washington Means by Policy Reform. In J. Williamson (Ed.), *Latin American Readjustment: How Much has Happened.* Washington: Institute for International Economics.

CHAPTER 5

Industrial Strategy During the *New Economy*

As described in the previous chapter, in the early 1990s several factors contributed to seriously change the political and economic global order: the fall of the Berlin Wall, in 1989, and the end of the Cold War; the establishment of the WTO; the trade agreement between the United States, Canada and Mexico (NAFTA) and other important regional agreements; the supranational integration in Europe; the rising of new global competitors, such as South Korea, Taiwan, Hong Kong, Singapore, Malaysia, Thailand, Indonesia and China. All these circumstances were radically changing the global institutional and competitive framework, creating room for the definitions of important structural reforms in developed and developing countries' policies. These changes had required a new approach to industrial development policy in many economies. Trade protectionism had to step down in favour of "freer markets", where national governments intervened mainly by negotiating the regulation of economic activity through multilateral and bilateral agreements. The effectiveness of this type of interventions in promoting national interest was basically anchored to the contractual power of the individual economies in the international and supranational arena.

Nonetheless, despite what the neoliberal rhetoric of those years was highlighting, an active role of governments remained also at national level. Indeed, public policies continued to promote improvements in productivity and technological innovation, in order to ensure competitiveness at the

M. Tassinari, *Capitalising Economic Power in the US*,
International Political Economy Series,
https://doi.org/10.1007/978-3-319-76648-5_5

international level. In this framework, science and technology policies remained a clear priority in many industrialized economies.

In Europe, the sovereignty of the single states in implementing industrial policies was declining, while the European Commission was increasing its influence. In this context, the promotion of innovation—especially in high-tech sectors—remained a high priority at a European level. For example, the programmes launched by the European Commission in the 1980s and 1990s subsidized R&D in particular strategic areas: in the first programme (1984–1987) the priorities were microelectronics and new materials; in the second (1987–1991) and third (1990–1994) greater importance was given to ICTs and biotechnology.[1]

In the United States, the end of the Cold War and the consequent pressure to reduce military expenditure (which represented the main way for promoting innovation in the American economic system) started to question the old approach to policies for science and technology. In particular, the Clinton administration promoted a "new approach" to industrial development. In this context, ICTs were considered a crucial area in order to address the need for continuous improvement in productivity in the US economy (ERP 2001). In the 1990s, the government role in this field was massive, with crucial repercussions on the competitiveness of this industry on international markets and on the organization of the entire national industrial system. The reach of the economic and social transformations induced by the development of the ICTs led to baptize this new economic setting as a "New Economy". This chapter shows the main changes introduced in the way in which the United States began to promote industrial and technological development at the national level within this new framework.

RHETORIC ON POLICIES FOR SCIENCE AND TECHNOLOGY IN THE 1990s

In 1989, George Bush Senior replaced Reagan at the White House. Since the beginning of his mandate, the rhetoric of the new President concerning policies for industrial development appeared in clear continuity with that of his predecessor:

> The Administration remains strongly opposed to any sort of industrial policy, which would involve second-guessing private investment decisions by selecting particular firms, industries, or commercial technologies for favorable tax treatment or direct subsidies. History provides strong support for the view

that private market participants, who have profits and jobs at stake, have sharper incentives and better information than government decision makers and, as a consequence, make sounder investment decision. (ERP 1990: 25).

In this context, greatest attention was paid to the flexibility of the markets in responding to structural economic changes. The government should not interfere with the natural process of structural adjustment of the economy, leaving the markets as flexible as possible:

> Flexibility enhances the ability of a market economy to respond to change and, thereby, enhances the rewards to innovation. [...] Such shocks may increase unemployment temporarily, but a flexible economy adjusts to new circumstances affectively and can return rapidly to full employment. [...] This reallocation of resources occurs without government planning. [...] the government is not nearly as good as the market at organizing the reallocation of resources that must accompany innovation. [...] Such qualitative changes are very difficult to predict, and government interference in market forces can suppress them without anyone even being aware of the loss. (ERP 1991: 111–112)

According to this perspective, changes in the structure of the production system should be guided by changes in market demand, consumers' preferences and the capacity of the private sector to stimulate and respond to such changes (ERP 1991). The ability of the economy to face the challenges posed by the competitive environment was described by the Bush administration as an issue entirely addressed within the market system:

> Some have argued for a broad new Federal role: choosing specific civilian technologies and financing their development or commercialization by special tax treatment or direct subsidy – a so-called industrial policy. Such an expansion of the current Federal role is strongly opposed by this Administration. (ERP 1990: 116)

In this context, a crucial policy was to remove any barrier to private saving and investment in physical, intellectual and human capital, by reducing the tax rate on capital gains (ERP 1990: 25, 109). According to this framework, the government should minimize its intervention in market dynamics, limiting, as far as possible, regulatory activities, as it was considered a source of inhibition of market flexibility:

The long-run growth rate of the U.S. economy is dependent on continued efforts both to eliminate government policies that inhibit flexibility and to resist pressure to reimpose unnecessary regulation on the economy. [...] Reduction in market flexibility is an important and often overlooked effect of regulation. (ERP 1991: 112–116)

However, the structural adjustment of the economy could also have negative consequences. The decline of some sectors that used obsolete technologies, and the unemployment of low-skill workforce were deemed too high social costs to bear. Concerning these issues, the Bush administration's approach was not interested in preventing these negative consequences, but it privileged an ex-post intervention, by alleviating the social costs that arose and by facilitating the re-training and re-employment of the workforce (ERP 1991). In this area, the administration supported a public unemployment insurance system and, in particular, interventions to improve the general level of education and of workforce's skills (ERP 1992).

Although primary and secondary education in the United States was a matter of local and state governments, at the beginning of its mandate, the Bush administration undertook some important initiatives with the goal of reforming the American school system (ERP 1990). In September 1989, the administration convened a summit with some members of the Cabinet and governors of the US states to discuss and establish the general objectives in primary and secondary education. These objectives—described in the report entitled *National Education Goals: A Report to the Nation's Governors*, of 1990—included, for example, the increase in the percentage of students with a high school diploma, the improvement of the quality of education in science, the improvement in adult literacy and the reduction of violence and drug use in schools (ERP 1991). As part of the strategy for achieving these goals—named America 2000, since the goals had to be achieved by the year 2000—the Bush administration proposed in Congress, in 1991, the Educational Excellence Act, a legislation aimed at allocating important funds for new American schools, supporting schools and teachers based on merit and providing assistance to states in developing alternative programmes for teacher certification and other programmes to improve the school system. The Congress, however, believed that with this legislation the federal government would play an excessive role in the management of the American school system, mainly of state competence, and the act was never approved (McAndrews 2006).

The training of workers was also considered by the Bush administration as a priority. The technological change in production processes created a growing demand for more and more specialized workforce. Alongside existing federal programmes—including the Economic Dislocation and Worker Adjustment Assistance programme, issued in 1988 by Reagan— the Bush administration launched a programme called Job Training 2000 (ERP 1992).[2] The programme had the general objective of coordinating over 600 committees involved in implementing federal vocational training programmes. In particular, the aim was to reform the field of vocational training, facilitate the transition from the welfare system to the labour market and improve the transition from school to work (ERP 1992).

Finally, another set of interventions promoted by the Bush administration was linked to policies aimed at the development of science and technology, but understood in a "horizontal" sense, with effects on a broad spectrum of sectors of the economy. These included the government's financial support for basic research, tax incentives for R&D to private companies and the protection of intellectual property rights. In this latter context, the role of the government was played, in particular, through the Uruguay Round negotiations on international protection of intellectual property, by influencing the adoption of uniform standards at international level for products and services and by continuing the support for the elimination of "unjustified" regulations (ERP 1990).

NATIONAL INNOVATION SYSTEM AND THE ISSUE OF DEFENCE CUTBACKS

The political rhetoric of the American government at the beginning of the 1990s emphasized the role of "free markets" in promoting technological advancement and innovation. In this context, public policies had to be *horizontal* as far as possible, limiting distortions to private incentives. Thus, the icon of public interventions in favour of scientific and technological progress in the United States could appear limited to education policies, workforce re-training and (rather marginal) R&D incentives for private companies, along with the protection of property rights. In this rhetorical framework, the American innovation system seemed far less structured than what it really was. Indeed, even in the 1990s, as in the previous decades, the main role in science and technology policies remained played by government agencies and departments, as part of their regular duties connected with the production and delivery of public services.

The "traditional" model of promotion of innovation in the United States was based on the demand for the development of new technologies, formulated by the various US public agencies (such as the DOD, the DOE, NASA, the NSF and the NIH) towards universities and government labs (see Chap. 3). The federal government also directly funded universities and laboratories for basic research activities, when they were not directly linked to the purposes of federal agencies. Newly developed technologies were later applied to new products or new production processes as spin-offs (ERP 1994). In this framework, technology transfer policies and incentives to ensure that publicly funded research results were spread to private industries became crucial, so that the government's research could be fully effective in terms of innovation in the private sector. In particular, it was the defence and security sector that played the main role for the advancement of science and technology in the United States. On the one hand, the weight that this sector had in the American economy alone was remarkable—in the late 1980s this industry accounted for about 6% of the US GDP. On the other hand, the interest for this sector was due to its effects on the overall industrial system, in terms of both technology *spill over* to companies operating in the civilian market and the development of production activities originating from the *public procurement* for products used for military purposes. In fact, the DOD commissioned and financed most of the government-sponsored research activities, and was, at the same time, the largest public purchaser of American products (Weiss 2008). As stated in the ERP of 1994:

> In this manner, the Federal Government supported the development and diffusion of jet aircraft and engines, semiconductor microelectronics, computers and computer-controlled machine tools, pharmaceuticals and biotechnology, advanced energy and environmental technologies, advanced materials, and a whole host of other commercially successful technologies. (ERP 1994: 193)

However, the change in the international political situation during the 1990s—basically the end of the Cold War—was building significant pressure to reduce military expenditures and, consequently, to reduce federal support to R&D (ERP 1994). The problem had already been introduced in the early 1980s, with the end of the Vietnam War (1955–1975), but Reagan, in the context of the Cold War needs, had been able to give new impetus to the national security-based innovation system and to raise military spending (see Chap. 3). The end of the Cold War in the late 1980s, however, raised the matter again. The consequence of cutting military spending was a general reduction in R&D expenditures that was supported by the US government during those years: "Federal civilian R&D spending has increased over this period, although government spending for defence-related research has declined somewhat" (ERP 1993: 239; Fig. 5.1).

While the conclusion of the Cold War and the emergence of the new global neoliberal order were functional to the implementation of the US foreign and trade policy strategy (see Chap. 4), they, at the same time, raised questions to the national innovation system, by reducing the reasons justifying such massive public funding for military purposes:

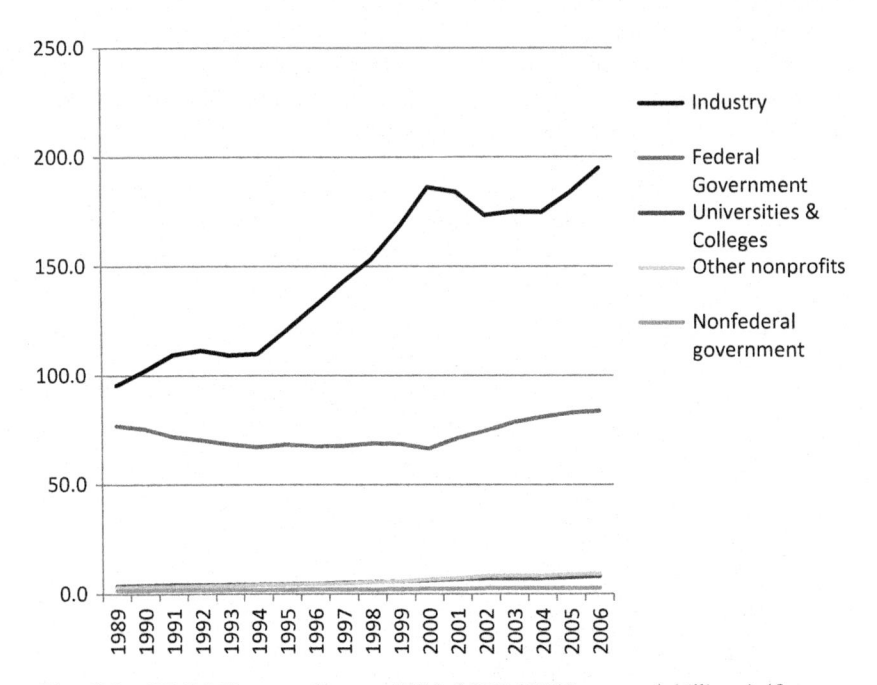

Fig. 5.1 US R&D expenditures: 1953–2007 (2000 const. $ billions) (Source: Author's elaboration based on data from National Science Foundation, Division of Science Resources Statistics, National Patterns of R&D Resources [annual series])

[…]the circumstances that allowed the United States to rely primarily on a defence-led model have changed. With the end of the cold war, demand for new defence systems is now less than it was. Commercial product spinoffs from military research have also diminished from their heyday of the 1950s and 1960s, and American companies face intense international competition from increasingly capable foreign firms. (ERP 1994: 193–194)

Indeed, as far as military spending as a percentage of the US GDP is concerned, the trend from the mid-1980s to 2001—the year in which Bush Junior embarked on the war in Afghanistan—showed a progressive reduction (Figs. 5.2 and 5.3).

However, in this apparent stalemate of the system of innovation based on military spending, it is important to note that the total consumption and investment in the defence sector (differently from the values assessed as percentage of GDP) remained at almost stationary absolute value, with limited repercussions in terms of structural adjustment of the economy. The DOD's activities, including R&D, continued de facto to be carried out regularly, albeit with a slight decrease. Indeed, despite the fact that the international threat of war had ceased, the idea that the US military superiority should be maintained over time remained of central importance:

One possible additional concern with cuts in defense spending is their potential effect on the defense industrial base and U.S. technological superiority. In managing the proposed spending cuts, the ability of the United

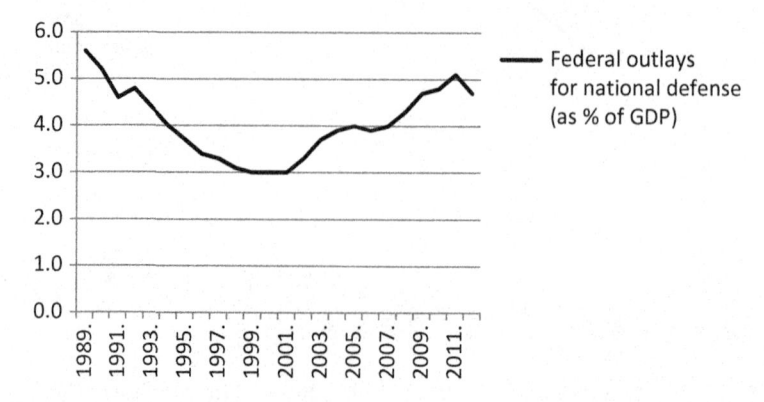

Fig. 5.2 Federal outlays for national defence (as % of GDP) (Source: Author's elaboration based on Table B–79 —E.R.P. 2013/Department of Commerce)

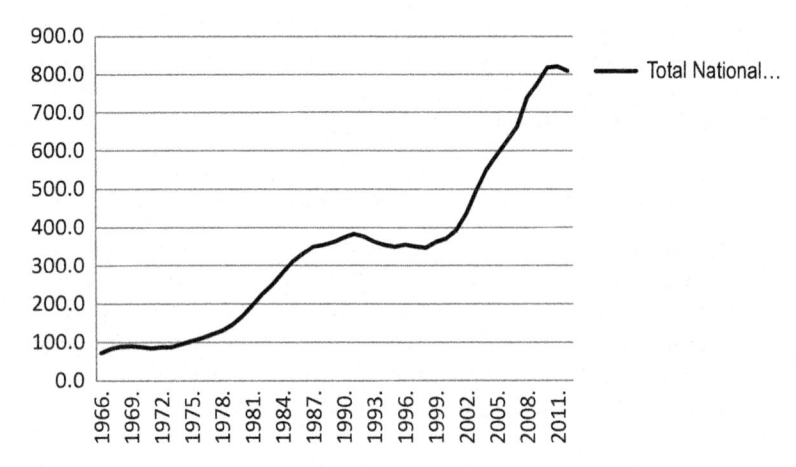

Fig. 5.3 Total national defence gov. consumption exp. and gross invest (billions of dollars, quarterly data at seasonally adjusted annual rates) (Source: Author's elaboration based on TABLE B–20—E.R.P.2013/Department of Commerce)

> States to continue to produce the equipment needed to fight future conflicts should be maintained. Furthermore, the advantage the Unite State has in defense technology should be protected thorough continued investment in research, although some of the priorities may be shifted. The defense technology base can also be protected by relaxing procurement regulations, particularly those that restrict the transfer of defense technology to civilian uses. (ERP 1991: 151)

Overall, therefore, the reduction in military spending during the 1990s was not such as to cause significant problems. Nevertheless, one of the major challenges of this historical moment was represented by the attempt of the United States to mitigate the role of the military sector as the main source of American scientific and technological progress. In particular, it was Clinton's administration (at the White House since 1993) to make the most significant steps forward. As stated in the ERP of 1994:

> The development and deployment of new technology have long been of interest to the government. But technology policy is especially critical in a period of large-scale defense cutbacks, because more than half of total Federal support for R&D has traditionally been related to national defense. With less need for research on weaponry, the Federal Government must now make a choice. Will we reduce total research support, or will we shift

the research dollars in to civilian technologies? The president believes that the latter is the wiser course, which is why the Administration is reorienting the research capabilities of the Defense Department and the national laboratories toward R&D partnerships with industry. (ERP 1994: 45)

A "NEW APPROACH" TO INDUSTRIAL DEVELOPMENT

The challenge posed by the need to change the role of the military sector and, more generally, by the rise of new emerging international competitors, prompted the Clinton administration to announce a "new approach" to innovation policy and industrial development. The element of novelty lied in an open declaration concerning the attempt to move federal spending on R&D from the military to the civilian sphere:

> The administration's technology initiatives are shifting the composition of Federal R&D from military to civilian concerns, and the composition of military R&D toward the development of so-called dual-use technologies – those with applications to both military and commercial products. (ERP 1994: 194)

This horizon gave the US government a clear strategic orientation, which directly assumed the task of stimulating and promoting the technological and industrial development of the American economic system. Once again, the central element that justified the role of the government was the need to provide those "public goods" that the private sector was unable to produce in optimum quantities. In this perspective, the public role remained conceived as complementary and "residual" to the market's ability to achieve adequate performance, and the government intervened to correct specific *market failures* (Bator, 1958) by promoting those R&D activities that private dynamics did not have the incentive to undertake:

> While the bulk of research and development (R&D) must and should be done by private industry, support for basic and generic research has long been recognized as a legitimate function of government because of informational externalities. New technology is expensive to discover but cheap to disseminate. So what one company learns passes quickly to others, making it impossible for the innovator to capture all the returns from its discovery. In fact, estimates find that innovating businesses capture less than half of the social returns to their R&D. (ERP 1994: 44)

However, what was clear—and what probably differentiated Clinton's administration from the governments of the previous decade—was that the emphasis on the promotion of technological innovation was conceived in the context of a more general and organized long-term industrial development strategy:

> This Administration is committed to a high-wage strategy to enable the United States to take advantage of the new opportunities and to meet the new challenges of the changing global marketplace. This strategy consists of two distinct but interrelated parts: trade policies that will promote trade and foster more-open markets both at home and abroad; and domestic policies that will help American companies remain the most skilled and productive in the world. This two-part strategy reflects the fundamental goal of the Administration's other economic policy initiatives: higher living standards for all Americans. Realizing this goal requires that America compete not on the basis of lower wages, but on the basis of superior productivity, technology, and quality. (ERP 1994: 206)

This strategy was structured as a double-leverage mechanism: on the one hand, the government action was exerting a massive influence, at international level, by promoting liberalization of foreign markets (as described in the previous chapter), and at the same time, on the other hand, it was promoting, at domestic level, technological innovation to increase the competitiveness of the American industries (as described in the next pages of this chapter). These are two complementary leverages of the American neoliberal strategy, adopted to maximize the gains achieved by the US industrial system in participating to the global economy.

In this framework, the policies implemented by the US government at national level were studied to improve the competitive performance of the American industries in the international markets. Along with policies for science and technology, other national initiatives strengthened this mechanism in a direct way during the Clinton administration.

The National Export Strategy, for instance, was a policy that accomplished this task. In September 1993, the Congress established the Trade Promotion Coordination Committee,[3] a committee formed by several major federal government agencies and departments to reduce the fragmentation of the US export promotion programmes. In particular, the Commission's objectives were to rationalize and combine various functions through agencies, strategically allocate resources, involve the private sector and state and local governments, effectively support the interests of the US exporters abroad, quantify results and reduce export control (ERP 1994). The work under this Commission led to the National Export Strategy, a "strategy" aimed at promoting the US exports through improved financial support to trade, support for the US companies in the global competition, aid to small- and medium-sized enterprises to enter the export market and promotion of the US export of environmental services and technologies (ERP 1995).[4]

Beyond the National Export Strategy, the goals of the American industrial strategy, combined with actions at national and international level, were related to the increase in productivity of the industrial system, economic growth, job creation, investment in technology and human capital, the opening up of foreign markets and the reduction of government deficit. It was clear to the Clinton administration that the improvement and maintenance of national prosperity were only achievable through a constant public commitment over time:

> The real measure of the success of any Administration's economic policies is not just today's economic statistics, but also the strength of the Nation's economy in 10 or 20 year' time. Today's economic policies will be judged favorably if, as result, growth is stronger, the environment cleaner, and the number of children growing up in poverty fewer. History will pronounce these efforts a success if, a generation from now, opportunity has been expanded in our cities, tomorrow's senior citizens are at least as economically secure as today's, and all our citizens have the education they need not just to cope with but to profit from the challenges of a changing world. If we can look back upon a record of such accomplishments, we will know that the last years of the 20th century laid a solid foundation for the 21st. (ERP 1997: 17)

In this context, Clinton was aware of the weaknesses and potential risks of *government failure*,[5] which required careful reflections on the efficiency and effectiveness of the interventions: "The Administration recognizes the need for change not only in what the government does, but also in how it does it" (ERP 1996: 33). Within this perspective, the administration promoted, during its two mandates, some initiatives to improve public action performance. For instance, The National Performance Review (NPR), later renamed The National Partnership for Reinventing Government, was launched in March 1993.[6] It was directed by Vice President Al Gore, with the specific task of reforming and streamlining the way the federal government operated:

The NPR identified 384 ways that the Federal Government could save money without reducing the level of service and, indeed, often while improving governmental performance. Its report concluded that, by shifting to a market-like focus on customer service, by introducing competition where possible, and by streamlining internal government processes to facilitate better management, we could have a government that "work better and costs less". (ERP 1994: 171)

The main "recommendations" emerged under the NPR focused, in particular, on improving the process through which public procurements were assigned, management control, services to customers, financial and human resources management, the integration of information technology (IT) systems in government affairs and on the improvement of the functions of each executive government branch (ERP 1994).

Overall, the economic strategy outlined by the US government during the 1990s appeared (at least in theory) consistent in its structure, by defining clear long-term goals and precise tools for intervention and for improving the performance of the system, a fact that could sound quite bizarre in a country that had always been defined as the land where the "antipathy for government, and the corresponding belief in individualism, competition, and the marketplace, go back to the days of the founding" (Etzioni 1983: 47).

ICTs as Strategic Sector

In the context of the American strategy outlined above, the ICTs sector was considered, by the Clinton administration, as a "key" area to provide a response to the need for continuous improvement in the productivity of the entire economy, by somehow compensating for a reduction in the role played by the defence sector (ERP 2001).

Between 1990 and 2000, the sector grew from 5.8% to 8.3% of the GDP. In 1995, the private investment in this sector grew by 28% per annum (ERP 2001). It was an important wave of technological innovations in the field of information and communication which revolutionized the organization of the economic activity (and the way of communicating within the society and of doing politics). The transformations introduced into the economic and social life by ICT led to baptize this new economic setting as "New Economy". The ERP of 2001 in this regard stated:

> At the heart of the New Economy lie the many dramatic technological innovations of the last several decades. Advances in computing, information storage, and communications have reduced firms' costs, created markets for new products and services, expanded existing markets, and intensified competition at home and abroad. [...] Indeed, the rapid growth of the information technology sector was one of the most remarkable of the 1990s. (ERP 2001: 95)

In those years, the Clinton administration, in an attempt to fully develop the opportunities offered by the scenario described above, promoted a series of initiatives to support the renewal process that was investing the IT industry.

First, an important measure to increase the competitiveness of telecommunications companies was the Telecommunications Act of 1996, through which the administration reformed the regulation of the national telecommunications sector (ERP 2000). Prior to 1996, the regulation of this industry was mainly related to the Communications Act of 1934. This was the first act that was issued for the communications sector, through which the Federal Communications Commission (FCC) was created as an agency to regulate the telecommunications networks (telephones, telegraphs, radios, internet, etc.), by setting the technical standards of the network and the access of new operators to the market and by monitoring the extension of the networks.

In this context, for the first time, the US Congress affirmed the principle of *universality* in telecommunications networks, sanctioning the importance of achieving basic connectivity for all American citizens through adequate access to radio and telephone equipment. Although the US government never decided to manage communications networks through public management (as it was the case in many other countries), the recognition of the *status* of *public good* of the ICTs sector provided important reasons for government regulation (Picot and Wernick 2007). Indeed, the important economic and social benefits associated with a widespread use of the telecommunications raised concerns about the "divide" between those who were connected to a network and those who did not have this opportunity. The idea that access to communication should be as secured as possible was an essential part of the policies that would affect the industry. In the following decades, the US government's policy did not substantially change its address, setting as its first goal the creation of a universal service system that did not exclude certain national geographic areas from interconnection benefits. In this context, AT&T—an American multinational telecommunications conglomerate—was the only entity capable of delivering services nationwide, by efficiently managing technological standardization of networks. As a result, AT&T during this period dominated the market, by controlling all communication infrastructures and by holding the monopoly of manufacturing dedicated to telephone equipment (Bazzucchi 2013).

Since the 1970s, the Court had forced the FCC to open both the communications and the telephone equipment market, so that AT&T, which had held a monopoly in both sectors, was attacked by competition from both fronts (Crandall 2005).

However, the introduction of a more substantial competition in the telecommunications market occurred only with the Telecommunication Act of 1996, introduced by the Clinton administration, which launched a process of expansion in the number of competitors. The Act essentially established a regulatory framework that promoted the spread of networks within competitive markets and sanctioned full freedom of entry into the market in all its areas. Among the operational precepts of the law there was the obligation of existing local companies (Bell, or Incumbent companies) to open their network to competitors at any technically possible point, and to rent part of their infrastructures to those companies that were trying to enter the market. The reason for requesting existing companies to share their network with new entrants was that some infrastructures were judged by FCC not replicable by competitors. Indeed, economies of density had prevented the possibility of duplicating certain sections of the network.

Although the law was not without criticism,[7] the government triggered an important process of restructuring of the industry, which attracted new entrants and stimulated innovation and capacity building in one of the most important sector for the American economy competitiveness.

Beyond the Telecommunication Act, during the 1990s, other public initiatives aimed at fostering the industry's development. The Internet Tax Freedom Act of 1998, for example, supported a suspension of fees charged on the Internet. Also, the signatures of the *WTO's* Information Technology Agreement and of the *WTO's* Basic Telecommunication Agreement were important steps for encouraging the opening of high-tech goods and services markets.

Finally, there were also interventions which directly affected the development of communication technologies. In this context, in 1999, the Information Technology for the 21st Century Initiative was launched as one of the most important interventions in the sector (ERP 2001). The initiative constituted a commitment of the federal government to fundamental research in IT. In 1999, this sector accounted for one third of US economic growth and employed 7.4 million Americans at wages that were more than 60%higher than the private sector's average. All sectors of the US economy could benefit from IT to compete in global markets. The document of the initiative clearly recognized the enormous potential of the development of the sector even beyond the economic sphere:

> Leading-edge information technology, due to its enormous and profound socioeconomic benefits, has, seemingly in a few short years, become critical to our Nation's continued well-being and prosperity. Information technology is also changing the way we live, work, learn, and communicate with each other. For example, advances in information technology can improve the way we educate our children, allow people with disabilities to lead more independent lives, and improve the quality of healthcare for rural Americans through technologies such as telemedicine. Information technology advances in supercomputers, simulations, and networks are creating a new window into the natural world, making high end computational experimentation an essential tool for path breaking scientific discoveries. Advances in weather and climate forecasting are providing early warnings of severe weather, which saves lives, lessens property damage, and helps business be more efficient. U.S. leadership in information technology is also vital to our national security. Our military strategy now relies on information superiority to gain advantage over our adversaries and to keep our troops out of harm's way.[8]

In the previous decades, federally sponsored high-end research in IT had led the development of prominent technologies such as the Internet, the first graphical web browser and advanced microprocessors. These efforts had helped to strengthen the American leadership in the IT industry. Following this trend, the Clinton administration planned significant new investments through the Information Technology for the 21st Century Initiative. It had a budget of $309 million in 2000 and $704 million in 2001, in order to increase investments in computing, information and communications research, and to help to expand the knowledge base in fundamental information science, advance the nation's capabilities in cutting edge research and train future researchers. The initiative integrated the public efforts conducted within the main existing programmes involved in developing information technologies in the United States, such as the DOE's Accelerated Strategic Computing Initiative (ASCI), High Performance Computing and Communications (HPCC), including the Next Generation Internet (NGI). It augmented the base HPCC programmes to fund critically needed extensions of some ongoing HPCC research agendas and expansions into entirely new research areas, as recommended by the President's Congressionally-chartered Information Technology (PITAC), with an explicit long-term horizon. The initiative also provided opportunities to address new, complementary R&D topics in three key areas: long-term IT R&D leading to fundamental advances in computing and communications; advanced computing infrastructure to facilitate scientific and engineering discoveries of national interest; research on the economic and social implications of the Information Revolution, and the training of additional IT workers at US universities.

Six agencies participated in the initiative: DoD (including the DARPA), DOE, NASA, NIH, National Oceanic and Atmospheric Administration (NOAA) and NSF.

Each agency was called to develop an appropriate subset of the R&D objectives of the initiative. Planned activities were closely coordinated to connect complementary efforts across research disciplines and funding agencies.[9]

Overall, the US government's actions in favour of the telecommunications sector implemented during the 1990s reveal an important public role played by the administration in the promotion of such a strategic industry, for the efficiency and competitiveness of the entire American economy.

PUBLIC-PRIVATE PARTNERSHIP AND OTHER TECHNOLOGY INITIATIVES

The role of the federal government in supporting scientific and technological progress in the United States was much wider than the specific interventions in the field of ICTs. Indeed, the "new approach" to science and technology policies launched by the Clinton administration provided for a substantial government commitment to promoting innovation within the American productive system, intensifying in particular civilian efforts (Shapira 2001). At this regard, the ERP of 1999 stated: "The Federal Government supports innovative activity in both direct and indirect ways. And it does so in no small measure." (ERP 1999: 172).

Data from 1997 show that US government agencies provided about 30% of all funds spent on R&D in the United States. In this context, several important initiatives were implemented, in the 1990s, by the US government.

One of the most important goals that led the government intervention was the improvement of partnerships between government and private sector in the field of R&D. In this area, several programmes that operated locally had already been launched in the 1980s, such as the Small Business Innovation Research programme (SBIR) and the Manufacturing Extension Partnership (MEP), started respectively in 1982 and 1988 (see Chap. 3). These programmes operated at a "meso" level, aimed at overcoming *network failures* (Whitford 2005; Whitford and Schrank 2011; Wade 2012) and favouring cooperation among a plurality of actors, such as companies, scientists, engineers, venture capitalists, local governments, state economic development agencies, private enterprise development centres, organizations that provided services for businesses and universities. These programmes played an important role in promoting innovation and development of small businesses by fostering cooperation and exchange of information among the agents of an increasing complex system of innovation and production (Wade 2012; Block 2008; Schrank and Whitford, 2009). During the 1990s this innovation framework was further strengthened.

The SBIR, which directly had been allocating a fraction of their research budget to support initiatives promoted by small private companies and to develop innovative start-ups, was integrated, in 1992, by the Small Business Technology Transfer programme (STTR). STTR, similar to the SBIR, had the goal of expanding funding opportunities in the federal innovation R&D arena. To this purpose, it promoted the expansion of the public-private sector partnership to include the joint venture opportunities for small businesses and non-profit research institutions. The main feature of the STTR programme was the requirement, for the small businesses, to formally collaborate with a research institution trying to bridge the gap between performance of basic science and commercialization of resulting innovations. In particular, the programmes pursued three main goals: stimulating technological innovation; fostering technology transfer through cooperative R&D between small businesses and research institutions; increasing private sector commercialization of innovations derived from federal R&D. In this context, government agencies with R&D budgets of $1 billion or more were required to set aside a portion of these funds to finance the STTR activity. Several agencies participated in the STTR programme, such as the DOD, the DOE, the Department of Health and Human Services, the National Aeronautics and Space Administration, the NSF. Each agency administered its own individual programme within guidelines established by Congress, and defined R&D topics by accepting proposals from small businesses.[10]

The MEP too was potentiated during the Clinton administration. The programme, sponsored by the National Institute of Standards and Technology (NIST), was launched in 1988 to improve productivity, competitiveness and technological capacities of American SMEs through the establishment of state and local centres. These hubs operated in order to foster the relationship between SMEs and innovation centres involved in R&D for manufacturing, by providing consultancy services related to, for example, access to new markets, financing, investment in physical capital and innovation and skilled workforce (Shapira 2001; Hallancher 2005). These centres were an excellent example of public-private partnerships because they involved the interest of a plurality of public and private actors, including individual states, the federal government, the scientific and university community in which they operated and the entrepreneurs to whom they offered service. Some of the US states where manufacturing tradition was more rooted—such as Michigan, Pennsylvania and Ohio—were particularly active in public intervention in favour of industry even before the federal government intervened in this direction. However, although the existence of MEP centres in some states dated back much before the late 1980s, their structure was only formalized at national level as a federal programme only in 1988, through the Reagan Omnibus Trade and Competitiveness Act (see Chap. 3).

The Clinton administration, during the 1990s, did a great deal to further develop the MEP programme, particularly by convincing the Congress of the effectiveness of the intervention and, hence, of the need to continue funding it (Hallacher 2005). Indeed, as it was occurring with many other federal programmes during the 1990s, the MEP's work was subjected to a rigorous performance monitoring system, implemented by the NIST. In this context, each contact of the centres with the clients was monitored by recording the cost of services and the remuneration received for the benefits provided. Since 1996, NIST also started submitting to companies participating in MEP programmes a survey to assess the impact of the programme in terms of performance achieved, staff improvements and savings. NIST also sought to evaluate the effect on the level of individual customers in terms of return on investment made by the federal government for each centre. In the course of the evaluation, a number of debates took place over the instruments that were most appropriate to measure the effectiveness of the programme. In fact, the assessment of the efficiency and effectiveness of MEP activities were rather difficult (Voytek et al. 2004). The reason was that the hubs were not confined to providing just monetizing services. Their impact on SMEs was also achieved through an important *relational capital* that created a network of relationships between the various actors in the area, benefiting economic development and innovation. This relational capital was hardly measurable, and this was one of the main problems in showing the real value of MEP activities and in seeking new funding for the programme in Congress. President Clinton was still quite effective in getting funds for the MEP in the 1990s. As the globalization processes advanced rapidly—exposing the American economy to international competition—the MEP worked to adapt the different territories and their manufacturing traditions to the new global context.

Furthermore, in the context of the programmes aim at promoting public-private partnership implemented during the 1990s, the Advanced Technology Program (ATP) was launched in 1991 by President Bush Senior and eventually implemented in 1995 by the Clinton administration. The programme was directed by the NIST and supported research projects aimed at meeting the technological advances of the US industry with a long-term horizon, on the basis of public-private partnerships: "Over 460 ATP awards – many of which have gone to cooperative ventures between firms and universities – have been made in fields as diverse as photonics, manufacturing, materials science, information technology, and biotechnology" (ERP 2001: 116). The ATP provided cost-shared funding to industry for high-risk R&D projects with high potential. It supported projects that the industry on its own could not fully sustain because of the technical risks involved. In several cases, ATP support was essential for the project to take place at all. The awards of the programme were made on the basis of a competitive review, considering scientific and technical merit for each proposal and its potential benefits to the US economy. For example, the ATP's 2000 competition attracted over 400 proposals representing a total of $1.6 billion in research funding. The selected projects targeted a broad array of technologies, including pharmaceutical design, tissue engineering, industrial catalysts, energy generation and storage, manufacturing technologies, electronics manufacturing, computer software and electro-optics. In this context, 54 projects were awarded, for a value of $274 million in private and federal funding.[11]

Another public-private partnership of those years occurred in the specific case of the automotive sectors. The Partnership for a New Generation of Vehicles (PNGV), founded in 1993, brought together the three major US automakers (Ford, Chrysler, General Motors), more than 300 car suppliers, universities and seven federal agencies in order to develop technologies for eco-friendly vehicles (ERP 2001).

More generally, during the 1990s, cooperations aimed at joint R&D activities were also stimulated by the antitrust regulation, which in the previous decades had raised some problems. Antitrust regulations were viewed as overly constraining to R&D cooperation. In 1984, the National Cooperative Research Act, introduced by the Reagan administration, had begun to provide less severe regulations, clarifying cases of interest for antitrust and related penalties. In 1993, the Clinton administration implemented the National Cooperative Research and Production Act, further liberalizing cooperation in research. About 740 joint ventures were registered in 1998, many of which in communication, electronic and the transport sector (ERP 2001).

During the 1990s, the Clinton administration also implemented policies for promoting science and technology by strengthening the budget of those agencies that in the United States were traditionally involved in R&D activities. For example, there was an increase of over 60% in eight years of funding for research conducted by the NSF and an increase of over 80% in eight years for research conducted by the NIH (principally in the biomedical field). There was also a 20% tax credit for expenditures on R&D carried out by private companies (ERP 2001). Finally, the Antitrust Guidelines for the Licensing of Intellectual Property of 1995 attempted to encourage the development and diffusion of new technologies through better regulation on the protection of intellectual property rights (ERP 1999).

ENVIRONMENTAL POLICIES DURING THE 1990s: INTERNATIONAL AND DOMESTIC ISSUES

In 1990s, environmental issues started to occupy an important position in the international political debate. International meetings to discuss problems related to *sustainable development* began in Rio de Janeiro in 1992 with the "Earth Summit". This was an unprecedented event involving 172 governments and 108 heads of state and government. The topics discussed were different, including an examination of production patterns to limit the production of toxins such as lead in diesel or poisonous waste; alternative energy resources to replace fossil fuel abuse, considered responsible for global climate change; public transport systems in order to reduce pollutant emissions from vehicles and increasingly problematic water scarcity.

This summit resulted in an agreement on the United Nations Framework Convention on Climate Change (UNFCCC). Even though the UNFCCC did not set mandatory limits for greenhouse gas emissions to individual nations, it however provided the possibility for the signatory parties to adopt formal protocols, which would impose mandatory emission limits. Following the entry into force of the Convention (on 21 March 1994), several Conferences of the Parties (COP) were held, with the purpose of defining the details of the adoption of the Protocols.[12]

In 1997, in the context of the third Conference of the Parties (COP3), the Kyoto Protocol was defined. The treaty provided for the obligation of industrialized countries to reduce emissions of polluting elements by no less than 5% compared to 1990 emissions, considered as a base year. As a condition, the treaty would come into force only when it had been ratified by no less than 55 signatory nations, responsible for at least 55% of polluting emissions (this condition was met only in November 2004, when Russia perfected its accession) (Harrison and Sundstrom 2010). The ratification phase of the protocol was particularly difficult in the context of the different COPs. Many countries struggled to sign the agreement because of the constraints that this imposed on the national level and the related political interests at stake.[13]

In the United States, which in 2001 accounted for 36.2% of world carbon dioxide emissions, President Bill Clinton (encouraged by Vice President Al Gore) signed the protocol during the last months of his mandate. American accession to the protocol was particularly affected by the dynamics of national politics. The adoption of multilateral agreements by the United States required a collective agreement between various interest-bearing centres, such as lobbies, American public opinion, Congress and the President. In this context, the discussion on environmental issues essentially put into question the balance of economic interests within the American economy, as it could potentially influence the development path of the productive structure. Indeed, the impact that public decision-making in the field of environmental regulation could have on investment decisions in particular sectors and technologies, the costs structure of companies and the structural adjustment of the US economy was enormous. The result of the complex dynamics of American politics on environment was that, shortly after the election of George W. Bush, the United States withdrew their membership from the Kyoto Protocol, initially signed by Clinton.

Even though Clinton's attempts to align the United States with international environmental agreements were not particularly effective after his mandate, in the context of domestic policies the 1990s saw some important actions in line with the need for change suggested by environmental issues.

In 1994, President Clinton's Executive Order 12898 established that every federal agency should, in its programmes, identify and address the disproportionate negative effects on humans and on the environment. The following year, Vice President Gore and Administrator Browner announced a series of 25 specific reforms within the US Environmental Protection Agency (EPA). One of these programmes was the Project XL ("Excellence and Leadership"), which launched 50 pilot projects to allow businesses to propose better alternatives to existing environmental regulations, which would allow higher levels of control on pollution at lower costs.

Furthermore, in 1995, EPA and states implemented the National Environmental Performance Partnership System (NEPPS). It was a performance-based system of environmental protection designed to improve the efficiency and effectiveness of state-EPA partnerships. By focusing EPA and state resources on the most pressing environmental problems, and taking advantage of the unique capacities of each partner, performance partnerships could help achieve the greatest environmental and human health protection.

Regarding air quality regulations, amendments were made to the Clean Air Act of 1990. Various methodologies for measuring air pollution were included in the legislation, along with various types of cost-benefit analysis for present and future investment in operations for environmental protection, specifically for air pollution.

Overall, Clinton's environmental initiatives in the 1990s show a will, though partly hindered by the dynamics of national politics, to steer the American economic system towards environmental goals.

CONCLUSION

This chapter has shown that, during the 1990s, policies to support technological innovation were particularly prominent. The increased political stability resulting from the end of the Cold War required the United States to reduce its military expenditures. Concerns about the possible negative impact on the technological and industrial development of the entire American economy of this retrenchment led the government to look for alternative ways to promote innovation. In particular, the Clinton administration was the one that proclaimed a "new approach" to the innovation policy. Specifically, ICT was considered by the government one of the priorities. This important wave of innovations in ICT, which marked the beginning of the so-called New Economy, was ridden by the American administration through a number of important initiatives to foster the development of the sector. Also, more general policies for the advancement of science and technology were actively implemented by the administration, with a particular commitment to improving the partnership between government and private sector. Finally, during those years, environmental issues entered the political debate at the international and domestic level, requiring from the government important efforts in an attempt to orient the American productive structure towards a sustainable development.

Overall, the scenario of the 1990s (described in this and in the previous chapter) shows that the United States was able, on the one hand, to exert a massive influence at the international level by promoting the liberalization of foreign markets, and, on the other hand, they also multiplied the benefits of that institutional framework by promoting selected key technologies and innovation policies. These are two complementary leverages of the American neoliberal strategy, which have operated in maximizing the gains achieved by the US industrial system in participating to the global economy. Indeed, while technology policies promote the competitiveness of American enterprises, the liberalization of foreign markets allows the United States to enforce this competitiveness abroad. This double-leverage mechanism has been made possible by the global institutional framework strategically established by the United States in the neoliberal era. This is the quintessence of the American industrial strategy in the neoliberal era, aimed at capitalizing the American economic power by paving the way for foreign markets and, on the other hand, by promoting the national industry.

NOTES

1. On the European case see Weiss (1997); Soete (2007). On the policies implemented by Japan in the same years see Nezu (2007), Buigues and Sekkat (2009), Chang et al. (2013).
2. See Bush G. H. (1992), *Remarks Announcing the Job Training 2000 Initiative in Atlanta*, 17 January 1992, George Bush Presidential Library and Museum. http://www.channelingreality.com/un/education/nationatrisk/bushlibrary_JT2000_Announce.pdf.
3. See The White House Archive, Executive Order 12870, Trade Promotion Coordinating Committee, 30 September 1993. http://govinfo.library.unt.edu/npr/library/direct/orders/tradepromotion.html.

4. One of the main results of the National Export Strategy was the elimination of unnecessary controls on exports of computers and telecommunications equipment, the process for obtaining export licences was streamlined and mandatory licences were reduced of about a third, and export assistance centres were set up for small businesses interested in obtaining financial information and support (ERP 1995).

5. See, for example, Schultze (1983), Datta-Chaudhuri (1990), Krueger (1990), Le Grand (1991), Chang (1994), Khan and Jomo (2000), Lerner (2009), Di Tommaso and Schweitzer (2013).

6. See *A Brief History of Vice President Al Gore's National Partnership for Reinventing Government During the Administration of President Bill Clinton 1993–2001.* http://govinfo.library.unt.edu/npr/whoweare/historyofnpr.html.

7. Despite the legislative efforts, the long-distance communication market (interstate) at the end of the 1990s was still heavily concentrated, with the first three network service providers holding more than 75% of the national market. The market power of the three companies and the high profitability of the services provided made the oligopoly solid for a long time (Crandall 2005). Only several years later the competition from wireless service providers was able to reduce the profits of the industry to the benefit of the consumers. In addition, some authors point out that at the end of the 1990s the deregulation process and the opening up of telecommunications networks to competition had created considerable confusion, both for existing companies in the market and for those who were new entrants, requiring, in 2003 and then in 2004, two review processes of the Telecommunication Act of 1996 (Bazzucchi 2013).

8. See National Science and Technology Council, IT Working Group (1999), on https://www.nitrd.gov/archive/it2/it2-ip.pdf (last accessed September 2017).

9. See National Science and Technology Council, IT Working Group (1999), on https://www.nitrd.gov/archive/it2/it2-ip.pdf (last accessed September 2017).

10. See the website of the initiative on https://www.sbir.gov/about/about-sttr (last accessed September 2017).

11. See NIST website on https://www.nist.gov/news-events/news/2000/10/nist-advanced-technology-program-launches-54-new-technology-rd-projects (last accessed September 2017)

12. The total number of COPs to date is 22, the 23rd will be held in Bonn in November 2017: 1992 Rio de Janeiro, 1995 Berlin, 1996 Geneva, 1997 Kyoto, 1998 Buenos Aires, 1999 Bonn, 2000 L'Aja, 2001 Marrakech, 2003 Buenos Aires, 2004 Milan, 2005 Montreal, 2006 Nairobi, 2007 Bali, 2008 Poznan, 2009 Copenhagen, 2010 Cancun, 2011 Durban, 2012 Doha, 2013 Warsaw, 2014 Lima, 2015 Paris, 2016 Marrakech.

13. The emission constraints imposed on countries by the protocol were not the same for all economies. The signatory states were divided into three groups: the countries of the Annex I (the industrialized countries), the countries of Annex II (the industrialized countries that pay for the costs of the developing countries) and developing countries. Each group faced different obligations. For example, countries in the Annex I had to reduce their emissions and if they did not succeed they would have to buy emission credits. By contrast, developing countries did not have immediate restrictions. For example, India and China, which ratified the protocol, were not required to reduce their carbon dioxide emissions because they were not among the major sources of greenhouse gas emissions during the industrialization period, which is believed to be causing today's climate change.

REFERENCES

Bazzucchi, L. (2013). *Industrial Policy 2.0: la frontiera del digitale, gli Stati Uniti e il dibattito sull'intervento di governo*. Tesi di Dottorato: Università degli Studi di Ferrara.

Block, F. (2008). *Swimming Against the Current: The Rise of a Hidden Developmental State in the United States*. Politics & Society, 36(2), 169–206.

Buigues, P. A., & Sekkat, K. (2009). *Industrial Policy in Europe, Japan and the USA. Amounts, Mechanisms and Effectiveness*. Basingstoke: Palgrave Macmillan.

Chang, H. J. (1994). *The Political Economy of Industrial Policy*. New York: St. Martin's Press.

Chang, H. J., Andreoni, A., & Kuan, M. L. (2013). *International Industrial Policy Experiences and the Lessons for the UK*, Policy Report for the UK Foresight Future of Manufacturing Project, UK Government Office of Science.

Crandall, R. W. (2005). *Competition and Chaos. U.S. Telecommunications Since the 1996 Telecom Act*. Washington, DC: Brooking Institution.

Datta-Chaudhuri, M. (1990). Market Failure or Government Failure? *Journal of Economic Perspectives, 4*(3), 25–39.

Di Tommaso, M. R., & Schweitzer, S. O. (2013). *Industrial Policy in America. Breaking the Taboo*. Cheltenham/Northampton: Edward Elgar.

ERP. (1990). *Economic Report of the President*. Washington, DC: United States Government Printing Office.

ERP. (1991). *Economic Report of the President*. Washington, DC: United States Government Printing Office.

ERP. (1992). *Economic Report of the President*. Washington, DC: United States Government Printing Office.

ERP. (1993). *Economic Report of the President*. Washington, DC: United States Government Printing Office.

ERP. (1994). *Economic Report of the President.* Washington, DC: United States Government Printing Office.

ERP. (1995). *Economic Report of the President.* Washington, DC: United States Government Printing Office.

ERP. (1996). *Economic Report of the President.* Washington, DC: United States Government Printing Office.

ERP. (1997). *Economic Report of the President.* Washington, DC: United States Government Printing Office.

ERP. (1999). *Economic Report of the President.* Washington, DC: United States Government Printing Office.

ERP. (2000). *Economic Report of the President.* Washington, DC: United States Government Printing Office.

ERP. (2001). *Economic Report of the President.* Washington, DC: United States Government Printing Office.

Etzioni, A. (1983). The MITIzation of America? *The Public Interest, 72*, 44.

Hallacher, P. (2005). *Why Policy Network Matter: The Advanced Technology Program and the Manufacturing Extension Partnership.* Lanhom: Rowman & Littlefield.

Harrison, K., & Sundstrom, L. M. (Eds.). (2010). *Global Commons, Domestic Decisions: The comparative Politics of Climate Change.* Cambridge, MA: MIT Press.

Khan, M., & Jomo, K. S. (2000). *Rents, Rent-Seeking and Economic Development: Theory and Evidence in Asia.* Cambridge: Cambridge University Press.

Krueger, A. O. (1990). Government Failures in Development. *The Journal of Economic Perspectives, 4*(3), 9–23.

Le Grand, J. (1991). The Theory of Government Failure. *British Journal of Political Science, 21*(4), 423–442.

Lerner, J. (2009). *Boulevard of Broken Dreams, Why Public Efforts to Boost Entrepreneurship and Venture Capital Have Failed and What to Do About It.* Princeton: Princeton University Press.

McAndrews, J. L. (2006). *The Era of Education: The Presidents and the Schools, 1965–2001.* Urbana: University of Illinois Press.

Nezu, R. (2007). *Industrial Policy in Japan,* Special Issue on the Future of Industrial Policy. Springer Science + Business Media, LLC.

Picot, A., & Wernick, C. (2007). The Role of Government in Broadband Access. *Telecommunication Policy, 31*(10–11), 660–674.

Schrank, A. J., & Whitford, J. (2009). Industrial Policy in the United States: A Neo-Polanyian Interpretation. *Politics and Society, 37*(4), 521–553.

Schultze, C. L. (1983). Industrial Policy: A Dissent. *The Brookings Review, 2*(1), 3–12.

Shapira, P. (2001). US Manufacturing Extension Partnership: Technology Policy Reinvented? *Research Policy, 30*, 977–992.

Soete, L. (2007). From Industrial to Innovation Policy. *Journal of Industry Competition and Trade, 7*(3–4), 273–284.

Voytek, K. P., Lellock, K. L., & Schmith, M. A. (2004). Developing Performance Metrics for Science and Technology Programs: The Case of the Manufacturing Extension Partnership Program. *Economic Development Quarterly., 18*, 174.

Wade, R. H. (2012). Return of Industrial Policy? *International Review of Applied Economics, 26*(2), 223–239.

Weiss, P. (1997). *Techno-globalism and Industrial Policy Responses in the USA and Europe. Springer in its Journal Intereconomics, 32*(2), 74–86.

Weiss, L. (2008). *Crossing the Divide: From the Military-industrial to the Development-Procurement Complex*. Presented at the Berkeley Workshop on the 'Hidden US Developmental State', 20–21 June 2008, San Francisco.

Whitford, J. (2005). *The New Old Economy. Networks, Institutions, and Organizational Transformation of American Manufacturing*. Oxford: Oxford University Press.

Whitford, J., & Schrank, A. (2011). The Paradox of the Weak State Revisited: Industrial Policy, Network Governance, and Political Decentralization. In F. Block & M. Keller (Eds.), *State of Innovation: The U.S. Government's Role in Technology Development*. Boulder: Paradigm Publishers.

CHAPTER 6

Incubating the Crisis: Bush Junior Back to the *Old Economy*

The international influence that the United States had begun to exert from the mid-1970s, with the creation of the neoliberal economic order, started in the years 2000s to meet some limit. Already during the 1990s, the international economic scenario began to note the presence of new emerging industrial powers.[1] During the 2000s, it became extremely clear that something in the American global power was changing. The rise of the BRIC and other manufacturing emerging countries, but in particular of China, started to create difficulties to the functioning of the neoliberal institutional structure. Indeed, the WTO system, as a regulatory framework of the international trade, began to struggle to impose its rules on the Southeast Asian economies. In this context, the Doha Round, which should have been an attempt to establish the neoliberal rules at international level once and for all, was in reality a fiasco. Generally, the US power to negotiate favourable trade conditions seemed to be, to some extent, changed.

Furthermore, on the side of the national policies, the election of Bush Junior opened a season of deregulation and spending cuts for new technologies. From Clinton's *New Economy*, aimed at fostering ICT, public-private partnership in R&D, and environmental friendly technologies, the American industrial strategy seemed to return to the *old economy* (Bianchi and Labory 2011), based on an economic growth driven by military public demand (and by a growing public debt). The 11 September 2011 attack, that marked the beginning of the fight against terrorism, was

© The Author(s) 2019   127
M. Tassinari, *Capitalising Economic Power in the US*,
International Political Economy Series,
https://doi.org/10.1007/978-3-319-76648-5_6

certainly a crucial factor in explaining the new shifting towards a military-driven economy.

As a result, the new economic conjuncture at international level and the policy orientation at domestic level during the 2000s had a crucial responsibility in incubating the crisis that would explode in 2007. Indeed, among other factors, the massive trade deficit with China and a high public debt generated by the military expenditures were the symptoms of an intrinsic weakness of the American economy, which led to one of the deepest recession since the 1929. This chapter describes the international context and the main changes in the American approach to industrial development during the Bush Junior administration, which led to the burst of the global financial crisis.

THE RISE OF CHINA AND THE CHALLENGES TO THE NEOLIBERAL ORDER

The growth of the BRIC, especially of China, at the beginning of the 2000s was already massive.[2] This situation had the consequence of inducing a change in the international economic equilibrium, undermining the basic neoliberal principles that governed the functioning of the WTO (Moran 2012; The Economist 2012). Since the early 1990s, China began to be an important trading partner for the United States, with the Bush Senior administration promoting the first bilateral agreements. In October 1992, a "Market Access Agreement" was signed between the United States and China, in order to provide "better export opportunities for the United States" (ERP 1993). The agreement essentially established the removal of Chinese barriers to import on hundreds of American products. Nonetheless, in 1997, American exports to China (at that time the fourth most important American trading partner) increased at an annual rate of 8%, while imports of Chinese products to the United States increased at an annual rate of 21%. In 1996, the US trade deficit with China amounted to about 39.5 billion dollars (ERP 1998). The cause of this situation was attributed by the US government to the barrier to trade imposed by China on American products. In an effort to mitigate these issues in subsequent years, the Clinton administration was strongly committed to negotiating China's access to WTO (ERP 1998: 233). As a part of this tortuous route—which begun in 1988 and was concluded only in December 2001 with the actual entry of China into the WTO—the Clinton administration undertook, during its two mandates, some legal actions aimed at removing the trade barriers that limited US exports. For example, the actions taken by the US government under Special 301, in June 1994, were intended to persuade China to negotiate on issues related to patents, copyright, trade secrecy, tariffs and restrictions to imports and transparency in health standards (ERP 1995). Despite the difficulties, American expectations on China's inclusion in the framework outlined by the international economic rules were extremely high in those years:

> The W.T.O. agreement will move China in the right direction. It will advance the goals America has worked for in China for the past three decades. And of course, it will advance our own economic interests. Economically, this agreement is the equivalent of a one-way street. It requires China to open its markets – with a fifth of the world's population, potentially the biggest markets in the world – to both our products and services in unprecedented new ways. All we do is to agree to maintain the present access which China enjoys. Chinese tariffs, from telecommunications products to automobiles to agriculture, will fall by half or more over just five years. For the first time, our companies will be able to sell and distribute products in China made by workers here in America without being forced to relocate manufacturing to China, sell through the Chinese government, or transfer valuable technology – for the first time. We'll be able to export products without exporting jobs. Meanwhile, we'll get valuable new safeguards against any surges of imports from China. We're already preparing for the largest enforcement effort ever given for a trade agreement.[3]

In reality, even after China's actual entry into the WTO in 2001, the Chinese economic growth continued to destabilize the international economic order. Prior to the full implementation of the WTO rules, China was granted a five-year adjustment period during which it would have to reduce the average tariff level from 24.6% to 9.4%, complying with the rules on Trade-Related Investment Measures (TRIMS), eliminate constraints and requirements on local content of foreign direct investment (FDI), increase intellectual property rights safeguards and open access to foreign companies for sale to state-owned enterprises (SOEs) (Kiely 2015: 47). Although some of these measures were partially implemented, China remained reluctant to liberalize in several areas (Fig. 6.1).

China continued de facto to adopt a strong interventionist approach to industrial development through the implementation of medium- and long-term structural adjustment plans (Di Tommaso et al. 2013; Barbieri

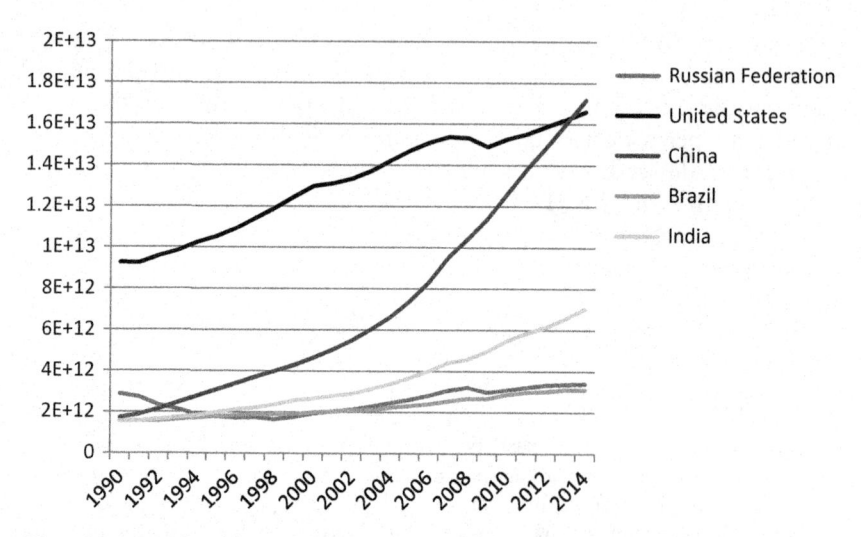

Fig. 6.1 BRIC and US GDP, PPP (constant 2011 international $) (Source: Author's elaboration based on data from IMF [UNdata])

et al. 2015). One of the predominant characteristics of the Chinese industrial policy was the implementation of selective (or "vertical") policies, according to a logic mainly oriented to the development of particular sectors.[4] In this context, the key industries that had to be promoted were clearly defined by the government's Five-Year Plans (Barbieri et al. 2015).

Indeed, the alignment of emerging economies with WTO rules, which should have come about through the negotiations under the Doha Development Round of 2001 (also known as the Doha Development Agenda)[5], was never fully realized. The trade negotiations started in Doha in 2001 were followed by repeated meetings over the subsequent years, and they were always marked by substantial failures in reaching a final agreement. The most controversial issues concerned the reduction of tariff and non-tariff barriers and agricultural regulations.[6] These issues highlighted the fact that the balances between global economies had now changed and that probably the conditions for continuing in a multilateral framework with the approach of the Clinton administration years were no longer there. The stalemate caused by the failure of the Doha agreements led the United States, in the 2000s, to an important commitment towards the implementation of bilateral trade agreements. The interventions had, on one side, the objective of liberalizing foreign markets and, on the other side, to protect the American companies from foreign competition (Ketels

2007). The Bush administration in those years was able to conclude numerous bilateral trade agreements. The words contained in the 2009 ERP confirm the central importance of market liberalization in the trade policy approach of the administration:

> In the past 8 years, U.S. policy has supported engagement in global free trade, which has been most evident in the increase in the number of U.S. free trade agreements (FTAs). [...] Before 2001, the United States had implemented FTAs with three countries. To date, the United States has concluded FTAs with 20 countries, including 16 in force, one approved by Congress but not yet in force, and three concluded but not yet approved by Congress. (ERP 2009: 132)

Data published in the ERP of 2009 reveal that in 2007 41% of US exports were directed to countries with which America had signed a trade agreement, but only 31% of the imports came from these countries (ERP 2009), indicating a substantial benefit derived from these agreements for the United States compared to the trade partners. The liberalization of foreign trade, which had been at the centre of the US trade policy in the 1980s and 1990s, continued in 2000s to massively foster the expansion of the flows of imports and export. Those years were characterized by an important expansion of trade relations between the United States and the rest of the world (see Fig 6.2 below).

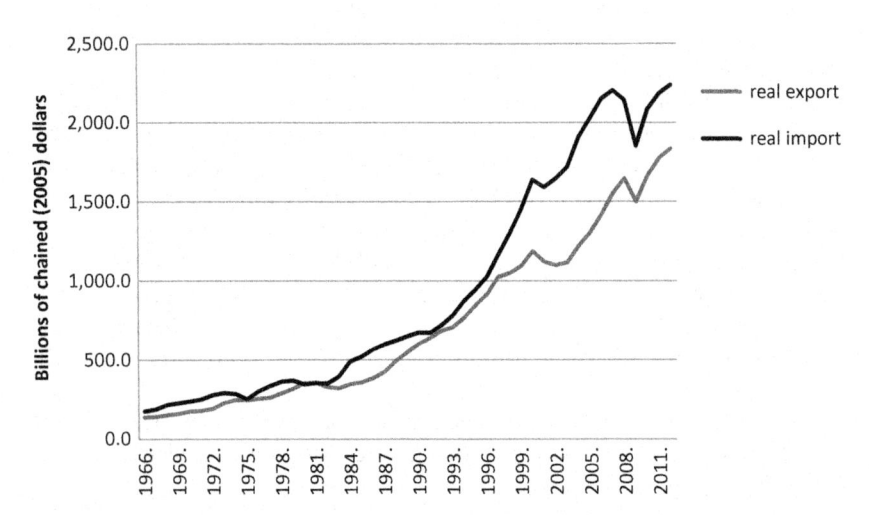

Fig. 6.2 Real import and export (billions of chained [2005] dollars) (Source: Author's elaboration based on TABLE B–2—E.R.P.2013/Department of Commerce)

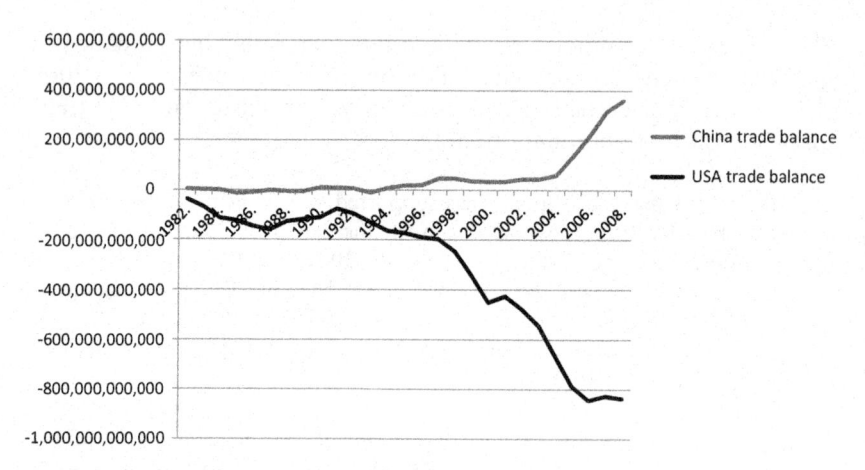

Fig. 6.3 US-China net export (1982–2008)—US dollar (Source: Author's elaboration based on data from IMF [UNdata])

However, the trend that characterized US foreign trade raised considerable concerns regarding the trade deficit that the United States was inexorably accumulating. More specifically, the US imports from China and Hong Kong grew from 5.7% to 15% of the total US imports from 1990 to 2005 and they were the major factors behind the growing US deficit (Schwartz 2009b). Indeed, the overall trend of the US trade deficit was, from the early 1990s, virtually mirroring the Chinese surplus. While the United States was importing more than they were able to export, China was expanding its importance in the international markets (Fig. 6.3).

Not all industrial sectors reacted to the dynamics of international trade in the same way (Kiely 2015; Dicken 2011; Schwartz 2009a). Observing the trade balance between the United States and China for the manufacturing sectors, among the industries that were able to maintain a substantial parity in trade balance during the 2000s were the pharmaceutical industry, beverages, tobacco and iron and steel (the latter however started to decline in 2009). The automotive industry recorded a growing trade deficit until 2008, when the trend started to improve, returning to deficit in 2015 (Fig. 6.4).

The electrical machinery industry, mechanical appliances, optical instruments, plastics and footwear recorded an increasing trade deficit since the early 1990s (Fig. 6.5).

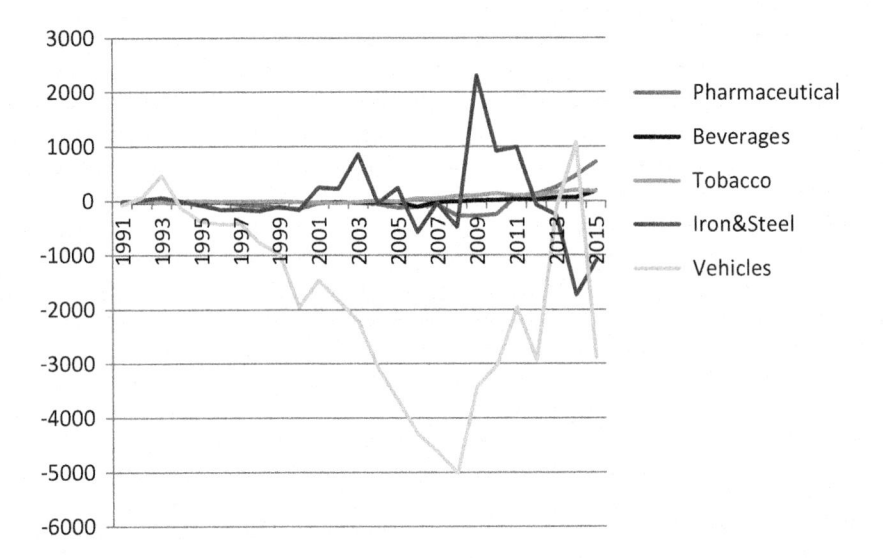

Fig. 6.4   US-China trade balance (million US$): industrial sectors (1) (Source: Author's elaboration based on data from UN Comtrade)

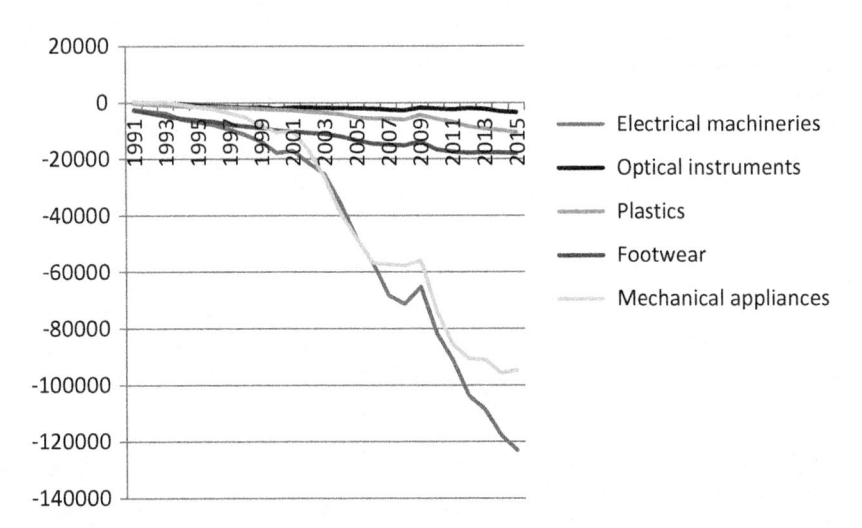

Fig. 6.5   US-China trade balance (million US$): industrial sectors (2) (Source: Author's elaboration based on data from UN Comtrade)

In this scenario, some attempts were made by the Bush administration to protect the American industry in the field of trade policies. This was the case, for example, of the iron and steel industries and textiles and timber industries, where the government applied protectionist tariffs on imported products. Also the agricultural sector needed important subsidies to compete with foreign productions (ERP 2009). These interventions were motivated by the Bush Junior administration as a response to unfair practices adopted by competing countries, but the US trade policy was highly contested at the international level. In 2003 and 2004, for example, the WTO imposed on the United States to remove tariffs on steel industry. Furthermore, in 2007 the Congress, under the growing international pressure, abolished the Continued Dumping and Subsidy Offset Act of 2000 (the "Byrd Amendment"), which stipulated that the revenues from import duties should be distributed to companies in difficulty (an amount of about 840 million dollars for the years 2001–2003). In 2002, the WTO also imposed on the United States the removal of the Foreign Sales Corporation, which reduced federal taxation on export profits, an export subsidy perceived as unfair (Ketels 2007).

This new international context that characterized the 2000s showed that the equilibrium of international trade was somehow changing. The neoliberal order promoted in the context of WTO by the United States, on the one hand, was struggling to impose its rules on emerging economies and, on the other hand, it began in some cases to impose on the United States market opening conditions that damaged the US economy. In other words, in the 2000s, the neoliberal order promoted by the United States in the previous decades seemed to backfire.

THE NEW WAVE OF MILITARY EXPENDITURES

Throughout the twentieth century the United States had been involved in a long list of conflicts all over the world, including the two World Wars, the War of Korea (1950–1953), the Vietnam War (1960–1975) and the Kuwait War (1990–91). By adding also the period of the Cold War to the list, it is possible to draw a line of continuity that shows the United States as engaged in a permanent state of war. As seen in the previous chapters, this military commitment had played a crucial role in promoting the domestic economic system. The public demand for private companies formulated by the DOD and other agencies involved in national security, and the continuous investment in new military technology had greatly supported the development and innovation of the American industrial system. In the 1990s, at the end of the Cold War, this mechanism seemed to somewhat slow down, giving greater scope to public engagement in civil matters. In this context, the Clinton administration had invested in the ICT sector, in public-private partnerships for technological advancement and in environmental sustainability.

The terrorist attack on the Twin Towers, on 11 September 2001, reversed once again this course. Immediately after this event, President Bush Junior's political priorities became the "global war on terrorism". In 2001, the United States began the armed intervention in Afghanistan in order to annihilate the Taliban regime and the Al Qaeda terrorist group, accused of carrying out the attacks. Furthermore, in 2003, the Iraq war began with the aim of overthrowing Saddam Hussein, accused of possessing weapons of mass destruction and supporting international terrorism. This intervention was defined by Bush as a "preventive war" to safeguard the global peace and order.

In this context, the military public demand returned to be a central factor in the growth dynamics of the US national economy (Ketels 2007; Weiss 2008; Buigues and Sekkat 2009). In those years, the budget allocated to the DOD increased from 15.6% of the total federal budget for 2001 to 19.9% of the 2008 total budget. [7] The impact on the national industry was once again impressive. American companies, protected from foreign competition, were able to provide enormous volumes of goods and services to the agencies and departments involved in national security by developing economies of scale and learning. Moreover, in the context of this new wave of military expenditures, the concept of "national security" assumed a different meaning from the past. In addition to the traditional military expenditures that responded to the direct needs of the US military engagement in war fronts, many other threats had to be addressed: pandemics and bacteriological attacks, terrorism, environmental crises, cyberattacks. This was a global war that was also fought within the national borders, a very wide front involving a long list of public agencies that required considerable investment in sophisticated and specialized research (Weiss 2014).

In 2003, a new department was created, the Department of Homeland Security, which had the task of anticipating, preventing and responding to national emergencies, especially concerning terrorist attacks. Within this department, a research agency was set up to develop new technologies for national security (called the Homeland Security Advanced Research

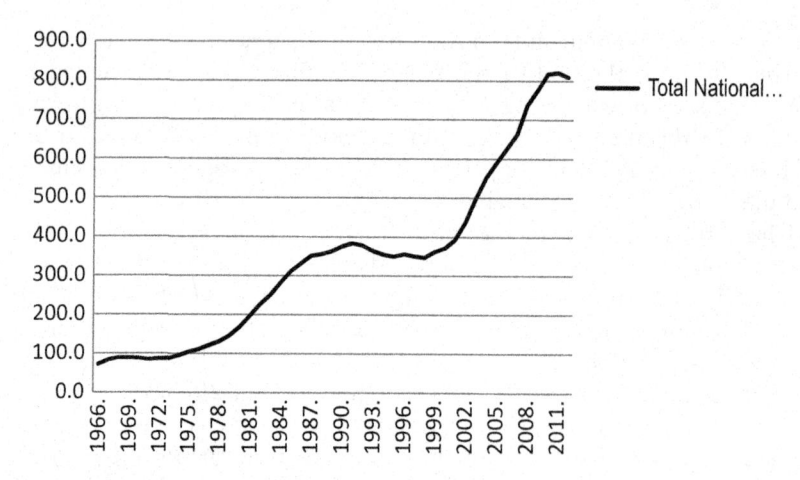

Fig. 6.6 Total national defence gov. consumption exp. and gross invest (Billions of Dollars, quarterly data at seasonally adjusted annual rates) (Source: Author's elaboration based on TABLE B–20—E.R.P.2013/Department of Commerce)

Projects Agency—HSARPA). In this context, there was a sharp increase in funds for R&D in the US army. Large public investments were also granted to the Advanced Research Projects Agency-Energy (ARPA-E) operating in energy sectors, which was of high strategic importance in the context of the world geopolitical equilibrium (Fig. 6.6).

The overall budget allocated to R&D activities under "national security" increased considerably in the 2000s. The HSARPA controlled a $6.6 billion budget during its first five years of operation. The NIH, the DOD and the NSF formed a biodefence consortium coordinating a $5 billion programme for vaccine development, purchase and storage (the Project Bioshield) (Weiss 2014: 48–49). Within the two mandates of the Bush Junior administration there were numerous special projects conducted by the agencies involved in "national security" issues. Particular activism was registered in the field of nanotechnology, robotics and renewable energy research (see Weiss 2014: 123).

Overall, the focus on national security issues interrupted the way the Clinton administration had embarked on when attempting to overthrow the military sector as the main pillar of the dynamics of technological and industrial development (Ruttan 2006). Indeed, the work of the Bush Junior administration for the promotion of science and technology for civil purposes was extremely weak. In this context, for example, in 2006 Bush launched the American Competitiveness Initiative (ACI). The plan, defined by the Office of Science and Technology Policy, requested to double the government investment in R&D over ten years, through an increase in funds allocated to some of the major federal agencies involved in research.[8] In reality, the initiative did not find enough support in Congress and was soon abandoned (Buigues and Sekkat 2009). The limited support provided by the Congress for civil science and technology programmes also manifested itself in the progressive reduction of the budget allocated to some of the major initiatives launched during the 1980s and 1990s. In this context, the budget for the Advanced Technology Program (ATP), managed by the NIST, was gradually reduced over the years, to eventually be terminated in 2007 (Wade 2014: 392). Environmental policies, which had marked Vice President Al Gore's commitment during the Clinton administration, also were critical during the Bush Junior administration. In particular, President Bush's decision, at the beginning of his mandate, to withdraw the United States from the Kyoto Protocol clearly outlined the administration's attitude towards environmental issues (Kennedy 2004).

As a result, the scenario of public intervention established by the Bush administration during the 2000s left little doubt: the United States had adopted an approach to industrial development that used a massive military public demand—formulated by the agencies involved in national security—to drive the growth of the US economy, denying de facto the need to respond to a long-term strategic vision on the future of the American industry. However, this growth model, centred on (military) public spending, had an intrinsic weakness in itself, which was reflected in the explosion, in those years, of the US public debt (Fig. 6.7).

THE OUTBREAK OF THE CRISIS

The outbreak of the crisis, in August 2007, was the result of long-standing dynamics.[9] As described above, in this context there was, first of all, the economic relationship with China. The more China was growing, the more it continued to show autonomy over the WTO and the requirements of the Washington Consensus (as witnessed by the repeated failures in the Doha negotiations begun in 2001). In this context, since the 1990s, China had begun to grow exponentially, and the United States continued to represent one of the major markets for Chinese products. It was a real

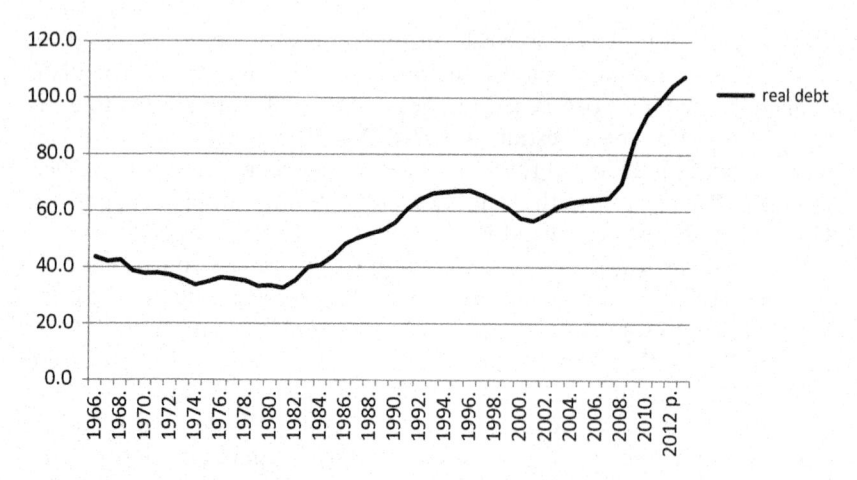

Fig. 6.7 US gross federal debt (as % GDP) (Source: Author's elaboration based on TABLE B-79—ERP 2013/Department of the Treasury and Office of Management and Budget)

invasion of the American market: China's expansion meant availability of low-priced products that fuelled the US consumption growth, driven by imports. The growth in the US imports led to a rapid increase in trade deficit in 2000s. In this context, the consumption growth in the US economy was not sustained, in those years, by an actual growth of income-generating capacity, but mainly by an increase in public and private indebtedness, which did not have adequate guarantees in the real economy. In other words, the Americans were consuming more than they were able to produce.

While the public debt growth served primarily to finance military spending and the global war on terrorism, the growing private indebtedness was driven by conditions that seemed increasingly favourable to the real estate market. The money borrowed from the Americans (at a cost that in the early 2000s was extremely favourable) was secured by mortgages on private homes, which were increasing their value, thanks to a growing real estate market. This situation encouraged investment and speculation in real estate through sub-prime mortgages. In this context, high domestic consumption, driven by cheap Chinese imports, was not sustained by the growth of the real economy and wages, but by real estate speculation and by the continuing contraction of new debts.

This condition became unsustainable over time. The growth in the value of housing could not go beyond a certain limit, since it was not possible to keep the demand and supply of the real estate market at an ever-expanding stage through the continuous involvement of new entrants, which were increasingly coming from low income groups. With the collapse of the real estate market bubble, the value of houses collapsed and, with it, the guarantees on which the US debt was based. In this condition, while inflation began to rise with the rising of Chinese products' prices, the interest rate on mortgages began to increase to levels at which many Americans were unable to repay their debts. The banks had lent loans without proper collaterals; many lenders began to fail, and the value of household savings collapsed.

In the end, the situation of extreme financial uncertainty and the impossibility of contract new debts led to a reduction in consumption, the fall of domestic demand, the collapse of domestic production and imports, with crucial repercussions for the countries exporting to the United States, including Europe. The crisis started in the American real estate market in the summer of 2007, to spread first to the other finance sectors and eventually affect the entire real world economy with the fall in global demand (Attali 2009; Krugman 2009; Stiglitz 2010; Bianchi and Labory 2011; Saad Filho 2011; Blanchard et al. 2012; Allen and Moessner 2012; Akyüz 2014; Evans 2015; Kiely 2015).

FINANCIAL BAILOUTS UNDER THE BUSH ADMINISTRATION

The outbreak of the financial crisis forced the Bush administration to intervene. The intervention in the real estate market was particularly significant. First of all, the Housing and Economic Recovery Act was promoted in July 2008. The purpose of the intervention was to save Fannie Mae (the Federal National Mortgage Association) and Freddie Mac (the Federal Home Loan Mortgage Corporation), two giants that together accounted for about $5 trillion of American mortgages. These were two government-sponsored enterprises (GSE) created respectively at the time of F.D. Roosevelt and Lindon B. Johnson, which, during the Clinton administration years, were particularly active in granting sub-prime mortgages to the US citizens, facilitating the purchase of housing even in cases of high bank risk. With the outbreak of the crisis, the two agencies found themselves in a state of extreme financial fragility, and the Bush administration decided to nationalize them. Under the protection of the Federal Housing Finance Agency, they received extraordinary government funding for a total of $187.5 billion dollars.[10] The immediate bailout was considered absolutely necessary in the name of national interest. In the words of Treasury Secretary Henry Paulson accompanying the announcement of the government intervention, the fundamental considerations underlying the decision of bailout were recalled:

> Fannie Mae and Freddie Mac are so large and so interwoven in our financial system that a failure of either of them would cause great turmoil in our financial markets here at home and around the globe. This turmoil would directly and negatively impact household wealth: from family budgets, to home values, to savings for college and retirement. A failure would affect the ability of Americans to get home loans, auto loans and other consumer credit and business finance. And a failure would be harmful to economic growth and job creation. That is why we have taken these actions today.[11]

In the following months, also Lehman Brothers, one of the largest American financial services companies, was hit by the crisis. On 15 September 2008, the bankruptcy procedure formally began. Lehman had 26,000 employees and a debt of about $613 billion. In this case the government decided not to save the financial colossus from collapse. Indeed, bailout operations undoubtedly collided with the administration's rhetoric of the past eight years, which, since the time of the first electoral campaign, had been opposed to government interference in the economy. Likewise, Republican candidate John McCain, who was conducting the electoral campaign against Obama, had ridden this neoliberal rhetoric, saying that he was happy that President Bush had decided not to use the money of taxpayers to save Lehman.

However, beyond the case of Lehman Brothers, the spread of the crisis to all the finance sectors led to an increasing political pressure for public intervention in order to limit the losses. This context forced the administration in the coming weeks to intervene in a structured way to save the entire financial and banking sector. The Republican President, however, made it clear that this intervention was legitimate only by the exceptionality of the moment. The fundamental neoliberal ideas that inspired the republican thought were clearly pointed out by President Bush:

> History has shown that the greater threat to economic prosperity is not too little government involvement in the market, it is too much government involvement in the market (...). While reforms in the financial sector are essential, the long-term solution to today's problems is sustained economic

growth. And the surest path to that growth is free markets and free people. (...) Free market capitalism is far more than economic theory. It is the engine of social mobility – the highway to the American Dream. (...) If you seek economic growth, if you seek opportunity, if you seek social justice and human dignity, the free market system is the way to go.[12]

In the context of the crisis that was rapidly hitting the world economy no protectionist temptation had to challenge the international pattern that had characterized the previous decades:

Just as important as maintaining free markets within countries is maintaining the free movement of goods and services between countries. When nations open their markets to trade and investment, their businesses and farmers and workers find new buyers for their products. Consumers benefit from more choices and better prices. Entrepreneurs can get their ideas off the ground with funding from anywhere in the world. Thanks in large part to open markets, the volume of global trade today is nearly 30 times greater than it was six decades ago – and some of the most dramatic gains have come in the developing world.[13]

In this scenario, it was clear to the Bush administration that the exceptionality of the moment demanded for an extraordinary government intervention. The intervention was required especially for banks and for the national industry. President Bush asked the Congress to approve a bailout programme with the utmost urgency. In October 2008, the Troubled Asset Relief Program (TARP) was launched.[14] The plan authorized the government to buy up to $700 billion of assets—mostly unprofitable and very risky mortgage-backed securities—whose value collapsed when the real estate market suddenly imploded. The programme funds were spent in the next few months at various stages, first by the Bush administration and later by the Obama administration (see next chapter). The two candidates for the upcoming elections—Obama and McCain—negotiated with Bush the conditions to support companies and banks within the TARP, in terms of amount of aid, list of beneficiaries and time of intervention. Obama and McCain gave their endorsement to Bush and he immediately was in the right position to intervene. About half of the TARP funds were eventually managed by the Bush administration, while the remaining part was subsequently distributed by the Obama administration (the so-called TARP II). In the few months before the end of his mandate, Bush utilized a huge amount of financial resources (about $350 billion) to save banks and financial institutions (Mishkin 2011).[15] An extensive list of the TARP beneficiaries is provided by the Department of the Treasury. There were about 300 credit institutions that received funds before the end of the Bush administration's mandate.[16]

The TARP was not limited solely to the bailout of the financial sector. An important part of the funds was directed to save the automotive industry, within the Automotive Industry Financing Program (AIFP). Among the companies which benefited from the loans were Chrysler[17] and General Motor (GM)[18], the two giants of the American automotive industry, which found themselves one step away from bankruptcy at the beginning of the crisis (see next section discussing this point). It was an intervention strongly demanded by Bush, who stated:

> Under ordinary economic circumstances, I would say this is the price that failed companies must pay, and I would not favor intervening to prevent the auto makers from going out of business. But these are not ordinary circumstances. In the midst of a financial crisis and a recession, allowing the U.S. auto industry to collapse is not a responsible course of action.[19]

Conclusion

The 2000s were marked by important changes in the global economic order. First, the rise of the South, in particular China, started to challenge the system of rules defined in the context of the WTO (as evidenced by the repeated failures of the Doha negotiations begun in 2001). Even after the formal inclusion in the WTO, China continued to adopt a strong interventionist approach to industrial development through the implementation of medium- and long-term structural adjustment plans (Di Tommaso et al. 2013; Barbieri et al. 2015), challenging the global hegemony of the American economic power that had characterized the 1990s. The Chinese expansion meant, for the US economy, the availability of low-priced products that fostered a growing consumption driven by imports, with a rapid increase of the trade deficit. One of the main problems that arose in this context was that the growth of the US economy in the 2000s was primarily supported by an increasing private and public debt rather than by an effective ability to generate income. Indeed, investments in the real economy were heavily overwhelmed by financialization dynamics, where the higher returns promised by financial and real estate assets reduced the incentives to invest in the real ability to produce goods and services.

In this context, also the public intervention for industrial development changed orientation considerably. From Clinton's New Economy, aimed at fostering ICT, public-private partnership in R&D and environmental friendly technologies, the American industrial strategy seemed to go back to the old economy (Bianchi and Labory 2011) based on an economic growth driven by military public demand and by a growing public debt. Some of the major technology initiatives of the 1980s and 1990s saw important budget cuts, and some of them were even extinguished.

In conclusion, the rise of emerging industrial powers, the resulting rebalancing of contractual powers in defining the influence of the international rules within the WTO, the weaker attention to industrial development in favour of the financialization of the economy, all these factors played a crucial role in the outbreak of the global crisis in 2007. The Obama administration's response to this scenario, as it will be shown in the next chapter, has to be regarded as an attempt, on the one hand, to restore a virtuous relationship between government and national industry and, on the other hand, to relaunch the American leadership on the international political and economic scene.

NOTES

1. As a part of this scenario that characterized the 1990s, there was, for example, the rise in the role played in the international productive network by South Korea, Taiwan, Hong Kong, Singapore (the so-called Asian tigers) and Malaysia, Thailand and Indonesia. And the rise of the BRIC, but China in particular, was at the door.
2. Concerning the factors that favoured the growth of the BRICs during the 2000s see, among others, Kiely (2015: 71–75).
3. President Clinton (2000), Speech on China Trade Bill, quoted in *The New York Times*, 9 March 2000, https://partners.nytimes.com/library/world/asia/030900clinton-china-text.html.
4. *Vertical* policies refer to those interventions aimed at promoting particular segments of the economy (specific companies, industrial sectors, technologies, clusters, value chains, geographic areas, etc.). In contrast, *horizontal* policies have a widespread and transversal effect on all segments of the economic system. See, in particular, Lall and Tuebal (1998).
5. See https://www.wto.org/english/tratop_e/dda_e/dda_e.htm.
6. The last round of negotiations (the tenth), which was held in Nairobi in December 2016, despite leading to the definition of some measures shared by developing countries, did not reach a comprehensive final agreement, putting

an end to the negotiations of Doha and leaving important uncertainties about the future role of the WTO. See *New York Times* (1 January 2016), http://www.nytimes.com/2016/01/01/opinion/global-trade-after-the-failure-of-the-doha-round.html?_r=0; Lester Simon, Is the Doha Round Over? The WTO's Negotiating Agenda for 2016 and Beyond, Free Trade Bulletin No. 64, Cato Institute. http://www.cato.org/publications/free-trade-bulletin/doha-round-over-wtos-negotiating-agenda-2016-beyond#full.

7. See *Budget of the United States Government: Historical Tables Fiscal Year 2010*.
8. See Ostp (2006), Ketels (2007).
9. For more details on the causes of Crisis see in particular Attali 2009; Krugman 2009; Stiglitz 2010; Bianchi and Labory 2011; Saad Filho 2011; Blanchard et al. 2012; Allen and Moessner 2012; Akyüz 2014; Evans 2015; Kiely 2015.
10. See Acharya et al. (2011); Frame et al. (2015); Wallison and Calomiris (2009).
11. See CNN, 7 Settembre 2008.
12. George W. Bush, Manhattan Institute Speech, 13 November 2008.
13. George W. Bush, Manhattan Institute Speech, 13 November 2008.
14. See, for example, Webel (2013); Nguyen and Enomoto (2009).
15. Particularly heated was the debate (and the controversy) on how public money should be allocated and on the transparency of the allocation criteria. See, for example, Forbes (19 dicembre 2008), http://www.forbes.com/2008/12/19/congress-tarp-paulson-biz-beltway-cx_bw_lm_1219tarp.html.
16. See the Department of the Treasury, https://www.treasury.gov/initiatives/financial-stability/reports/Pages/TARP-Investment-Program-Transaction-Reports.aspx.
17. See Webel and Canis (2012); Anginer and Warburton (2010).
18. Canis et al. (2010), Helper and Henderson (2014).
19. *Wall Street Journal*, 20 December 2008.

References

Acharya, V. V., Richardson, M., Van Nieuwerburgh, S., & White, L. J. (2011). *Guaranteed to Fail: Fannie Mae, Freddie Mac and the Debacle of Mortgage Finance*. Princeton: Princeton University Press.

Akyüz, Y. (2014). *Crisis Mismanagement in the United States and Europe: Impact on Developing Countries and Longer-Term Consequences*. UN-DESA Working Paper, No. 132.

Allen, W. A., & Moessner, R. (2012). *The International Propagation of the Financial Crisis of 2008 and a Comparison with 1931.* Financial History Review, 19, 123–147.

Anginer, D., & Warburton, A. J. (2010). *The Chrysler Effect: The Impact of the Chrysler Bailout on Borrowing Costs.* World Bank Policy Research Working Paper, No. 5462.

Attali, J. (2009). *La crisi e poi?* Roma: Fazi editore.

Barbieri, E., Di Tommaso, M. R., & Tassinari, M. (2015). *Politiche industriali selettive e settori strategici. Lo scenario e le scelte di Pechino.* l'Industria, 36(3), 403–434.

Bianchi, P., & Labory, S. (2011). *Industrial Policies after the Crisis. Seizing the Future.* Cheltenham: E. Elgar.

Blanchard, O., Romer, D., Spence, M., & Stiglitz, J. (Eds.). (2012). *In the Wake of the Crisis: Leading Economists Reassess Economic Policy.* Cambridge, MA: MIT Press.

Buigues, P. A., & Sekkat, K. (2009). *Industrial Policy in Europe, Japan and the USA. Amounts, Mechanisms and Effectiveness.* Basingstoke: Palgrave Macmillan.

Canis, B., Webel, B., & Shorter G. (2010). *General Motors' Initial Public Offering: Review of Issues and Implications for TARP.* Congressional Research Service Report for Congress, Report R41401, November 10.

Clinton, B. (2000). *Speech on China Trade Bill,* citato in "The New York Times", 9 marzo 2000, https://partners.nytimes.com/library/world/asia/030900 clinton-china-text.html.

Di Tommaso, M. R., Rubini, L., & Barbieri, E. (2013). *Southern China: Industry, Development and Industrial Policy.* Milton Park Abingdon: Routledge.

Dicken, P. (2011). *Global Shift* (6th ed.). London: Sage.

ERP. (1993). *Economic Report of the President.* Washington, DC: United States Government Printing Office.

ERP. (1995). *Economic Report of the President.* Washington, DC: United States Government Printing Office.

ERP. (1998). *Economic Report of the President.* Washington, DC: United States Government Printing Office.

ERP. (2009). *Economic Report of the President.* Washington, DC: United States Government Printing Office.

Evans, T. (2015). *The Crisis of Finance-Led Capitalism in the United States of America.* Institute for International Political Economy Berlin, Working Paper 51. http://www.ipe-berlin.org/fileadmin/downloads/working_paper/ipe_ working_paper_51.pdf.

Frame, W.S. Fuster, A., Tracy J., & Vickery, J. (2015). *The Rescue of Fannie Mae and Freddie Mac.* Federal Reserve Bank of New York Staff Reports, No. 719.

Helper, S., & Henderson, R. (2014). *Management Practices, Relational Contracts, and the Decline of General Motors.* Journal of Economic Perspectives, 28, 49–72.

Kennedy, R. F., Jr. (2004). *Crimes Against Nature.* New York: Harper Perennial.

Ketels, C. H. M. (2007). *Industrial Policy in the United States. Journal of Industry, Competition and Trade, 7,* 147–167. Springer Science, Business Media, LLC.

Kiely, R. (2015). *The BRICs, US "Decline" and Global Transformation.* Basingstoke: Palgrave Macmillan.

Krugman, P. (2009). *How Did Economists Get It So Wrong,* September 2, New York Times online article: www.nytimes.com/2009/09/06/magazine/06Economic-t.html?_r=1&emc=eta1.

Lall, S., & Teubal, M. (1998). *Market-Stimulating' Technology Policies in Developing Countries: A Framework with Examples from East Asia. World Development, 26*(8), 1369–1385.

Mishkin, F. S. (2011). *Over the Cliff: From the Subprime to the Global Financial Crisis. Journal of Economic Perspectives, 25,* 49.

Moran, M. (2012). *The Reckoning.* Basingstoke: Palgrave.

Nguyen, A. P., & Enomoto, C. E. (Eds.). (2009). *The Troubled Asset Relief Program (TARP) and the Financial Crisis of 2007–2008. Journal of Business & Economics Research, 7*(12), 91–106.

OSTP (Office of Science and Technology Policy). (2006). *American Competitiveness Initiative: Leading the World in Innovation.* Domestic Policy Council, Office of Science and Technology Policy, February.

Ruttan, V. W. (2006). *Will Government Programs Spur the Next Breakthrough? Issue in Science and Technology, 22*(2), 55–61.

Saad-Filho, A. (2011). Crisis in Neoliberalism or Crisis of Neoliberalism?. *Socialist Register, 47,* www.socialistregister.com.

Schwartz, H. (2009a). *Sub-prime Nation.* Ithaca: Cornell University Press.

Schwartz, H. (2009b). *Origins and Consequences of the US Subprime Crisis.* In H. Schwartz & L. Seabrooke (Eds.), *The Politics of Housing Booms and Bust* (pp. 188–207). Basingstoke: Palgrave.

Stiglitz, J. (2010). *Freefall: America, Free Markets, and the Sinking of the World Economy.* London: Allen Lane.

The Economist. (2012). *The Rise of the State Capitalism,* January 21, 2012.

Wade, R. H. (2014). *The Paradox of US Industrial Policy: The Developmental State in Disguise.* In J. M. Salazar-Xirinachs, I. Nübler, & R. Kozul-Wright (Eds.), *Transforming Economies: Making Industrial Policy Work for Growth, Jobs and Development.* International Labour Office: Geneva.

Wallison, P. J., & Calomiris, C. W. (2009). The Last Trillion-Dollar Commitment: The Destruction of Fannie Mae and Freddie Mac. *Journal of Structured Finance, 15*(Spring), 71–80.

Webel, B. (2013). *Troubled Asset Relief Program (TARP): Implementation and Status.* Congressional Research Service, 27 June.

Webel, B., & Canis, B. (2012). *TARP Assistance for Chrysler: Restructuring and Repayment Issues.* Congressional Research Service Report for Congress, September 7.

Weiss, L. (2008). *Crossing the Divide: From the Military-industrial to the Development-procurement Complex.* Presented at the Berkeley Workshop on the 'Hidden US Developmental State', 20–21 June 2008, San Francisco.

Weiss, L. (2014). *America Inc.? Innovation and Enterprise in the National Security State.* New York: Cornell University Press.

CHAPTER 7

The Great Recession and Recovery Under the Obama Administration

In January 2009, at the outset of the Obama administration, the government's main aim was to bring about recovery to the American economy from the threat of a truly catastrophic economic recession.

During the 2000s, something in the American international economic and political leadership had progressively changed. The established industrial strategy based on the US ability to *capitalize their economic power—* namely to exert a global influence able to open foreign markets and, at the same time, to protect and promote American industrial interests—seemed to be questioned. Among the structural causes of the American "stagger", as we discussed in the previous chapter, there was the economic boom of China in 1990s and 2000s, which had brought the "US-guided" WTO system to struggle in the attempt to impose its regulatory framework on the emerging powers. Furthermore, the election of Bush Junior had opened a season of deregulation and spending cuts for new civilian technologies. From Clinton's *New Economy*, aimed to foster ICT and environmental friendly technologies, in 2000s the United States went back to the *old economy* (Bianchi and Labory 2011), mainly based on an economic growth driven by the military public demand and by a growing public debt (justified with the 11 September 2001 attack). As a result, the 2000s had seen an economic growth "drugged" by a high public demand (especially from the DOD) and *financialization*, which were followed by a massive trade deficit, and finally by the Great Recession in 2008 (Kiely 2015; Bianchi and Labory 2011).

© The Author(s) 2019   149
M. Tassinari, *Capitalising Economic Power in the US*,
International Political Economy Series,
https://doi.org/10.1007/978-3-319-76648-5_7

The interventions of the Obama administration to recover the US economy must be conceived as an answer to this complex context. This chapter describes the main actions of the administration as an attempt, in the short term, to address the problems raised by the crisis, but also as an effort to address the more structural problems that were distressing the US global leadership. In the next chapter, we will discuss how the changes that have taken place in the international arena in the post-crisis period could affect the ability of the United States to restore an effective American neoliberal strategy.

OBAMA'S INTERVENTIONISM IN RESPONSE TO THE CRISIS

The crisis, which started in the mortgage market in 2007 and spread to the entire financial sector, has quickly flooded the real economy leading the United States, in 2009 to a fall of 3.1% of the real GDP and to an unemployment rate of 9.3% (data from the ERP 2013).

Obama's political campaign of 2008 was intensely conducted by politically managing the many uncertainties that the crisis was raising concerning the future of the American economy. When faced by a dramatic circumstance, as the crisis was, the interventionist hand of the American government (often *hidden* by a neoliberal rhetoric) has always surfaced; in the specific case of the Obama administration this was mastered brilliantly. Massive programmes of public intervention to recover the economy started to have extensive visibility on blogs, websites and public speeches. With excellent oratory skills, President Obama won the elections, thanks to a rhetoric that claimed to radically break with the past and totally take the distance from the Bush administration. Ironically, it can be argued that Obama was able to win the elections, thanks to the word *change*, which, during his campaign, had resounded as an icon thousands of times in his public speeches. Perhaps not coincidentally, the Democratic Party's campaign approach found many Americans ready to welcome it. Faced by the increasing unemployment, inequalities and more than a pessimistic vision of the future of the American society, there were little doubts that the civil society would be looking for a *change*.[1]

In February 2009, at the very beginning of his mandate, Obama signed his first and massive action to recover the US economy, reduce unemployment and promote the American industry. A "stimulus package" of 787 billion dollars was implemented through the ARRA of 2009, as "the largest countercyclical fiscal action in American history" (ERP 2010: 52). The actions promoted by Obama through the ARRA were characterized, on the one hand, by short-term interventions to address emergency situations and, on the other hand, by measures driven by a more long-term vision concerning the structural adjustment of the US economy, towards sectors considered in some way *strategic*[2] (ERP 2010). Concerning the latter kind of interventions, the ERP of 2010, for example, stated:

> (...) the Administration has also focused special attention on certain areas where particular national needs are urgent. These include investments in building a "smart grid" to enhance the reliability, flexibility, and efficiency of the electricity transmission grid; research on renewable energy technologies like wind, solar, and bio fuels; and support for research into advanced vehicle technologies. These investments are motivated not only by the perception that technological breakthroughs are possible and would be highly valuable, but also by the enormous potential benefits that such breakthroughs could have in terms of enhancing national security, mitigating pollution, and stemming climate change. These are also investments that have a direct impact on creating high-paying, durable jobs - something that is particularly valuable at a time of high unemployment. (ERP 2010: 272)

The more active and strategic presence of the government in the economy was therefore, at least at a rhetorical level, the initial distinguishing element of the Obama administration and, indeed, the idea of a public action guided by a long-run vision seemed to remain stable also in the post-crisis speeches. In July 2013, for example, the President asserted:

> What we need is not a three-month plan, or even a three-year plan; we need a long-term American strategy, based on steady, persistent effort, to reverse the forces that have conspired against the middle class for decades. That has to be our project. (Obama 2013)

Concerning the ARRA, initially the plan allocated approximately $90 billion for short-term "emergencies", by financing health insurances, unemployment-support initiatives and basic assistance programmes, including, for example, the Supplemental Nutritional Assistance Program. Furthermore, about a third of the budget of the Act was made available also in the form of tax cuts to households and businesses. The Making Work Pay programme of 2009 and 2010, for example, reduced taxes for an "average" family by about $800 per year. About $14 billion were also allocated to support elderly, veterans and people with disabilities. Another important part of these funds—about $140 billion—was made available in the form of tax relief for several states, in order to avoid an excessive decrease in their level of public expenditure or an increase in the states' tax burden (ERP 2010).

Finally, approximately one-third of the total resources available through the ARRA were earmarked for financing particular segments of the economy by promoting a long-term development of sectors and industries considered to be "strategic" for the country. On one side, the Act included funding for traditional government investment projects, such as infrastructures. Indeed, as highlighted by the Keynesian theory, transport infrastructures have always played a key role for the recovery in times of crisis, and the Obama administration exploited the need to modernize the Interstate Highway System and the railways in order to reduce unemployment and increase the level of investment. However, the government promoted also *innovative* infrastructures that have today an enormous impact on the productivity and efficiency of the economy, such as the broadband access for the movement of digital information. In this latter area in particular, the ARRA allocated approximately 7 billion dollars. On the other side, the ARRA funded initial investments to jump-start private investment in emerging new areas, such as health information technology, a smart electrical grid, clean energy technologies, nanotechnologies and robotics (ERP 2010).

Generally, the recovery from the crisis in the United States was characterized by a massive influence of the government in selected areas of the economy, both within the ARRA initial plan and through other subsequent actions implemented during the two presidential mandates. In this context, the manufacturing industry was one of the main targets of the administration, in order to keep up with the general "rejuvenation of industrial policy" that was characterizing all the major global economies (Stiglitz and Lin 2013; Wade 2012). For example, in 2010 the German federal government began to encourage a technological revolution by releasing the "German high-tech Innovation Strategy 2020" and by putting forward the implementation of the "Industrie 4.0". Likewise, on 19 May 2015, China's State Council issued the "Made in China 2025" strategic plan, emphasizing the challenge that China's manufacturing industry was facing from developed and some developing countries.[3]

In the United States, after the ARRA, in December 2009, the Obama administration released "A framework for revitalizing American manufacturing",[4] in August 2010 enacted the United States Manufacturing Enhancement Act, in June 2011 launched the Advanced Manufacturing

Partnership (AMP) plan,[5] investing and implementing tax cuts as a reindustrialization strategy. The hope was to make America a "magnet" for manufacturing companies.[6]

In this scenario, the administration highlighted the central role that back-shoring policies had to play in encouraging the return of high-value-added companies to the United States. In this area, for example, in 2011 the government launched the SelectUSA initiative, which aimed at encouraging FDI in the United States (ERP 2014). In this programme global teams were formed, led by American ambassadors in 32 key countries, to encourage foreign investment, thereby establishing a "coordinated process" for networking potential investors with senior American officials. The initiative offered a number of tools, including a list of various federal and state programmes available to foreign investors, in order to facilitate investment in the United States (Jackson 2013).

Although this new "interventionist" approach was at its peak at the onset of the Obama administration and progressively reduced its intensity in the following years due to a decline of consent for the Obama's strategy, there are no doubts that the crisis damped down the neoliberal aura of the US government, calling for an active role of the administration in the relaunch of the American industrial leadership at international level. As a part of the US response to the global changes that are still threatening the American supremacy (see the Chap. 8), there was the effort to establish strategic trade alliances in different world regions. In this context, several initiatives were undertaken by the Obama administration with the aim of promoting trade and investment with Europe and Asia. As an attempt of the US government to regain its influence on international trade rules, one of the main elements was to move the focus from the WTO system towards big regional agreements. Specifically, the administration started the negotiations within two regional initiatives, the Trans-Pacific Partnership Agreement (TPP), which included several countries in Asia, and the Transatlantic Trade and Investment Partnership (TTIP), with the European Union. In this context, although there was a change in the modalities of intervention, the American industrial strategy seemed to maintain its attitude to "capitalize the US economic power", by influencing the international order to favour the American industrial interests.

The next pages recall in more details the main actions of the Obama administration towards several areas of economic and industrial interest.

THE FINANCIAL SECTOR AS EPICENTRE OF THE CRISIS

The financial sector was the driving force of the 2008 economic crisis.

Since the 1980s, the lack of a comprehensive and robust regulation of the international financial system has progressively produced a massive growth in the volume and complexity of the financial products, leading to the *financialization* of the global economy. As carefully analysed (see, e.g. Stockhammer 2004; Fine 2010, 2013; Onaran et al. 2011), at a general level this conformation of the financial system explains the surprising speed through which the crisis was able to spread from the US mortgage market to the global real economy (or at least to a considerable part of it).[7]

In this context, the extremely high lobbing capacities of the financial sector, along with concerns about the consequences of a definitive collapse of the financial system, triggered an immediate response of the US government to "bail-out" those who had ingeniously created a hole in their own boat. Immediately after the bankruptcy of Lehman Brothers, in September 2008, the American government was ready to intervene to prevent the collapse of the entire banking system, through the bailout of numerous banks (ERP 2010). The first actions in this direction were conducted by the Bush administration through the TARP, within the Emergency Economic Stabilization Act of 2008. The government gave the United States Treasury the authority to purchase $700 billion worth of mortgage-backed securities. In March 2011, more than 900 banks received TARP funds (Di Tommaso and Schweitzer 2013).[8] Subsequent interventions were promoted by the Obama administration. The Financial Stability Plan, which was approved by the Congress in February 2009, allocated $2 trillion to buy mortgages from the banks in order to supplement liquidity in the banking system. These measures, however, had a limited effect. Banks did not grant new loans, mainly because of pessimistic expectations towards the economy; thus this cash infusion to the banks did not have the hoped-for effect on the economic growth (Di Tommaso and Schweitzer 2013).

Beyond the direct financial support to the sector, the administration also pursued the goal of providing more general regulatory reforms of the financial system, in order to promote the future stability of the sector. In particular, the objective was, on the one hand, to promote greater responsibility of the banks to avoid new bailouts and, on the other hand, to increase the transparency of the financial transactions. The main law was the Dodd-Frank Wall Street Reform and Consumer Protection Act of

2010, which established the Financial Stability Oversight Council, a centre responsible for monitoring the stability of the entire financial system. The law also imposed rules to protect the security and transparency of financial products, to increase the protection of investors, and to strengthen the power of the supervisory authority in the investigation of financial frauds. However, even though these measures introduced more constraints in the system, they have not been able to impose the more radical reform that was expected (as evidenced by the protest movements against the hegemonic power of international finance, like the Occupy Wall Street movement).

NEW OLD BAILOUTS: THE CASE OF CHRYSLER AND GM

As we have seen in the previous chapters, American auto industry has always had a powerful influence in recalling the attention of the government, and not only in crisis times. This was true at the beginning of the twentieth century, when the *infant* auto industry needed to be protected and subsidized by the government, during the two World Wars, and the sector grew, thanks to the military public demand. The same in the 1970s and 1980s, when the Carter and Reagan administrations decided for the bailout of Chrysler to avoid its bankruptcy (see Chaps. 2 and 3).

On the wave of this trend, at the beginning of the financial crisis in 2008, the sector was one of the main subjects of the government "thoughtfulness". Chrysler and General Motors (GM) in particular, two of the three largest American automakers, were clearly risking bankruptcy. Due to the high number of people employed, the huge weight of the industry in the American economy and, in general, the substantial amount of stakeholders involved in the sector, the two companies were considered—according to the recurrent term used in these cases—*too big to fail*.

The government intervention in this industry started with the Bush administration, which decided to directly act in order to save the two companies. According to the data from the Congressional Research Service (2009), the American automotive industry as a whole employed, in 2008, about 500,000 workers. The bailout, regulated by the Loan and Security Agreement, happened in different ways for the two companies.

In the case of GM, the US government became the largest owner of the company, by acquiring most of its assets. The funds for the operation were initially provided by the Bush administration as part of the TARP, established by the Emergency Economic Stabilization Act of 2008. The TARP allocated to the automotive industry a total of 17.4 billion dollars for the two companies (13.4 billion for GM and 4 billion for Chrysler). In addition to the financial assistance, the Obama administration's approach to the bailout of GM was to promote the change of the management that had led to the bankruptcy. In this area, the actions included: the replacement of the CEO of the company, the renewal of the Board of Directors, the elimination of certain production lines and the reduction of the number of auto dealers. Thus, it can be argued that the rationale that generally led the government intervention in this area was not merely to provide financial assistance to a company whose management had shown contestable capacities; on the contrary, it was an attempt to promote a more radical structural adjustment of the company, with the effect of consolidating the industry in the long run.

Also in the case of Chrysler, the government played a key role in the bailout and in the organizational renewal of the company. In this context, however, the modalities of intervention were different than those used for GM. The government, in fact, did not acquire the ownership of the company, but it directly participated in the negotiations that allowed FIAT to acquire Chrysler.

However, looking at the long and troubled history of the auto industry in America, a couple of questions may spontaneously arise: why did the Obama administration once again bail out this sector? Why so much concern for carefully monitoring and controlling the bailout processes?

Naturally, the political power of the stakeholders involved in this industry could be enough to answer the first question. At any rate, it is important to say that in the case of the US auto industry, *mere* lobbing pressures have been able to stabilize for more or less a century a special "partnership" between government and private manufacturers. Thus, some more considerations deserve to be developed. Indeed, the long-run effectiveness of the automakers in "speaking" with the government can be reasonably explained by the complex structure that constitutes the auto industry. The level of *interdependence* between the sector and the other economic activities is extremely high. In these cases, as pointed out by Hirschman (1958), a sector that bears high upstream connections, which buys inputs from many other sectors, assumes a *strategic* significance for its capacity of increasing overall economic production by stimulating demand for the related sectors.[9] In our case, the high level of interconnections of the auto industry in the US economy implies an extremely high negative impact, in case of bankruptcy, for all subcontractors. More generally, the *weight* (or the *strategic* significance) of the auto industry has always discouraged structural adjustments of the US economy towards more "competitive" sectors, due to the economic and social costs that such adjustments would require (in terms of, e.g. unemployment and retraining of workers for a possible transition to other sectors) (see, e.g. Chang 2003; Whitford 2005; Di Tommaso and Schweitzer 2013). Thus, the automotive industry has de facto found itself to play a key role in the economic and political history of the United States.

Some might, however, argue that this is a story that belongs to the past. Indeed, if the relevance of the auto industry depends essentially on its vertical integration in the US economy, it could be argued that today—where interconnections between sectors are developed within *global value chains*—there is no industry vertically integrated in a *national* economy. Therefore, the prevailing idea of global markets' liberalization, emerged during the last decades, has largely emphasized the promotion of the domestic firms' ability to enter the global networks of suppliers and customers, at the expense of the *overall* development of a national industrial system.[10]

However, one of the effects of the crisis has been to challenge, to a certain degree, the idea of a development based on global value chains, recognizing the peculiar role that manufacturing industries play in the economic growth dynamics, in terms of high labour productivity (and high-wage jobs), economies of scale, technological change and innovation, and positive externalities (Tregenna 2009, 2014; Chang et al. 2013; Andreoni and Scazzieri 2014; Di Tommaso et al. 2017). From this point of view, it is not surprising that Obama, in his State of the Union speech, in January 2014, stated: "the best measure of opportunity is access to a good job. With the economy picking up speed, companies say they intend to hire more people this year. And over half of big manufacturers say they're thinking of in-sourcing jobs from abroad. So let's make that decision easier for more companies" (Obama 2014).

Thus, to answer our second question, in times in which the necessity to reconstruct the manufacturing base of an economy was at its peak, it seems reasonable to assert that the *economic power* of the US economy was in urgent need for maintaining so "heavy" an industry, such as the automotive, on American *soil*. In this context, Obama's concern for carefully monitoring and controlling the bailout processes appears to have been an effective way of "fertilising" the US field, by preparing the legal and economic conditions for ensuring the Americans their "jewel".

HEALTHCARE REFORM

At the onset of the Obama administration, the launch of the so-called healthcare reform had a great echo in the public opinion, giving the President an enormous visibility at a national and international level. The reason for this is to be found in the social and economic impact that the reform was expected to produce.

Indeed, a healthcare reform was long overdue in the United States, and several attempts had already been made in the past by other American presidents. Obama had to invest a great part of his initial presidential "political capital", given the opposition that the new law found in the Congress. In fact, the health system involved—beyond the final users—a number of significant stakeholders, such as pharmaceutical industry, insurance companies, employers and so on, not all ready to change the status quo. Thus, considering the political context that characterized this area, the Obama administration got a significant success when finally a law was signed.

The healthcare reform was founded on two legislative actions: the Patient Protection and the Affordable Care Act (PPACA) (more generally known as the Affordable Care Act—ACA) and the Health Care and Education Reconciliation Act, both approved in Congress in 2010. These interventions aimed at extending health insurance coverage by basically making it mandatory for most employers and individuals. The health reform was expected to improve social equity, thanks to the universality of health care coverage, and to have also a broad economic impact. First, the reform was expected to trigger an increase in the demand for health insurance, which would stimulate the insurance sector itself, and also those industries that are part of the health care system, such as pharmaceutical, biomedical, biotechnology, medical devices and health services in general. A second goal of the reform was to reduce the health care costs, and to produce a "bend" of the cost curve, substantially higher in the United States than in other countries. One of the hoped-for results of this manoeuvre was a reduction in the insurance policies costs, thanks to a greater sharing of risk, which could produce an overall decrease in employment costs, normally a substantial part of medical insurance costs. The health reform was also aimed at increasing the health provider efficiency by creating innovative forms of care delivery and providing payers and patients with more and better information about providers and treatments. Furthermore, the new law was also hoped to ensure greater speed and security in data acquisition in the industry, to improve health care quality (Di Tommaso and Schweitzer 2013).

ICT AND BROADBAND

Since the Clinton administration, ICT industries had started to occupy a central position in the US economy, deserving special attention from the government. The rapid development of ICTs, in the 1990s, had prompted the administration to reform the industry through the Telecommunications Act of 1996, which essentially fostered the transition from a monopolistic market (characterized by the presence of AT&T) to a competitive one, enabling new operators to enter the industry and also implementing direct measures for technology development (ERP 2000). The objective was essentially to develop the competitive potential of companies, in an industry that was growing fast at national and international level (ERP 2000). Led by a similar rationale, during the 2000s, the Bush administration had reformed the industry, further increasing its degree of liberalization.

With the outbreak of the crisis, the sector returned to be a target of the government's policies. In this regard, the main action implemented by the Obama administration was the National Broadband Plan of 2010 (Federal Communications Commission 2010). In the context of the strategic response to the crisis, the intervention on ICT was aimed at expanding the coverage and quality of Internet connections through a strong public investment in broadband. There was no doubt that this investment had the goal of improving an infrastructure of crucial importance for the overall growth and competitiveness of the American economy:

> Expanding broadband across the nation will build a foundation of sustained economic growth and the widely shared prosperity we all seek. [...] My Administration will build upon our efforts over the past year to make America's nationwide broadband infrastructure the world's most powerful platform for economic growth and prosperity, including improving access to mobile broadband, maximizing technology innovation, and supporting a nationwide, interoperable public safety wireless broadband network.[11]

In this perspective, ARRA allocated a total of $7.2 billion through two new programmes: the Broadband Technology Opportunities Program (BTOP),[12] managed by the US Department of Commerce, and Broadband Initiatives Program (BIP),[13] managed by the US Department of Agriculture (Fig. 7.1).

After the ARRA's investments in the framework of the National Broadband Plan, in the subsequent years, the administration also launched the ConnectEd programme, to further promote a greater spread of high-

Agency	Program	Description	Annual funding amount
Federal Communications Commission	Universal Service Fund	Provides funding for companies serving high-cost areas, low-income consumers, rural health care providers, and schools and libraries.	$8.7 billion (FY2010)
National Telecommunications and Information Administration	Broadband Technology Opportunities Program	Grant program to promote deployment and adoption of broadband throughout the country, particularly in unserved and underserved areas. Priority in the second Notice of Funding Availability (NOFA) will be given to middle-mile broadband infrastructure projects that offer new or substantially upgraded connections to community anchor institutions, especially community colleges.	$4.7 billion (one-time ARRA)—includes at least $2.5 billion for infrastructure, $250 million for adoption, and $200 million for public computing centers.
Rural Utilities Service	Broadband Initiatives Program	Loan, loan guarantee and grant program to increase broadband penetration and adoption, primarily in rural areas. Priority in the second NOFA will be given to last-mile projects, and middle-mile projects involving current RUS program participants.	$2.5 billion (one-time ARRA)—includes at least $2.2 billion for infrastructure.
Rural Utilities Service	Telephone Loans and Loan Guarantees Program	Provides long-term, direct and guaranteed loans to qualified organizations, often telephone companies, to support investment in broadband-capable telephone networks.	$685 million
Rural Utilities Service	Rural Broadband Access Loans and Loan Guarantees Program	Provides loans and loan guarantees to eligible applicants—including telephone companies, municipalities, non-profits and Tribes—to deploy broadband in rural communities.	$298 million
Institute of Museum and Library Services	Library Services and Technology Act Grants	Provides funds for a wide range of library services including installation of fiber and wireless networks.	$164 million
Multiple agencies	Other programs[18]	Multiple purposes	$49 million
Total			$17.1 billion

Fig. 7.1 Existing sources of federal support for communications connectivity (Source: Federal Communications Commission 2010: 139)

speed Internet connections (ERP 2014). For this last initiative, another $2 billion were allocated over two years by the FCC, and additional investments by private partners.

The Obama administration's interventions in the field of ICTs acted in particular on digital divide, to reduce the disparities in the possibility of internet access (ERP 2016: 241). These interventions targeted a specific sector but, at the same time, had a cross-cutting impact on the American economy and society as a whole. The universal spread of high-speed connections was sought as having important effects on the development of business competitiveness, with a positive impact on productivity, innovation, organizational models, access to information and markets (ERP 2016: 239). At the same time, government investment in ICT was proposed as improving the opportunities for job creation and for citizen education, reducing social inequalities and favouring fuller participation in civil and political life (ERP 2016).

ENERGY SECTOR AND "GREEN INDUSTRIES"

In recent decades, the energy and ecological problems have gradually assumed a central position both in the public opinion and in the political debate, in many industrialized and emerging economies. As well known, the main concerns are related to the scarcity and increasing costs of non-renewable energy sources (fossil fuels in particular) and the environmental impact caused by their use (first of all *global warming*). At an international level, several initiatives have been undertaken as an attempt to mitigate these problems. A first response was the creation, within the United Nations (UN), of the International Panel on Climate Change (IPCC), which built the base for the adoption of a protocol for greenhouse gas emission reduction (initially signed in Rio de Janeiro in 1992, and then amended and approved in Kyoto in 1997). To this, a series of UN conferences to discuss the problem of climate change and to negotiate the terms of international agreements on the environment followed (among the others, in Bali in 2007, in Copenhagen in 2009 and several others, up to the most recent ones in Lima, in December 2014 and in Paris, in November and December 2015).[14]

Generally, despite the number of conferences and initiatives undertaken, the concrete results in terms of environmental sustainability of the economic development have been rather poor. The differences in political and economic "constraints" among the countries potentially involved in the agreements have usually hindered the adoption of spread and effective measures to contrast environmental degradation. In the specific case of the United States, for example, while Vice-President Al Gore was signing the Kyoto Protocol in 1997, it was clear that the driving force within the US Congress would have never allowed its ratification.

Ambitiously, Obama's first political campaign announced the administration's commitment to reduce carbon emissions by 80% below the 1990s levels by 2050; to reach the 25% share of electricity from renewable sources by 2025; to reach quota 30% of the electricity used by the federal government from renewable sources by 2020; and to make all new buildings "carbon neutral" (with zero emissions) by 2030.

Energy sector and *green* industries had a central position in the policy for science and technology in the Obama administration. Approximately $90 billion ($60 billion in direct incentives to industries and $30 billion as tax credits) were invested by the administration through the ARRA, involving numerous industries. For example, with regard to renewable energies (solar, wind and geothermal) the investment amounted to \$23 billion. In the transport sector, including plug-in hybrid vehicles, electric vehicles and the infrastructure necessary for their operation, the administration invested \$16 billion. In particular, the government invested \$2.4 billion to build the plants producing batteries and components for electric vehicles. Another 300 million dollars were invested through the General Services Administration for purchasing energy-efficient vehicles produced in America (Di Tommaso and Schweitzer 2013). Furthermore, \$400 million were spent for the establishment of the ARPA-E, an agency in charge of carrying out scientific research in the field of advanced energy technologies (ERP 2010).

In order to reduce the national consumption of electrical energy, the government promoted the construction of a modern *smart grid*. The investment in this area has been \$4 billion. The ARRA provided also a tax credit from \$500 to \$1500 in 2010 for the renovation of private homes in line with energy efficiency standards (Di Tommaso and Schweitzer 2013).

Furthermore, the administration launched the "Cap and Trade programme", included in the American Clean Energy and Security Act of 2009 (ERP 2010). The cap and trade system would have set an overall limit on emissions of gases responsible for the greenhouse effect, and divided that amount in "allowances" (corresponding to the right for a company to emit one ton of pollutant gases in the atmosphere). These allowances would have then been allocated to companies through an auction and the companies would have been free to market them to each other. The total amount fixed on gas emissions would have been limited by the number of allowances available and, according to supply and demand, it would have determined the price, hence creating a market for the allowances. In this manner, the system would have ensured that a certain level of pollution would have not been exceeded and the companies involved would have been encouraged to adopt the most effective technologies to reduce carbon emissions, by boosting incentives to innovate in this area (ERP 2010: 248–249). However, after the loss of the majority in the House, following the 2010 mid-term elections, the programme was never approved by the Congress.

Naturally, energy sector and green industry have not been targeted merely for their capacity to respond to environmental problems and to a demand of quality of life. The race to develop a competitive advantage through innovation in a capitalist global economy is always ongoing in many sectors, and the first to arrive is probably the one who gets the future economic leadership. International competition, especially against China, is aggressive in these promising industries and it is easy to suppose that the Obama administration wanted to win the gold medal.[15]

However, the relevance of these sectors goes even beyond a "single competition". More generally, the energy sector involves crucial economic and geopolitical dimensions, such as the reduction in the dependence on foreign oil and in energy costs, improvement of industrial efficiency and international competitiveness, creation of quality jobs and so on (ERP 2010). These rationales explain how strategic these industries are for the overall ability of the United States to maintain their economic supremacy in the future, and the massive efforts to promote them are also to be read in the light of a wider industrial strategy aimed at maximizing and capitalizing the US economic power.

POLICIES FOR SCIENCE AND TECHNOLOGY

Naturally, in a context characterized by a "rejuvenation of industrial policy" (Stiglitz and Lin 2013), both at a national and international level, the advancement of science and technology played a central role. Initially, the ARRA of 2009 allocated to this field—including support for education and basic research—a total of about $100 billion (ERP 2010). These investments resulted in an increase in the budget of the main research government agencies, such as the NIH, the NSF, the Office of Science of the Department of Energy, the NIST of the Department of Commerce and the DOD (EPR 2010). In this context, the federal budget of 2011, for example, provided $1.8 billion for the National Nanotechnology Initiative for the advancement of science and technology in the field of nanotechnology.

Similarly, the America Invents Act of 2011 was important in order to promote basic research with public funding, to support the creation and commercialization of innovative products through the support of start-ups, and to provide greater protection of intellectual property rights (ERP 2012).

Other relevant interventions focused on education and on the development of workforce skills. The American Graduation Initiative was launched in 2009 to support educational programmes at the local level, in particular by promoting education in those fields where skills are lacking in comparison with the demand coming from the labour market. In 2010, the government also created the Early Learning Challenge Fund, sponsored by the Department of Education, which encouraged the development of new educational models and programmes for teacher training. With the objective of improving university education, the Obama administration tripled the funds for the NSF's Graduate Research Fellowship and for scholarships aiming to support students during their doctoral studies. Other programmes also provided financial support to job training in health care. In 2009, for example, the government allocated $200 million through the Health Resources and Services Administration. The Administration was also committed to make the American Opportunity Tax Credit permanent, which provided tax support for education costs, and to fund the New College Access and Completion Fund 2009 (ERP 2010).

More recently, one of the major initiatives included in the budget for the fiscal year 2015 was the Opportunity, Growth and Security Initiative, which allocated $56 billion for additional investments in areas such as education, research, infrastructure and national security (ERP 2014). In particular, the funds destined to this initiative, were equally shared between the civilian and the military area, to finance, among others, primary education and early childhood education, work training, basic research in the health field, applied research in technologies for energy efficiency and renewable energy (including electric motors, batteries and ultra-light materials for electric vehicles), creation of a national network for innovation in the manufacturing sector (with the goal of launching 45 new centres in the country), modernization of the state electricity grids, modernization of the national aviation system and improvement in the efficiency and effectiveness of public administration. Generally, federal spending in R&D for 2015 grew by approximately 1.2% compared to the previous year. Overall, in 2015 the budget allocated about $135 billion for research, $2.2 billion for advanced manufacturing (12% more than in 2014), $325 million for the transition to clean-energy (as part of the $5.2 billion allocated for the Clean Energy Technology programme), $2.5 billion for the US Global Change Research Program in response to climate change, $30.2 billion for the NIH (of which a portion is earmarked for research against cancer and Alzheimer's disease, as part of the BRAIN Initiative) and $7.3 billion for the NSF.

In this context, naturally, the role of the DOD in the advancement of the US science and technology continued to be crucial, as it was during the previous Bush administration. Some important technology breakthroughs, related for example to robotics and nanotechnology, were developed, thanks to a prominent role of this Department (Weiss 2014). This could suggest a substantial continuity with the past, and Obama's approach could not be as "interventionist" or as "rejuvenating", as the rhetoric during the crisis would want us to believe. Even federal funding for R&D, compared to that provided by the Bush Junior administration, declined during the Obama presidency (ERP 2016: 224).

Nevertheless, an innovative element of the Obama intervention in science and technology might be found not as much in the *quantity* of spending as rather in its *quality*. Indeed, Obama's strategy was also aimed at directly targeting sectors that can be considered strategic, for economic reasons and for their ability to promote a more socially sustainable development, such as automotive, healthcare, energy and green industries, infrastructure, ICT and broadband (as we have discussed in the previous pages of this chapter). Taken together, these interventions show how the United States, during the Obama administration, was de facto oriented to spring forward in the global competition for technological leadership.

SMALL BUSINESS AND LOCAL DEVELOPMENT

In the United States, as already discussed in the previous chapters, a key role in promoting industrial development was also played by several agencies that operated at a local level through development centres located throughout the national territory. In this context, the most important agencies that operated in promoting small business and local development were the Small Business Administration (SBA), the Economic Development Administration (EDA), the Department of Agriculture (DoA) and the Department of Housing and Urban Development (HUD).

These agencies, to a certain degree, were able to mitigate the problems of *inconsistency* and the *network failures*[16] that could characterize politico-institutional systems with a strong separation of powers between executive, legislative and judiciary, and between federal, state and local levels, such as the American one (Wade 2014; Ketels 2007; Hall and Soskice 2001; Mann 1997).[17] Since the 1980s, some agencies started to implement specific programmes aimed at overcoming and favouring cooperation among a plurality of actors, such as companies, scientists, engineers, venture capitalists, local governments, state economic development agencies, private enterprise development centres, organizations that provided services for businesses, universities and so on. Programmes such as the Small Business Innovation Research (SBIR) and the Manufacturing Extension Partnerships (MEPs) started to foster cooperation and exchange of information among the agents of an increasing complex system of innovation and production (Wade 2012; Block 2008; Schrank and Whitford 2009).

During the Obama administration, albeit with some of the past major programmes still active, the role of agencies that operated in promoting small business and local development evolved according to the necessity of the economy and, especially, in order to respond to the crisis.

In the context of the crisis, for example, the SBA played a key role in supporting small businesses, by improving access to capital through guarantees on loans, credit and micro-credit granting.[18] In 2008, with a budget of about $570 million, the agency approved around 69,434 guarantees on loan (for a total of 12.7 billion dollars), 8883 loans (for a value of 5.3 billion US dollars) and micro-credit granting for a total of about 31 million dollars to more than 2650 entrepreneurs. In the following years, the ARRA allocated about $730 million to the SBA to help small businesses address the financial crisis. Funds were $255 million in loans and $375 million directly allocated to the SBA to facilitate access to the financial capital. The Export Working Capital Program (EWCP) and the Dealer Floor Plan (DFP) are examples of programmes implemented by the SBA in order to extend guarantees on loans for small businesses. Other initiatives undertaken by the SBA to support small business were the Export Market Entry Training Program (EMETP) and the Export Trade Assistance Program (ETAP), aimed at promoting American exports (Di Tommaso and Schweitzer 2013). In early 2011, the Congress expanded the Small Business Jobs Act, providing $2 billion of new tax incentives for the creation of new businesses and start-ups. Other initiatives to support small businesses were the State Small Business Credit Initiative and the creation of a Small Business Lending Fund, managed by the Treasury (ERP 2012). Finally, the Congress passed the Consolidated Appropriations Act, through which the budget for the Small Business Investment Company (SBIC) venture capital programme, aimed at promoting access to capital, was increased from $3 to $4 billion (Dilger 2014).

In the field of regional development, the EDA, an office of the Department of Commerce, had the main objective of promoting the development of regions or localities economically distressed, through structural adjustment programmes and trade-related assistance.[19] In 2010, the budget for the EDA allocated a $50 million fund—called Regional Planning and Matching Grants—to improve living conditions in economically backward areas. During the years of the financial crisis, support to local communities was also provided through the National Emergency Plan for Communities and Regions, a programme of the Department of Labour set up by the Obama administration in 2010 to subsidize job training for the long-term unemployed (Di Tommaso and Schweitzer 2013).

TRADE POLICY AND THE BIG REGIONAL AGREEMENTS

One of the main effects of the crisis at an international level has been to encourage a sort of global reorganization process that calls, to some extent, for a redefinition of the global trade equilibrium (see the next chapter). In order to address this emerging context, the United States reacted by continuing with specific trade actions to protect and promote the American economy.

For example, during the first term, the Obama administration took legal actions in the WTO to remove barriers towards American exports of automotive spare parts into the Chinese market. The final verdict forced China to change its trade policy by opening its market. The administration has also launched an appeal against the use of subsidies and tax forgiveness by China, to reduce the production costs of domestic companies. In 2009, another measure of the administration was to add Canada in the Priority Watch List of the Special 301 process (measures controlling the protection and enforcement of intellectual property rights) (ERP 2010). Furthermore, some new bilateral trade agreements were concluded with Korea in 2010 (the Korea-United States free trade agreement [FTA]) and with Colombia and Panama in 2011. Other agreements were negotiated with several countries, including Australia, Chile, Malaysia, New Zealand, Peru, Singapore and Vietnam (ERP 2012). In addition, other initiatives were conducted at an international level within the WTO system. These include the International Services Agreement, for the liberalization of the services market, the agreements related to exchange of technologies and information related to the environment and, in 2013, the negotiations for the Trade Facilitation Agreement (ERP 2014). This latter global agreement was aimed at speeding up the movement of goods and services by increasing the cooperation between customs and by standardizing the import-export procedures.

However, one of the most important efforts of the Obama administration to strategically influence the international trade arena was the attempt to establish big regional agreements. Specifically, the administration continued the negotiations within two regional trade initiatives, the TPP, which included several countries in Asia, and the TTIP, with the European Union.

The TPP included 12 countries (Australia, Brunei, Canada, Chile, Japan, Malaysia, Mexico, New Zealand, Peru, Singapore, Vietnam and the United States). After seven years of negotiations, an agreement was signed on 5 October 2015, and the ratification of national parliaments should have taken place in the next two years. This could have been particularly important in order to carry out trade relations with Asia within a single regulatory framework. Such relations were, in fact, characterized by a large number of individual Preferential Trade Agreements. The TTP could have facilitated the entry of the United States into Asian markets, while the other signatory countries hoped to gain a preferential access to the US market (Capling and Ravenhill 2011). The signatory countries of the TPP had already signed trade agreements with the United States and among themselves, whilst the TPP would have touched the deepest aspects of the national regulations and, therefore, it would have represented an important transfer of sovereignty (Fergusson et al. 2013; Williams 2013). However President Trump signed a Presidential memorandum to withdraw the United States from the TPP on 23 January 2017 and the direct involvement of the United States in the initiative has vanished.

The TTIP concerned the reduction of tariff and non-tariff trade barriers, access to public procurement, regulation of FDI and the definition of technical standards shared in some industries (EC 2013). The debate on the impact of this partnership involved a wide range of areas, such as the consequences, in terms of GDP growth and employment, in the two areas, the relationship between corporations and national governments, the impact on the sustainability of environmental systems, up to considerations related to possible influences on inequality, social stability and global competitive dynamics (Raza et al. 2014). Many studies were carried out that tried to analyse the different bargaining power between the two parties, the impact that the agreement could have had on the world trade, on the power of the WTO and on the countries outside the agreement (Rubini et al. 2015; Venhaus 2015; Fontagné et al. 2013; Felbermayr and Larch 2013; ECORYS 2009; Beghin et al. 2014; EC 2013; Manrique Gil et al. 2015). Indeed, it was very difficult to predict the future impact of the agreement, as its contents were still evolving and kept secret. The idea of a transatlantic trade partnership dated back to the late 1990s. However, the crisis intensified the negotiations, since it showed the creation of a large transatlantic free trade area as an opportunity to support growth and jobs in the two areas, as well as a possible solution to counter the rise of China and other emerging countries (Felbermayr and Larch 2013; Eliasson 2015). The EU-US Summit, in November 2011, was concluded with the establishment of a joint working group (the High-Level Working Group) aimed at identifying measures to increase transatlantic trade and investment flows.

In July 2013, the negotiations started (Akhtar and Jones 2013). Initially the agreement should have been sealed by 2014. However, the complexity and the numerous different aspects touched by TTIP protracted the signing of the agreement (Venhaus 2015; Felbermayr and Larch 2013). Both parties, during the tenth round of negotiations, held in Brussels in mid-July 2015, said that they would give a strong acceleration in the negotiations in order to conclude the agreement by the end of the mandate of President Obama. However, when Donald Trump won the elections the TTIP had not yet come to a conclusion. The new President had stated since the electoral campaign that he would not support this trade initiative, and even the TTIP was lost. Europe and the United States had already put in place a number of bilateral agreements with many countries; the signing of TTIP, however, would have created the largest free trade area in the world. In the face of 11.4% of the world population, this area would have represented almost 50% of the global economic output, 30% of the world trade volume, as well as 57.4% of incoming flow of FDI and 75.6% of output flow (Rubini et al. 2015). Indeed, these agreements should not have been confused with mere FTAs. As it will be discussed in the next chapter, the strategic decisions of the United States concerning their role in the international trade arena have a crucial impact on the rules of the global economic order and on the future distribution of economic power among the world economies.

Conclusion

This chapter has described the main actions of the Obama administration to address the problems raised, in the short term, by the crisis, as well as the efforts to restore an effective American industrial strategy by addressing the more structural problems that were questioning the US global leadership. Generally, the analysis has shown how the recovery from the crisis has been characterized by a more "interventionist" approach, based on the definition of clear priorities, the selection of industrial targets able to address them and a *vision* concerning the future of the American industrial system.

Indeed, the international crisis, since its very beginning in 2008, immediately called for what was defined as a "rejuvenation of industrial policy". In this context, the US government—bypassing the neoliberal rhetoric that had characterized the previous decades—implemented the ARRA. Not only was this massive government intervention—a stimulus package worth a total of $787 billion—oriented to address short-run social and economic emergencies, but it was also meant to foster a more radical development of the American productive structure in a long-term perspective. About a third of the total resources available through the ARRA were earmarked for financing particular segments of the economy—primarily the financial sector, but including also industries, such as automotive, healthcare, energy and green industries, infrastructures, ICT and broadband. Other actions were also directed to education, science and technology and regional and small businesses development. After these interventions, the US economy started to regrow and the rate of unemployment started to decrease.

A *change*, compared to the previous Bush administration—as Obama's first campaign stressed he would implement—perhaps occurred for the American society. Whilst the DOD has continued to play a crucial role for American growth and competitiveness, the Obama's strategy also aimed at directly targeting additional sectors that could be considered *strategic*, for economic reasons and for their ability to promote a more socially sustainable development.

Furthermore, two important initiatives—the TPP and the TTIP—were undertaken by the Obama administration, with the aim of promoting trade and investment with Europe and Asia. These could be considered as an attempt of the administration to regain influence on international trade rules by moving the focus from the WTO system towards big regional agreements. However, the new Trump administration has opted for the withdrawal of the United States from the initiatives.

Generally, the intervention of the Obama administration in economic dynamics, albeit some differences in tools and modalities of action, compared with the past, seems to preserve the US inclination to adopt an industrial strategy based on the power of maintaining technology leadership and control of the global trade system. Yet, a question remains, which is going to open the next chapter: how will this industrial strategy continue to be effective in the future? Indeed, after the emergency raised by the crisis, a declining consent for a strategic role of the government in economy (along with budgetary constraints[20]), could limit the public action at a domestic level, while important changes in the international arena in the recent post-crisis context are casting doubts about the future US global influence.

Notes

1. The Obama's commitment to distancing himself from his predecessor seemed initially to go well beyond the mere economic sphere. His approach to the foreign policy and international diplomacy, for example, gave Obama an enormous national and international visibility, crowned by the winning of the 2009 Nobel Peace Prize. Naturally, this created important dissents among the sceptical observers of the US management of the problems associated with the wars in Iraq and Afghanistan.

2. As reported by *The Economist*, according to President Obama the crisis required "strategic decisions about strategic industries" (The Economist 2010).

3. In this context, it appeared to be a growing interest for a *sectoral* approach to promote key segments of the economy. China, of course, confirmed a vertical approach to industrial development in the 12th Five-Year Plan (2011–2015). The "key industries" promoted were equipment manufacturing, shipbuilding, automobile, iron and steel, non-ferrous metal, building materials, petrochemical, light industry and textile (Di Tommaso et al. 2013; Barbieri et al. 2015). Also, the European Union moved some steps towards a selective approach. Under the general aims of bringing industry back to contribute to 20% of GDP, to promote growth and competitiveness and ensure the creation of jobs, a number of key documents were produced. The main policy document identifying the priorities for industrial policy in the European Union was the European Commission "Industrial Compact" (European Commission 2014). Together with the precedent communication on Industrial Policy (2012), it identified the actions for "transversal" strategic sectors: advanced manufacturing, KET, bio-products, clean vehicles and ships, sustainable constructions and raw materials, smart grids and digital infrastructures. However, as pointed out (Pianta 2014), despite the novelty of concentrating on fast growing, high-value-added sectors, no additional funds were offered to support such policies, which were mainly financed by existing tools, such as the Horizon 2020 R&D program, the Competitiveness of Enterprises and Small and Medium-sized Enterprises (COSME) and the Structural Funds (European Commission 2014). Parallel to the above-mentioned "Industrial Compact", there were a number of other policy initiatives that involved targeting specific industries. The European Commission issued the Investment Plan for Europe which, together with the European Fund for Strategic Investment, was mainly directed at supporting infrastructures with impact on industries such as energy and transports. It also issued the Plan for a Circular Economy, with specific actions for targeted sectors, where recycling/waste was particularly relevant. This latter plan had a

major focus on regulations and legislation, but it also provided financial tools. In its political guidelines then, President Junker referred to the need to ensure that EU would maintain its leadership in strategic sectors with high-value jobs: automotive, aeronautics, engineering, space, chemicals and pharmaceuticals. The DG Internal Market, responsible for implementing industrial policy, set specific action plans for strategic sectors including chemicals, automotive, tourism, textiles and clothing, fashion high-end and creative industries, raw materials, electrical engineering, food and drinks, healthcare, biotechnology, aeronautics, maritime industries.

4. See https://www.whitehouse.gov/sites/default/files/microsites/20091216-maunfacturing-framework.pdf (last accessed March 2016).

5. See https://www.whitehouse.gov/the-press-office/2011/06/24/president-obama-launches-advanced-manufacturing-partnership (last accessed March 2016).

6. See The White House, Office of the Press Secretary, 13 Feb. 2013 on https://www.whitehouse.gov/the-press-office/2013/02/13/fact-sheet-president-s-plan-make-america-magnet-jobs-investing-manufactu   (last accessed March 2016).

7. On the causes of the financial crisis see the Chap. 6. See also Stiglitz (2010), Saad Filho (2011), Blanchard et al. (2012), Allen and Moessner (2012), Akyüz (2014), Evans (2015), Kiely (2015).

8. For the list of banks that received government funds and the corresponding amount, see the US Treasury Department website: http://www.treasury.gov/initiatives/financial-stability/reports/Pages/TARP-Investment-Program-Transaction-Reports.aspx (last accessed October 2017).

9. See also Laumas (1975), Schultz (1977), Meller and Marfán (1981), Hewings (1982), Cella (1984), Oosterhaven (1988), Dietzenbacher and Van Der Linden (1997), Los (2001), Chang et al. (2013), Andreoni and Scazzieri (2014).

10. See Pack and Saggi (2006), Gereffi et al. (2005), Gibbon et al. (2008), Pietrobelli and Rabellotti (2011), Elms and Low (2013).

11. Statement from the President on the National Broadband Plan (16 March 2010), The White House Office of the Press Secretary, https://obamawhitehouse.archives.gov/the-press-office/statement-president-national-broadband-plan (last accessed October, 2017).

12. See https://www.ntia.doc.gov/category/broadband-technology-opportunities-program (last accessed October, 2017).

13. See https://www.sbc.senate.gov/public/_cache/files/f/0/f0fc95ef-18ef-4f1b-a1cc-0cab31394b1c/11824FA937892AEF65A916A2803681F3.bip-grant-guide.pdf (last accessed October, 2017).

14. See http://unfccc.int/2860.php.
15. In this context, for instance, the case of Solyndra, a US company producing solar panels, shows how hard the competition between China and the United States was. Solyndra was funded by the US government with a huge amount of money, but its inability to compete with Chinese competitors soon led to the failure of the company (see for more details Mazzucato 2013).
16. Whitford 2005; Whitford and Schrank 2011; Wade 2012.
17. See the discussion on these topics in the Chap. 3.
18. See http://sba.gov/index.html.
19. *Economic Development Administration*—http://www.eda.gov/.
20. Since the beginning of Obama administration's second term, considerable attention has been devoted to problems related to public debt (caused, e.g., by the fiscal cliff in early 2013) and to the establishment of measures aimed at its reduction over the long term. In this context, particular emphasis has been given to the promotion of practices for evaluating the impact of public programmes in order to increase efficiency and reduce administrative costs (ERP 2014). For further details see the next chapter.

REFERENCES

Akhtar, S. I. & Jones, V. C. (2013). *Proposed Transatlantic Trade and Investment Partnership (TTIP): In Brief.* Washington, DC: Congressional Research Service.

Akyüz, Y. (2014). *Crisis Mismanagement in the United States and Europe: Impact on Developing Countries and Longer-Term Consequences.* UN-DESA Working Paper No. 132.

Allen, W. A., & Moessner, R. (2012). *The International Propagation of the Financial Crisis of 2008 and a Comparison with 1931. Financial History Review, 19*, 123–147.

Andreoni, A., & Scazzieri, R. (2014). Triggers of Change: Structural Trajectories and Production Dynamics. *Cambridge Journal of Economics, 38*(6), 1391–1408.

Barbieri, E., Di Tommaso, M. R., & Tassinari, M. (2015). Politiche industriali selettive e settori strategici. Lo scenario e le scelte di Pechino. *l'Industria, 36*(3), 403–434.

Beghin, J. C., Bureau, J.-C., Gohin, A. e altri (2014). The Impact of an EU-US Transatlantic Trade and Investment Partnership Agreement on Biofuel and Feedstock Markets. Working Paper 552, Center for Agricultural and Rural Development, Iowa State University.

Bianchi, P., & Labory, S. (2011). *Industrial Policies after the Crisis. Seizing the Future.* Cheltenham: E. Elgar.

Blanchard, O., Romer, D., Spence, M., & Stiglitz, J. (Eds.). (2012). *In the Wake of the Crisis: Leading Economists Reassess Economic Policy*. Cambridge, MA: MIT Press.

Block, F. (2008). Swimming against the Current: The Rise of a Hidden Developmental State in the United States. *Politics & Society, 36*(2), 169–206.

Capling, A., & Ravenhill, J. (2011). *Multilateralising Regionalism: What Role for the Trans-Pacific Partnership Agreement? The Pacific Review, 24*(5), 553–575.

Cella, G. (1984). The Input-Output Measurement of Interindustry Linkages. *Oxford Bulletin of Economics and Statistics, 46*(1), 73–84.

Chang, H.-J. (2003). Trade and Industrial Policy Issues. In H.-J. Chang (Ed.), *Rethinking Development Economics*. London: Anthem Press.

Chang, H. J., Andreoni, A., & Kuan, M. L. (2013). *International Industrial Policy Experiences and the Lessons for the UK, Center for Business Research* (Working Paper N. 450). Cambridge: University of Cambridge.

Congressional Research Service. (2009). *US Motor Vehicle Industry: Federal Financial Assistance and Restructuring*, Report No. R40003, January, on: http://www.fas.org/sgp/crs/misc/R41154.pdf

Di Tommaso, M. R., & Schweitzer, S. O. (2013). *Industrial Policy in America. Breaking the Taboo*. Cheltenham/Northampton: Edward Elgar.

Di Tommaso, M. R., Rubini, L., & Barbieri, E. (2013). *Southern China: Industry, Development and Industrial Policy*. Milton Park Abingdon: Routledge.

Di Tommaso, M. R., Tassinari, M., Bonnini, S., & Marozzi, M. (2017). Industrial Policy and Manufacturing Targeting in the US: New Methodological Tools for Strategic Policy-Making. *International Review of Applied Economics, 31*(5), 681–703.

Dietzenbacher, E., & Van Der Linden, J. A. (1997). Sectoral and Spatial Linkages in the EC Production Structure. *Journal of Regional Science, 37*(2), 235–257.

Dilger, R. J. (2014). *Small Business: Access to Capital and Job Creation*. Washington, DC: Congressional Research Service.

EC (European Commission). (2013). Impact Assessment Report on the Future of EU-US Trade Relations. *Commission Staff Working Document, 12*(03), 2013.

ECORYS. (2009). *Non-tariff Measures in EU-US Trade and Investment: An Economic Analysis*. Final Report Prepared for the European Commission, Rotterdam.

Eliasson, L. J. (2015). *The Transatlantic Trade and Investment Partnership: Interest Groups and Public Opinion*. Presented at the 14th Biennial Meeting of the European Union Studies Association, Boston, 5–7 March.

Elms, D. K., & Low, P. (Ed.). (2013). *Global Value Chains in a Changing World*. Fung Global Institute (FGI), Nanyang Technological University (NTU), and World Trade Organization (WTO).

ERP. (2000). *Economic Report of the President*. Washington, DC: United States Government Printing Office.

ERP. (2010). *Economic Report of the President*. Washington, DC: United States Government Printing Office.

ERP. (2012). *Economic Report of the President.* Washington, DC: United States Government Printing Office.

ERP. (2013). *Economic Report of the President.* Washington, DC: United States Government Printing Office.

ERP. (2014). *Economic Report of the President.* Washington, DC: United States Government Printing Office.

ERP. (2016). *Economic Report of the President.* Washington, DC: United States Government Printing Office.

European Commission. (2014). For a European Industrial Renaissance. COM: 14/2.

Evans, T. (2015). The Crisis of Finance-Led Capitalism in the United States of America, Institute for International Political Economy Berlin, Working Paper 51.

Federal Communications Commission. (2010). *Connecting America: The National Broadband Plan.* Retrieved http://www.broadband.gov/downloadplan/.

Felbermayr, G. J. & Larch, M. (2013). The Transatlantic Trade and Investment Partnership (TTIP): Potentials, Problems and Perspectives. *CESifo Forum, 14,* 49. Institut für Wirtschaftsforschung (Ifo).

Fergusson, I. F., Cooper, W. H., Jurenas, R., & Williams, B. R. (2013). *The Trans-Pacific Partnership Negotiations and Issues for Congress.* Washington, DC: Congressional Research Service.

Fine, B. (2010). Locating Financialisation. *Historical Materialism, 18*(2), 97–116.

Fine, B. (2013). Financialization from a Marxist Perspective. *International Journal of Political Economy, 42*(4), 47–66.

Fontagné, L., Gourdon, J., Jean, S. et al. (2013). Transatlantic Trade: Whither Partnership, Which Economic Consequence. CEPII, Policy Brief, 1.

Gereffi, G., Humphrey, J., & Sturgeon, T. (2005). *The Governance of Global Value Chains.* Review of *International Political Economy, 12*(1), 78–104.

Gibbon, P., Bair, J., & Ponte, S. (2008). *Governing Global Value Chains: An Introduction.* Economy and Society, *37*(3), 315–338.

Hall, P., & Soskice, D. (Eds.). (2001). *Varieties of Capitalism.* Oxford: Oxford University Press.

Hewings, G. J. D. (1982). The Empirical Identification of Key Sectors in an Economy: A Regional Perspective. *The Developing Economies, 20*(2), 173–195.

Hirschman, A. (1958). *The Strategy of Economic Development.* New Haven/London: Yale University Press.

Jackson, J. K. (2013). *Foreign Direct Investment in the United States: An Economic Analysis.* Washington, DC: Congressional Research Service.

Ketels, C. H. M. (2007). Industrial Policy in the United States. *Journal of Industry, Competition and Trade, 7,* 147–167. Springer Science, Business Media, LLC.

Kiely, R. (2015). *The BRICs, US "Decline" and Global Transformation.* Basingstoke: Palgrave Macmillan.

Laumas, P. S. (1975). Key Sectors in Some Underdeveloped Countries. *KYKLOS, 28*(1), 62–79.

Los, B. (2001). Endogenous Growth and Structural Change in a Dynamic Input-Output Model. *Economic Systems Research, 13*(1), 3–34.

Mann, M. (1997). Has Globalization Ended the Rise and Fall of the Nation State? *Review of International Political Economy, 4*(3), 472–496.

Manrique G. M., Lerch M., & Bierbrauer E. (2015). The TTIP's Potential Impact on Developing Countries: A Review of Existing Literature and Selected Issues. Report Prepared for the European Parliament, April

Mazzucato, M. (2013). *The Entrepreneurial State. Debunking Public vs. Private Sector Myths.* UK and USA: Anthem Press.

Meller, P., & Marfán, M. (1981). Small and Large Industry: Employment Generation, Linkages and Key Sectors. *Economic Development and Cultural Change, 29*(2), 263–274.

Obama, B. (2013). *Remarks by the President on the Economy*, Knox College, July 24, 2013, Galesburg.

Obama, B. (2014). *State of the Union Address*, January 28, 2014.

Onaran, Ö., Stockhammer, E., & Grafl, L. (2011). Financialisation, Income Distribution and Aggregate Demand in the USA. *Cambridge Journal of Economics, 35*(4), 637–661.

Oosterhaven, J. (1988). On the Plausibility of the Supply-Driven Input-Output Model. *Journal of Regional Science, 28*(2), 203–217.

Pack, H., & Saggi, K. (2006). Is There a Case for Industrial Policy? A Critical Survey. *World Bank Research Observer, 21*(2), 267–297.

Pianta, M. (2014). An Industrial Policy for Europe. *Seoul Journal of Economics, 27*, 3.

Pietrobelli, C., & Rabellotti, R. (2011). *Global Value Chains Meet Innovation Systems: Are There Learning Opportunities for Developing Countries? World Development, 39*(7), 1261–1269.

Raza, W., Grumiller, J., Taylor, L., Tröster, B., & von Arnim R. (2014). ASSESS_TTIP: Assessing the Claimed Benefits of the Transatlantic Trade and Investment Partnership. Relazione Tecnica 10, Policy Note, Austrian Foundation for Development Research (ÖFSE).

Rubini, L., Tassinari, M., & Di Tommaso, M. R. (2015). The Transatlantic Trade and Investment Partnership (TTIP). Some Insights on the Implications for the European and the American Industry. *Economia Marche – Journal of Applied Economics, XXXIV*(1), 51–71.

Saad Filho, A. (2011). Crisis *in* Neoliberalism or Crisis *of* Neoliberalism? *Socialist Register, 47*, 242–259.

Schrank, A. J., & Whitford, J. (2009). *Industrial Policy in the United States: A Neo-Polanyian Interpretation. Politics and Society, 37*(4), 521–553.

Schultz, S. (1977). Approaches to Identifying Key Sectors Empirically by Means of Input-Output Analysis. *Journal of Development Studies, 14*(1), 77–96.

Stiglitz, J. (2010). *Freefall: America, Free Markets, and the Sinking of the World Economy.* London: Allen Lane.

Stiglitz, J. E., & Lin, J. Y. (2013). *The Industrial Policy Revolution I: The Role of Government Beyond Ideology.* New York: Palgrave Macmillan.

Stockhammer. (2004). Financialisation and the Slowdown of Accumulation. *Cambridge Journal of Economics, 28*(5), 719–741.

Tregenna, F. (2009). Characterising Deindustrialisation: An Analysis of Changes in Manufacturing Employment and Output Internationally. *Cambridge Journal of Economics, 33*(3), 433–466.

Tregenna, F. (2014). A New Theoretical Analysis of Deindustrialisation. *Cambridge Journal of Economics, 38*(6), 1373–1390.

Venhaus, M. (2015). An Unequal Treaty – Tip and Inequality in Europe. Working Paper 01, Berlin Forum on Global Politics (BFoGP).

Wade, R. H. (2012). *Return of Industrial Policy? International Review of Applied Economics, 26*(2), 223–239.

Wade, R. H. (2014). The Paradox of US Industrial Policy: The Developmental State in Disguise. In J. M. Salazar-Xirinachs, I. Nübler, & R. Kozul-Wright (Eds.), *Transforming Economies: Making Industrial Policy Work for Growth, Jobs and Development.* International Labour Office: Geneva.

Weiss, L. (2014). *America Inc.? Innovation and Enterprise in the National Security State.* New York: Cornell University Press.

Whitford, J. (2005). *The New Old Economy. Networks, Institutions, and Organizational Transformation of American Manufacturing.* Oxford: Oxford University Press.

Whitford, J., & Schrank, A. (2011). The Paradox of the Weak State Revisited: Industrial Policy, Network Governance, and Political Decentralization. In F. Block & M. Keller (Eds.), *State of Innovation: The U.S. Government's Role in Technology Development.* Boulder: Paradigm Publishers.

Williams, B. R. (2013). *Trans-Pacific Partnership (TPP) Countries: Comparative Trade and Economic Analysis.* Washington DC: Congressional Research Service.

CHAPTER 8

Trumponomics Facing a New Global Governance: Is the American Neoliberal Strategy Still Viable?

The Obama administration's response to the issues raised by the economic crisis had been basically consistent with the strategic approach to industrial development that had characterized the previous decades: on the one hand, to intervene at the national level with policies to support techno-logical innovation and industrial development and, on the other hand, to promote the opening up of foreign markets to American products through trade agreements.

With President Trump coming to the White House, this American neo-liberal strategy seems to be seriously questioned. Trump's victory in the 2016 election against Democratic candidate Hillary Clinton, who had ben-efited from Obama's support during the campaign, seems to mark an important loss of consensus accorded to the American *establishment* and to the neoliberal strategic line that had characterized the previous administra-tions. Indeed, the anti-globalization setting held by Trump's rhetoric dur-ing the electoral campaign represents what a substantial part of the American electorate—the "rural America"—chose to pursue by voting the republican candidate (Auerback 2017). Trump as President represents the conviction from a large part of the American electorate to break up with the neoliberal past. While the neoliberal era had been favouring the US industrial interests, it had also been giving the chance to Trump to leverage on the inequalities that it had created and win the elections (Stiglitz 2012).

© The Author(s) 2019   179
M. Tassinari, *Capitalising Economic Power in the US*,
International Political Economy Series,
https://doi.org/10.1007/978-3-319-76648-5_8

Despite the United States retaining considerable economic and political power over the international stage, America's participation in global economic dynamics no longer enjoys the undisputed leadership that allowed it to fully benefit from the neoliberal regime by capitalizing on its economic power (Kissinger 2014). In other words, the neoliberal approach is experiencing a loss of effectiveness as a tool that has allowed levels of prosperity able to preserve the interest of the dominant industrial class and, at the same time, to keep the social system in a sort of equilibrium during the last decades (Di Tommaso and Tassinari 2017). Although it should not be confused with the prospect of an imminent decline in the US leadership, the rebalancing in the distribution of economic power at the international level, unfavourable to the United States (and in favour of emerging powers, especially China), is the cause of a certain instability in the consensus accorded to the neoliberal approach.

This chapter goes through the essential elements of American industrial strategy in the neoliberal era, as they emerged from the historical reality of the last 40 years, in order to locate them in the recent post-crisis international context. The main aim of this chapter is to assess the actual space for the United States to continue to implement a neoliberal industrial strategy in the future.

It shows how current global transformations, essentially a shift in the distribution of international economic power and a change in key formal and informal institutions, are gradually limiting the American economic power and hence its ability to adopt a neoliberal strategy that is able to open the international markets and, at the same time, to protect and promote the national industry. Since the redistribution of international economic power has reduced the American influence in the definition of global economic rules, the decline of the American industrial strategy could correspond to a change of paradigm in global governance, where the old international institutions created from Bretton Woods are losing their effectiveness as a global regulatory system. This "global confusion" seems to promise an epochal transformation that leaves room for a new international paradigm.

Peculiarities of the American Industrial Strategy in the Neoliberal Era

This book has analysed how, in the neoliberal era, the United States has been capitalizing its economic power by implementing an identifiable industrial strategy. During the last four decades, three interconnected elements can be identified at the base of the American economic power, which—with different effectiveness over time—have made it possible to implement the American industrial strategy in the neoliberal era.

First, a spread and almost unconditioned consensus accorded to the "free market" regime all around the world, as the predominant economic model. In this regard, the American traditional rhetoric has played a crucial role since the beginning of the neoliberal era.[1] It has served to informally create legitimization and consent at national and international level for an economic order congenial to the interest of the most competitive industries in the United States, which could benefit from a laissez-faire system over weaker competitors. The role of this rhetoric has been to make the neoliberal prescriptions seductive, even among the domestic and international groups that would subsequently suffer from this regime: liberalization, privatization, fiscal austerity and demonization of the term "industrial policy" have been the drugs that the neoliberal rhetoric has promoted as the panacea for every evil all around the world.

Second, the US ability to formally determine the rules of the international game, by capitalizing on the bargaining power in trade and public procurement agreements. In this context, the United States during the neoliberal era has been able to negotiate favourable conditions for the American industry in bilateral and multilateral agreements. This has been a key leverage in determining and managing the effective American competitive advantage against other world economies.

During the 1980s, the strategy of the Reagan administration was basically to negotiate "voluntary" export restraints to protect the American economy when European and Japanese manufacturers made serious inroads into national markets. Also, on the side of export promotion, Reagan's commitment was punchy. The literature on the topic shows how the American government adopted an "aggressive unilateralism" strategy: the United States exercised pressure on foreign governments to reduce barriers to American exports and investments through trade threats, without any reciprocal concession.

During the 1990s, the American government played a major role as a regulator, in particular by actively participating in the definition of supranational and international rules. The establishment of a number of multilateral and bilateral trade agreements was at the centre of the American political agenda. There were the negotiations in the Uruguay Round, which led, in 1994, to the creation of the WTO. Even if the negotiations for the establishment of economic rules under the WTO were formally carried out at the multilateral level, the United States benefited from an undisputed political and economic leadership and was therefore in a stronger bargaining position than any other country. Indeed, there is little doubt that the birth of the WTO coincided with a historical period characterized by a substantial identity of views between the American government and the international institutions. As part of this scenario, several others trade initiatives took place during the 1990s: the NAFTA, the APEC programme, aimed to increase economic cooperation between the United States and Asian economies, and the FTAA, for the establishment of a free trade area among the countries in the Western Hemisphere. Other initiatives were primarily motivated by the desire of the American government to promote the transition to a market economy in the countries of the Soviet bloc and to support institutional reforms in the countries that needed to renegotiate their loans with Western banks. Overall, the trade policy initiatives undertaken by the American government during the 1990s show how the influence of the US government in the definition of the rules of the international economic game had an almost global reach.

The same approach (even if with weaker effectiveness) also characterized the Bush Junior administration through its commitment to further expand the WTO's influence over emerging economies and through the promotion of numerous bilateral agreements. Later, the Obama administration continued to follow the same rationale by attempting to establish big regional agreements, namely TTIP and TPP.

Third, the ability, in several circumstances, of "deceiving" at domestic level the same (formal and informal) rules that the United States had been promoting at international level. In this context, despite the anti-government rhetoric and the actions to promote free(er) markets at international level, many areas of intervention have been documented, in which the public role has supported and protected the national industrial system, such as public procurement, science and technology policies, protectionist trade policies, industrial bailouts. The DOD, along with other agencies, has continuously played a central role by actively supporting the "dual-use" of industries and technologies. By pursuing the goal of national security, they contributed to the innovation and development of the industries operating in the civil market. Even during the 1990s, when the increased stability resulting from the end of the Cold War required from the United States to reduce its military expenditures, policies to support technological innovation remained particularly prominent. Concerns about the possible negative impact on the technological and industrial development of the entire American economy of the military cutbacks led the government to look for alternative ways to promote innovation. In particular, the Clinton administration was the one that proclaimed a "new approach" to the innovation policy. ICT was considered by the government as one of the priorities. This important wave of innovations in ICT, which marked the beginning of the so-called New Economy, because of its massive impact on the entire economy, was ridden by the American administration through several important actions to further push the development of the sector. In the same years other important policies and programmes started to play a crucial role for the American industrial development. Public-private partnerships were promoted through, for instance, the launch of the ATP, directed by the NIST. Also, other programmes continued to exert a direct and effective influence on the US economic dynamic, such as, the SBIR programme, the STTR programme and the MEP.

During the 2000s, military expenditures regained an important role in the American economy. The beginning of the "war on terror" led again to an economic growth driven by military public demand and by a growing public debt, with important spending cuts to civilian technology programmes. At the same time, new emerging industrial powers (China in the first place) began to redefine the international trade equilibrium, with significant repercussions on the US trade deficit. This context marked the outbreak of the global crisis in 2008. At the outset of the Obama presidential administration (approximately a year after the financial crisis began), the government's main aim was to bring about recovery to the American economy from the threat of a catastrophic economic recession. Towards this goal, the central action was represented by the ARRA, enacted early in 2009. Not only was this massive government intervention—a stimulus package worth a total of $787 billion—oriented to address short-term social and economic emergencies, but it was also meant to foster a more radical development of the American productive structure in a long-term perspective. About a third of the total resources available through the ARRA were earmarked for financing particular segments of the economy—primarily the financial sector, but including also those industries which were considered "strategic" for the country, such as automotive, healthcare, energy and green industries, infrastructure, ICT and broadband. Other actions were also directed to education, science and technology, trade policy and regional and small businesses development. During the crisis, the American industrial strategy seems to have been characterized by a more interventionist approach, based on the definition of clear priorities and on the selection of industrial targets able to address them.

Overall, the three elements of the US industrial strategy—the unconditional trust in the neoliberal prescriptions all around the world, the US ability to formally determine the rules of the international game and the capacity of the American government to act at domestic level in support of the national industry—have been creating an (formal and informal) institutional framework whereby the American economy has been able to take advantage from the global system. In this context, the United States has been capitalizing its economic power, by paving the way for the international markets and promoting the domestic industry. The neoliberal institutional framework and the *global governance* model of the last 40 years have been, to a large extent, the outcome of the US economy's strategic interest, which has impacted the life within the economies all around the world.

Notwithstanding this long-lasting setting of the global order, several elements of novelty seem to characterize the post-crisis period compared to the past. Important changes have occurred in the international economic and institutional order and—along with the *Trumponomics*—in the American domestic economic policy. In particular, the three above-mentioned elements of the American economic power have to be reconsidered in light of this new contemporary context.

Is the US Neoliberal Rhetoric Still Effective?

President Trump's election seems to open a completely new season in the US political economy. Indeed, the main points announced by the Republican candidate during the electoral campaign seemed to radically break with the logic that had characterized the previous decades. Riding the populist horse, Donald Trump had promised to look at the domestic scenario by considering "America first". The rhetorical idea behind this slogan has been to redefine the US economic policy within an *isolationist* framework, basically aiming at making America autonomous from the international dynamics. In this context, *Trumponomics* was immediately outlined by rhetorically disrupting some of the fundamental political continuity lines carried out by the Obama administration. This radical break with the past has been evident in Trump's announcements concerning, for instance, the decisions of extinguishing and cutting on programmes related to Social Security, Medicare and the Affordable Care Act (the Obama's Healthcare Reform), to environmental protection, to trade regional agreements, up to a drastic change in the US foreign relations (especially with Mexico, Russia, China, South and North Korea). Overall, one of the main roles played by Trump's rhetorical stance has been to clearly bring out the latent contrasts within the American electorate: on one side, those groups endowed of high skills, competence and technologies able to compete in international markets, which could benefit from the participation to global production networks (the "winners" of the globalization); on the other side, those groups of the American society that have been suffering unemployment, marginalization and stagnation because they were excluded from the processes of economic growth (the "rural America" that has—eventually—decided to vote for Donald Trump). The fundamental result of the 2016 American election has been that the neoliberal consensus that had reigned sovereign over the past 40 years has been seriously questioned by nationalist and anti-globalization proposals. The United States is not an exception in the contemporary international stage. Similar phenomena had before also affected Great Britain with *Brexit*. More generally, several upheavals have taken place in many parts of Europe: nationalist sentiments have been vigorously emerging, for instance, in France, Italy and up to the recent elections in Germany. Such cracks in the consent accorded to the globalized order potentially open a space for alternative regulatory regimes, since the "discontents" of the globalization are raising their *voice* and exerting—when possible— their right to *exit* from the international dynamics (Hirschman 1970).

In the United States, there is no doubt that Trump's proposals suggest to the Americans a rather different industrial development path. Environmental policies represent an emblematic case. After Obama's commitment and signing of the Paris Climate Agreement of 2015, President Trump has soon declared the withdrawal of the United States from the accord. Consistently with this position, just a few months after his election, Trump has again contrasted the Obama administration's intervention by launching the Energy Independence Policy Executive Order.[2] The impact of this executive order could be irruptive. It aims at deleting the Clean Power Plan launched in 2015 by Obama to promote clean energy production. In this framework, the consequence of Trump's executive order is that the US EPA will change the rules on greenhouse gas emissions, not only for existing power plants but also for those to be built. The Obama administration's rules virtually made it impossible to build new coal-fired power plants, because they required that every new plant should have a system (very expensive and only recently developed) to store carbon dioxide underground. Trump's EPA could rewrite these rules by softening its terms. Another prescription that Trump might erase in the light of the Energy Independence is the reduction of methane losses in the atmosphere during mining and refining of oil and natural gas (Obama had decided to reduce them by 2025 of 40% compared to 2012 levels). Furthermore, Trump's executive order would revise the current estimations of the social cost of emissions: under the new laws, EPA could lower these estimates by considering, for example, only the emissions which damage the United States, with no consideration given to the whole planet. Finally, one of the few measures contained in Trump's executive order that could have an immediate effect is the elimination of Obama's moratorium on federal land-use concessions for coal mining, which was established to discourage the opening of new mines.

This approach tends by definition to "isolate" the United States from the rest of the world, and not just from an ecological point of view. Environmental protection is a crucial field in determining the structural adjustment of the American economy. It involves future technological breakthroughs, incentives to invest in new promising sectors and the development path of the productive structure. The current decisions on environment have an impact on the future ability of the United States to compete at an international level in some crucial areas. This context aggravates the contrast between the *old economy*, linked to the industrial interests in oil and coal, and the most dynamic America, oriented to the new technologies and to compete in international markets.

Breaking with the neoliberal past has been also manifested in the administration's announcements concerning the substantial withdrawal from the main trade regional agreements conducted by Obama: the TPP, which included several countries in Asia, and the TTIP, with the European Union (see Chap. 7). Regardless of the effective magnitude and impact on the level of international trade, these episodes reveal a change in the consent accorded to the globalized economic system.

Trump's election resounds consistent with an emerging international request for withdrawal from the globalization processes, request that comes from an ever-growing part of the world population.

Is the United States Still Able to Control the Rules of the International Economic Game?

During the time span of the crisis, while the United States and the European Union struggled to limit the losses in the financial markets and in the real economy, a number of emerging and frontier markets have attracted capital and wealth which had previously been concentrated in the North (Gourinchas et al. 2012). The "Rise of the South" since the 1990s (e.g. NICs, BRICS and some more recent African markets, but especially of China) has come to overshadow the power of the industrialized North (HDR 2013; Abdenaur and Fonseca 2013). There is no doubt that the redistribution of economic power between different national states is energizing those economic and cultural contexts that had beforehand no influence in defining the rules of the international economic game. This context is allowing the flowering of different national economic regimes and *varieties of capitalism* alternative to the neoliberal one (Nolke 2014; Overbeek and Apeldoorn 2011). In this heterogeneity of national regulatory frameworks, the "American model" of global governance (despite it still having a significant influence) is increasingly becoming unstable, being it unable to respond to the differences in country preferences and in abilities to compete in international markets (Wade 2009). As a consequence of this fact, the United States risks to lose control on the *traditional* global economic mechanisms, which have, so far, allowed the American hegemonic strategy to be effective.[3]

In this context, the growth of new economic powers has had the consequence of inducing a change in the international economic equilibrium, undermining the basic neoliberal principles that governed the functioning of the WTO (Moran 2012; The Economist 2012). Since the negotiations under the Doha Development Round of 2001, the alignment of some emerging economies with WTO rules has been unachievable. The Doha's negotiations were followed by repeated meetings over the subsequent years, and they were always marked by substantial failures in reaching a final agreement. The most controversial issues concerned the reduction of tariff and non-tariff barriers and agricultural regulations. This issue highlights the fact that the balance between global economies has changed and that, probably, the conditions for continuing in a multilateral framework with the American neoliberal approach are no longer there (see also the Chap. 6).

As a part of this global transformation, the crisis has also encouraged new "alliances", which are progressively leading to the formation of new "regional blocks" characterized by an economic magnitude potentially able to further threaten the undisputed US economic power of the twentieth century.[4] New regionalisms are currently fostered by a substitution of the north-south axis in favour of an east-south preferential channel, in the direction of resource flows and productive relations (Pieterse 2011; Shaw 2015). This new economic axis, along with the financial constraints that may ensue for the countries involved, marks the strategic liaison between the emerging industrial powers, especially China and India, and the African frontier markets. Other several circumstances can be briefly recalled as feeding these regional integration processes.

First of all there is the Chinese "Belt and Road" initiative. It is a development strategy launched by Xi Jinping in 2013 that aims at connecting China, by land and by sea, with countries located on the Silk Road Economic Belt (SREB) and on the Maritime Silk Road (MSR) in Asia, Europe and Africa, which account for 64% of the world population and 30% of the world GDP. The project focuses on massive investments in infrastructure (i.e. railways and highways) and related sectors (construction materials, real estates, power grid, automobile, iron and steel) in order to expand the China's network of trade and economic relations. It is not limited to infrastructure development, since it also focuses on policy dialogue, unimpeded trade, financial support and people-to-people exchange. This initiative is supposed to give China a preferential access to many important markets by massively increasing exports, investments and economic influence in Asia, Europe and Africa. In this framework, the "Belt and Road" project is going to further reinforce the competitive position of China at the international level (Huang 2016).

Secondly, there is the foundation of the BRICS, New Development Bank (NDB), entered into force in 2015. It could further reinforce financial and economic cooperation among the five emerging markets in the future. It was explicitly created [...] *as an alternative to the existing US-dominated World Bank and International Monetary Fund,*[5] stressing the decline of the Washington Institutions' international influence. The NDB would fund long-term investments in infrastructure by playing a complementary role with existing development banks. Despite the challenges that this initiative is facing in the start-up phase, it shows the existing commitment for enhancing the influence of BRICS and other developing countries in the international development architecture (Griffith 2014).

Finally, we have the Regional Comprehensive Economic Partnership (RCEP), launched in 2012. It is an FTA between ASEAN countries and China, Japan, South Korea, India, Australia and New Zealand, that aims to foster trade in goods and services, economic and technical cooperation, and to address other issues related to intellectual property, competition and dispute settlement among the signatory countries. The RCEP countries constitute 46% of the global population and are worth 24% of the global GDP. This agreement, if approved, will create one of the world's largest free trade zones and could further strengthen a regional block capable of contrasting the old industrial powers.[6]

In this context, the Obama administration, as an attempt to counter a possible decline of the American international influence, had continued to carry forward an approach aimed at strengthening the US trade partnerships around the world. One of the most important efforts in this direction was the commitment to establishing important trade and political agreements with Europe and Asia. Specifically, the United States had negotiated two regional initiatives: the TTIP, with the European Union, and the TPP, which included 12 countries in the Pacific region (see the Chap. 7 for details).

These agreements should not be confused with mere FTAs. The rise of China inevitably involves a challenge to the rules of the international game and to the established order, threatening the US international leadership. Not surprisingly, for example, at the end of the negotiations for TPP, on 5 October 2015, Obama stated:

> When more than 95 percent of our potential customers live outside our borders, we can't let countries like China write the rules of the global economy. We should write those rules, opening new markets to American products while setting high standards for protecting workers and preserving our environment.[7]

Nevertheless, Trump administration seems to have radically modified the strategic approach to the US international leadership. On 23 January 2017 he signed a presidential memorandum to withdraw the United States from the TPP and he also denied his support to the TTIP. These developments could have significant repercussions on the US capacity to counterbalance the rise of China and emerging partner economies. In this context, the American international leadership is therefore challenged by a changing global order, whereby the US-dominated Bretton Woods Institutions are losing their hegemonic stance in defining the rules of the international economic system.

IS AMERICAN DOMESTIC ECONOMIC POLICY KEEPING UP WITH THE FOURTH INDUSTRIAL REVOLUTION?

During the 1990s, the ICT industries started to experience a massive and rapid development. Since those years, the Internet has progressively spread globally, becoming a key infrastructure that has revolutionized social communication, the availability of information on the World Wide Web and the processes of creating economic value. In recent years, the centrality in the economic and social life of technological innovations in this field has been further consolidated, to the point that the impact of these technological breakthroughs has been defined as the Fourth Industrial Revolution. In reality, this definition consecrates advances in ICT that have been going on for several decades, but that are now clearly recognized as the fundamental field on which future industrial, economic and social development will be based.

More specifically, the Fourth Industrial Revolution is associated with the integration, in a massive part of human activities, of *Cyber-Physical Systems* (CPS), which are based on the *internet* and digital interconnection between the biological sphere and physical machineries and devices. The Forth Industrial Revolution involves "[...] fields such as artificial intelligence, robotics, the Internet of Things, autonomous vehicles, 3-D printing, nanotechnology, biotechnology, materials science, energy storage, and quantum computing" (Schwab 2016). The impact of this new technological sphere is going to revolutionize the relation between industries and costumers, by fostering a system of *Mass Customization*, whereby the production will combine the flexibility and personalization of custom-made products with the low unit costs associated with mass production (Bianchi and Labory 2017). In this context, central to the growth and competitiveness of the industrial system is, on the one hand, a continuous relationship with the market demand to rapidly interpret changes in consumers' preferences, and, on the other hand, to rapidly respond with cutting-edge technology solutions. Competition is mainly based on the ability to identify and meet emerging needs in efficient terms, namely on the ability to collect and process the data concerning the needs to be met and the data for programming the new digital technology. Barriers to entry into markets become the *big data*'s control, to directly obtain information about consumer preferences and needs and the ability to combine different technologies in a way that they can communicate with each other. In this framework, the competitiveness of the enterprises is essentially created at the system level, since it is based on the ability to bring together different disciplines and technologies by linking the production system with the scientific community to respond to a complex market demand. The role of the institutions becomes crucial to govern these processes of continuous technological innovation, by defining common goals and strategic lines for the actors involved (Bianchi and Labory 2017).

The competition in this new industrial order is going to surprisingly accelerate the changes in the international division of labour and in the allocation of global economic resources. It will markedly define the threshold in the distribution of global economic power between those who will operate on the technological frontier of the Fourth Industrial Revolution and those who will lag behind. The race to develop and integrate CPS in industrial systems has already started, and the first to arrive will probably be the ones who will have economic and technological global leadership in the near future, since the Forth Industrial Revolution is supposed to disrupt "almost every industry in every country" (Schwab 2016).

In 2010, the German federal government began to encourage this technological revolution by releasing the "German high-tech Innovation Strategy 2020" and putting forward the implementation of the "Industrie 4.0". A budget of EUR 8.4 billion was allocated for the period 2012–2015 to implement the various measures of the action plan and to push all major science and technology centres in the country to an effort towards common goals. It is a country strategy where the government has provided a long-term strategic line and a unitary framework for the new development perspective.[8]

Likewise, on 19 May 2015, China's State Council issued the "Made in China 2025" strategic plan, emphasizing the challenge that China's manufacturing industry faces from developed and developing countries. It is an initiative to comprehensively upgrade the Chinese industry by drawing direct inspiration from Germany's "Industrie 4.0" plan. The guiding principles, goals and tools of the Made in China 2025 plan are clearly defined. It aims at promoting an innovation-driven manufacturing by emphasizing quality over quantity and achieving green development. The plan identifies the goal of making the Chinese industry more efficient and integrated in a way that it can occupy the highest parts of global production chains. In this context, ten priority sectors have been identified by the government: new advanced information technology, automated machine tools and robotics, aerospace and aeronautical equipment, maritime equipment and high-tech shipping, modern rail transport equipment, new-energy vehicles and equipment, power equipment, agricultural equipment, new materials and biopharma and advanced medical products.[9] In this context, of course, there is a significant role played by the government in providing an overall framework, utilizing financial and fiscal tools, and supporting the creation of manufacturing innovation centres.

In the United States, the Executive Office of the President's Council of Advisors on Science and Technology (PCAST) issued, in 2011, a *Report to the President on ensuring American Leadership in advanced manufacturing*.[10] Here a clear emphasis is given to the role of the US manufacturing in sustaining American prosperity:

> The United States has long thrived as a result of its ability to manufacture goods and sell them to global markets. Manufacturing activity has supported our economic growth, leading the Nation's exports and employing millions of Americans. The manufacturing sector has also driven knowledge production and innovation in the United States, by supporting two-thirds of private sector research and development and by employing scientists, engineers, and technicians to invent new products and introduce innovations in existing industries. (Council of Advisors on Science and Technology, 2011)

The report also highlighted the crucial challenge that the United States has been experiencing in limiting the decline of its manufacturing system due to the competition with other industrialized economies:

> The Nation's historic leadership in manufacturing, however, is at risk. Manufacturing as a share of national income has declined, as has manufacturing employment, and our leadership in producing and exporting manufactured goods is in question. The loss of U.S. leadership in manufacturing, moreover, is not limited to low-wage jobs in low-tech industries, nor is it limited to our status relative to low-wage nations. The United States is lagging behind in innovation in its manufacturing sector relative to high-wage nations such as Germany and Japan, and has relinquished leadership in high-tech industries that employ highly skilled workers. Our trade balance in advanced technology manufactured products—long a relative strength of the United States—shifted from surplus to deficit starting in 2001, and a trade deficit of $17 billion in 2003 further widened to $81 billion by 2010. In addition, the United States has been steadily losing the research and development activity linked to manufacturing—and associated high-skilled jobs—to other nations, as well as our ability to compete in the manufacturing of products that were invented and innovated here—from laptop computers to flat panel displays and lithium ion batteries. As U.S. manufacturing leadership is waning, other nations are investing heavily in growing and revitalizing their manufacturing sectors and are crafting policies to attract and retain production facilities and multinational companies within their borders. (Council of Advisors on Science and Technology 2011)

To mitigate this negative trend in the US competitiveness in manufacturing, the Obama administration had launched the AMP and a number of other programmes in the framework of the US Advanced Manufacturing Initiative, such as Materials Genome Initiative (with a $100 million budget), National Robotics Initiative (with a $70 million budget), Hollings MEP and Advanced Manufacturing Technology Consortia (AMTech). These programmes were mainly coordinated by the NSF and the NIST.[11] Overall, the administration proposed $2.2 billion in advanced manufacturing R&D in FY13 Budget, a nearly 20% increase over the prior year (President's Council of Advisors on Science and Technology, 2014: 46). The initiatives aimed at creating a fertile environment for innovation, by encouraging firms to locate R&D and manufacturing activities in the United States.

Despite the importance for competitiveness in manufacturing recognized by the Obama administration to the Advanced Manufacturing Initiative, the overall budget allocated was rather modest compared to the main international competitors.[12] With the election President Trump, the funds allocated to advanced manufacturing initiatives are expected to be even decreasing. Indeed, President Trump's fiscal year 2018 budget request proposes to reduce funding for the NIST by 23% below the fiscal year 2017 enacted level. Currently funded at just under $1 billion, NIST is one of the most important institutes to promote US innovation and industrial competitiveness.[13]

In this scenario, the challenge the United States is addressing against the global competitors of the Fourth Industrial Revolution is extremely severe. The new global economic arena requires from the United States to deal with stable and structural capacities of foreign governments to promote technological and industrial development. The ability to answer to this competitive context and to the emerging economies' strategies could require from the United States a more steady national consensus towards policies aimed at directly promoting industrial innovation, which would have not been necessary to survive to competition a couple of decades ago. However, ideological constraints and national psychology with strong anti-government planning elements may not be conducive to pursuing such a more interventionist approach in the United States. Furthermore, the United States has accumulated an important public debt that could preclude the possibility of ambitious investments in new technologies, which the need to keep up with the Fourth Industrial Revolution will require.

Today China is already operating on the technological frontier along with the other major industrialized economies, and the ability of the United States to maintain its global technological leadership is seriously questioned at the time of "disruptive politics" and severe public budget cuts.

CONCLUSION

This chapter has, first of all, recalled the essential elements of the American industrial strategy in the neoliberal era, as they have been identified in the different chapters of the book: the unconditional trust in the neoliberal prescriptions all around the world, the US ability to formally determine the rules of the international game, and the capacity of the American government to act at domestic level for supporting the national industry. Through these three elements the United States have been *capitalizing their economic power* by promoting an institutional framework able, on the one hand, to pave the way for foreign markets and, on the other hand, to protect and promote the national industry. From this perspective, the US industrial strategy has had an international relevance, through the creation of a formal and informal institutional framework able to impact many economies and the life of many societies. The US industrial strategy in the neoliberal era has had a crucial influence in establishing the *global governance* model for the last 40 years. Is this strategy still viable?

The main aim of this chapter has been to reconsider the three above-mentioned elements in light of the recent post-crisis international scenario. In this context, several factors of novelty seem to characterize the post-crisis period compared to the past. Important changes have occurred in the international economic and institutional order. Indeed, one of the effects of the crisis has not been merely to foster a possible change in the distribution of economic power among different national states, but it has also been to push a transformation of the institutional channels through which international economic relations were conducted. Particularly from the post-crisis period, the global regulatory framework, which had allowed the American industrial strategy to be effective, seems to be under renovation.

President Trump's election has sounded as a request, coming from an important part of the American electorate for withdrawal from the globalization processes. Similar phenomena had before also affected Great Britain, with *Brexit*, and other upheavals have been taking place in Europe. In this context, the US "traditional" neoliberal rhetoric, which had created a spread consensus for market liberalization policies, has lost part of its influence, making room for alternative regulatory regimes.

Furthermore, BRICS have gradually increased their influence in the international economic and institutional system. The influence of new varieties of capitalism and new regionalisms are challenging the US hegemonic stance in defining the rules of the international economic system.

Finally, the challenge that America is facing from the global competitors of the Fourth Industrial Revolution is extremely severe, and the ability of the United States to intervene at domestic level in order to maintain their global technology leadership is seriously questioned by anti-government positions and public budget cuts.

As a result, the post-crisis period raises important doubts about the future ability of the United States of implementing an industrial strategy based on the global influence of their economic power. The decline of American influence in the definition of global economic rules opens the door to important transformations in future global governance. The old system of the international institutions created by Bretton Woods is losing its effectiveness as a global regulatory system. The world is currently asking for a new global paradigm: how will the community of nations be able to answer this question?

NOTES

1. See, for example, Mirowski and Plehwe (2009), Harvey (2005).
2. See https://www.whitehouse.gov/the-press-office/2017/03/28/president-trumps-energy-independence-policy (last accessed October, 2017).
3. On issues related to new form of transnational governance see, for example, Dingwerth (2008), Hale and Held (2011), Brown (2011, 2013), Harman and Williams (2013), Weiss and Wilkinson (2014), Shaw (2015).
4. A number of analysis has attempted to outline the emerging world; see, for example Shaw (2015), Zakaria (2011), Khanna (2009).
5. See http://ndbbrics.org/.
6. See CNN, January 26, 2017, http://edition.cnn.com/2017/01/24/asia/tpp-rcep-nafta-explained/index.html.
7. See https://www.whitehouse.gov/the-press-office/2015/10/05/statement-president-trans-pacific-partnership (last accessed October 2017).
8. See http://industrie4.0.gtai.de/INDUSTRIE40/Navigation/EN/Topics/Why-germany/why-germany-policy.html (last accessed October 2017).
9. See https://www.csis.org/analysis/made-china-2025 (last accessed October 2017).
10. See https://obamawhitehouse.archives.gov/sites/default/files/microsites/ostp/pcast-advanced-manufacturing-june2011.pdf (last accessed October 2017).

11. For details on the mentioned programmes and other initiatives related to manufacturing see https://www.manufacturing.gov/programs/ (last accessed October 2017). See also the Chap. 7.
12. See NAMRI/SME Position Paper, Advanced Manufacturing Initiatives: A National Imperative, https://www.sme.org/namri-position-paper/ (last accessed October 2017).
13. See https://www.aip.org/fyi/2017/nist-science-down-13-trump-budget.

REFERENCES

Abdenur, A. E., & de Fonseca, J. M. E. M. (2013). The North's Growing Role in South-South Cooperation: Keeping the Foothold. *Third World Quarterly, 34*(8), 1475–1491.

Auerback, M. (2017). Explaining the Rise of Donald Trump. *Real-world Economics Review*, Issue No. 78.

Bianchi, P., & Labory, S. (2017, forthcoming). Manufacturing Regimes and Transitional Paths: Lessons for Industrial Policy. *Structural Change and Economic Dynamics.*

Brown, S. (Ed.). (2011). *Transnational Transfers and Global Development.* London: Palgrave Macmillan.

Brown, S. (2013). *The Future of US Global Power: Delusions of Decline.* London: Palgrave Macmillan.

Council of Advisors on Science and Technology. (2011). Report to the President on Ensuring American Leadership in Advanced Manufacturing, https://obamawhitehouse.archives.gov/sites/default/files/microsites/ostp/pcast-advanced-manufacturing-june2011.pdf. Accessed October 2017.

Council of Advisors on Science and Technology. (2014). Accelerating U.S. Advanced Manufacturing: *Report to the President,* https://www.manufacturingusa.com/sites/prod/files/amp20_report_final.pdf. Accessed October 2017.

Di Tommaso, M. R., & Tassinari, M. (2017). Industria, Governo, Mercato. Lezioni americane, Il Mulino, Bologna.

Dingwerth, K. (2008). Private Transnational Governance and the Developing World. *International Studies Quarterly, 52*(3), 607–634.

Gourinchas, P. O., Rey, H., & Truempler, K. (2012). The Financial Crisis and the Geography of Wealth Transfers. *Journal of International Economics, 88*(2), 266–283.

Griffith, J. S. (2014). *A BRICS Development Bank: A Dream Coming True?, United Nations Conference on Trade and Development (UNCTAD) Discussion Paper.* UNCTAD: Geneva.

Hale, T., & Held, D. (Eds.). (2011). *Handbook of Transnational Governance.* Cambridge: Polity.

Harman, S., & Williams, D. (Eds.). (2013). *Governing the World: Cases in Global Governance*. Abingdon: Routledge.

Harvey, D. (2005). *A Brief History of Neoliberalism*. New York: Oxford University Press.

HDR – Human Development Report. (2013). *The Rise of the South: Human Progress in a Diverse World*. New York: UNDP.

Hirschman, A. O. (1970). *Exit, Voice, and Loyalty. Responses to Decline in Firms, Organizations, and States*. Cambridge, MA: Harvard University Press.

Huang, Y. (2016, September). Understanding China's Belt & Road Initiative: Motivation, Framework and Assessment. *China Economic Review, 40*, 314–321.

Khanna, P. (2009). *The Second World: How Emerging Powers are Redefining Global Competition in the Twenty-First Century*. New York: Random House.

Kissinger, H. (2014). *World Order*. New York: Penguin Press.

Mirowski, P., & Plehwe, D. (2009). *The Road from Mont Pèlerin. The Making of the Neoliberal Thought Collective*. Cambridge, MA/London: Harvard University Press.

Moran, M. (2012). *The Reckoning*. Basingstoke: Palgrave.

Nolke, A. (Ed.). (2014). *Multinational Corporations from Emerging Markets: State Capitalism 3.0*. London: Palgrave Macmillan.

Overbeek, H., & van Apeldoorn, B. (Eds.). (2011). *Neoliberalism in Crisis*. London: Palgrave Macmillan.

Pieterse, J. N. (2011). Global rebalancing: Crisis and the East-South turn. *Development and Change, 42*(1), 22–48.

Schwab, K. (2016). *The Fourth Industrial Revolution*. Geneva: World Economic Forum.

Shaw, T. M. (2015). From Post-BRICS' Decade to Post-2015: Insights from Global Governance and Comparative Regionalisms. *Palgrave Communications*. https://doi.org/10.1057/palcomms.2014.4.

Stiglitz, J. E. (2012). *The Price of Inequality: How Today's Divided Society Endangers Our Future*. New York: W.W. Norton.

The Economist. (2012). The Rise of the State Capitalism, January 21, 2012.

Wade, R. (2009). From Global Imbalances to Global Reorganisations. *Cambridge Journal of Economics, 33*, 539–562.

Weiss, T. G., & Wilkinson, R. (Eds.). (2014). *International Organization & Global Governance*. Abingdon: Routledge.

Zakaria, F. (2011). *The Post-American World: Release 2.0, Updated and Expanded Edition*. New York: Norton.

CHAPTER 9

Conclusion: The Illusion of the Economic Power

> I confess I am not charmed with the ideal of life held out by those
> who think that the normal state of human beings is that of
> struggling to get on; that the trampling, crushing, elbowing, and
> treading on each other's heels, which form the existing type of social
> life, are the most desirable lot of human kind, or anything but the
> disagreeable symptoms of one of the phases of industrial progress.
> [...] the best state for human nature is that in which, while no one is
> poor, no one desires to be richer, nor has any reason to fear being
> thrust back by the efforts of others to push themselves forward.
> *(Mill, John Stuart, 1848, Book IV, Chapter VI).*

This book has considered the economic power at the centre of the analysis as the main force that has guided the US political action over the last 40 years. The United States has capitalized its global economic power in order to promote the interest of its national industry. The analysis conducted in the various chapters of this book has shown how the American industrial strategy was implemented. At a general level, the United States was capable of influencing the creation of an international institutional framework able, on the one hand, to open up the foreign markets to the American products and, on the other hand, to intervene at domestic level for promoting the competitiveness of the national industries, through policies designed to support technological innovation and industrial development.

© The Author(s) 2019   199
M. Tassinari, *Capitalising Economic Power in the US*,
International Political Economy Series,
https://doi.org/10.1007/978-3-319-76648-5_9

In this context, the United States has acted first of all at a rhetorical level. The American political rhetoric of the past decades has served to informally create legitimization and consent at national and international level for a "free market" regime, as the predominant economic model. Since the 1980s, President Reagan in the United States (and Prime Minister Thatcher in the UK) began a campaign of clear opposition to public intervention by enforcing the neoliberal arguments. In this way, the most competitive industries of the United States could benefit from a laissez-faire regime over weaker competitors.

Despite the neoliberal stance embodied by the United States at a rhetorical level, this book has also clearly shown how the role of the American government has been crucial, during the past 40 years, in order to promote the national industrial system. The US ability to formally influence the rules of the international economic game has been a decisive feature of the American industrial strategy. In this context, the capacity of negotiating favourable conditions for the US industry in many bilateral and multilateral agreements has been a key leverage in determining and managing the effective American competitive advantage. Furthermore, at domestic level, many areas of intervention in which the government has supported and protected the national industrial system have been documented in the book: public procurement, science and technology policies, industrial bailouts and protectionist trade policies.

All these circumstances have exerted an influence over the conformation and results of the global economic system, by determining the allocation of its productive resources and impacting on the life style and on the development *status* within the world societies.

However, as discussed in the previous chapter, the international context is now changing. Despite the American influence in the global economy being still significant, ongoing global transformations are gradually restricting the American economic power and hence its ability to adopt a neoliberal industrial strategy. In this context, the United States is no longer the only hegemonic power. China and, more generally, emerging economic powers have been eroding the American international leadership of the past decades. New regionalisms and new varieties of capitalism oppose the ability of the United States to influence the rules of the global system through multilateral agreements. The WTO system, after the failures of the 2001 Doha Round, did no longer work with the same effectiveness as it used to in Clinton's days. And the American ability to impose "voluntary export restraints" on foreign competitors, as President Reagan did in the 1980s, no longer exists. The capital has partly shifted from the West to the

East. The financial capacity of the emerging economies is such that they are now able to invest significantly to promote technological innovation and therefore, to drive the dynamics of the Fourth Industrial Revolution. In this scenario, the new emerging powers have significant potential to threaten the US technology leadership, by defining clear, long-term industrial development strategies at national level.

This new scenario has raised important questions for the United States in the post-crisis. At a national level, the American system, which has been structured to meet the benefits of being the dominant industrial power, is struggling to find those "surpluses" to keep the social system in equilibrium, risking a social breakdown. The neoliberal system of the last 40 years has begun to generate strong dissatisfaction among the weakest groups of the American economy. In this context, conflicting forces coexist at national level. On the one hand, strong and technologically advanced industrial powers, which have the most to gain from their ability to compete in a globalized system, push the American system to the continuation of a neoliberal regime in foreign policy. On the other hand, Trump's election represents a prominent demand for isolationism and withdrawal from global dynamics. Similar phenomena are also characterizing other Western nations, where important parts of the electorate are manifesting their disappointment towards globalization. Great Britain, with *Brexit*, is the most blatant example. More generally, nationalist sentiments have been vigorously emerging in many parts of Europe, such as France, Italy, up to the recent elections in Germany.

The international and national scenarios described above weaken the US ability to define global economic rules. From this point of view, the decline of the American industrial strategy could open the door to a new paradigm in global governance, in which the old system of international institutions created by Bretton Woods is losing its effectiveness as international regulatory system.

In this context, a dangerous road seems to loom on the horizon. The political dynamics of the different nations, pushed by the populist stream, risk to seek consensus in nationalistic policies, closed to external issues (e.g. environment and immigration), establishing, by so doing, a corporative and authoritarian system focused on the interests of individual states. This system is critical to fuel the struggle for global resources, in a competition between isolated national states that promote their interest and states claiming their right to adequate living standards. Marginalization, non-integration, rejection of diversity can only fuel global conflicts and the climate of terror that is already so evident in our societies. This would be a tragic result of the excess of neoliberal global competitive dynamics. The discontent generated by the inability of the neoliberal system to promote fairness and justice at national and international level risks to generate fighting for survival, forming closed groups that feel threatened and conflicting with the outside.

This "global confusion" does not have to be surprising. It is the logical consequence of the dissatisfaction of some actors of the system for the results they achieved, which inevitably generates conflicts, tensions and new expectations on the outcome to be pursued, pushing the change in the fundamental institutions and in economic power distribution. The rise of new powers and the decline of the American neoliberal hegemony, like the fall of other empires in history, are the results of structural conditions of the system. They are consistent with an economic system based on the *struggle to get on* and on the *fear of being thrust back by the efforts of others to push themselves forward.*

These structural conditions reveal the deep illusion that lies behind the economic power: economic supremacy and prosperity will be elusive and without real foundation until they are used to obtain individual benefits rather than used to construct an economic and social result shared by the members of the community. So, in reality, who the next hegemonic power in history will be has scarce relevance. We do not want to replace a hegemonic power with another one. True human progress today needs a profound renewal of the formal and informal global institutions, where those who hold the economic power use it to pursue the common good. These institutions should be based on listening, dialogue and shared actions to address the major global issues. The overwhelming technological advances and the enormous productive potential announced by the Fourth Industrial Revolution will be worthless if they will not be guided by international governance towards achieving global development goals.

Building such a governance is, first and foremost, an individual responsibility. It means using our personal power, even if scarce, to serve the collective development. It means suggesting new parameters of private and public debate to educate each other on better ideals for the attainment of shared collective goals. The moment of profound crisis and transformation that the present world is facing is a precious opportunity for individual and collective renewal towards a new identity worthy of being called *human.*

REFERENCE

Mill, J. S. (1848). *Principles of Political Economy* (7th edn., 1909). London: Longmans, Green and Co.

Index[1]

---

[1] Note: Page numbers followed by 'n' refer to notes.

© The Author(s) 2019
M. Tassinari, *Capitalising Economic Power in the US*,
International Political Economy Series,
https://doi.org/10.1007/978-3-319-76648-5

CPSIA information can be obtained
at www.ICGtesting.com
Printed in the USA
LVOW13*1924300518
578995LV00012B/340/P